Riding to the Rescue
The Transformation of the RCMP in Alberta and Saskatchewan, 1914–1939

The Mountie may be one of Canada's best-known national symbols, yet much of the post-nineteenth century history of the Royal Canadian Mounted Police remains unexamined, particularly the years between 1914 and 1939, when the RCMP underwent enormous transformation. The nature of this transformation as it took place in Alberta and Saskatchewan – where the Mounties have traditionally dominated policing – is the focus of Steve Hewitt's *Riding to the Rescue*.

During the period covered, the nineteenth-century model of the RCMP evolved into a twentieth-century version, and the institution that emerged responded to a nation that was being transformed as well. Forces such as industrialization, mass immigration, urbanization, and political radicalism compelled the Mounties to look away from the frontier and toward a new era.

Incorporating previously classified material, which explores the RCMP both in the context of its ordinary policing role and in its work as Canada's domestic spy agency, Hewitt demonstrates how much of the impetus behind the RCMP's transformation was ensuring its own survival and continued relevance. *Riding to the Rescue* is a provocative and incisive look behind one of Canada's enduring icons at the cusp of the modern era.

(The Canadian Social History Series)

STEVE HEWITT is a lecturer in the Department of American and Canadian Studies at the University of Birmingham.

Riding to the Rescue

The Transformation of the RCMP in Alberta and Saskatchewan, 1914–1939

Steve Hewitt

UNIVERSITY OF TORONTO PRESS
Toronto   Buffalo   London

Reprinted 2016

ISBN-13: 978-0-8020-9021-8 (cloth)
ISBN-10: 0-8020-9021-4 (cloth)

ISBN-13: 978-0-8020-4895-0 (paper)
ISBN-10: 0-8020-4895-1 (paper)

Printed on acid-free paper

Library and Archives Canada Cataloguing in Publication

Hewitt, Steve
Riding to the rescue : the transformation of the RCMP in Alberta and
Saskatchewan, 1914–1939 / Steve Hewitt.

(Canadian social history series)
Includes bibliographical references and index.
ISBN-13: 978-0-8020-9021-8 (bound)
ISBN-13: 978-0-8020-4895-0 (pbk.)
ISBN-10: 0-8020-9021-4 (bound)
ISBN-10: 0-8020-4895-1 (pbk.)

1. Royal Canadian Mounted Police – History.   2. Intelligence service –
Alberta – History – 20th century.   3. Intelligence service – Saskatchewan –
History – 20th century.   I. Title.   II. Series.

HV8158.7.R69H48 2006   363.2'32'0971209049   C2005-906171-5

University of Toronto Press acknowledges the financial assistance to its publishing
program of the Canada Council for the Arts and the Ontario Arts Council.

University of Toronto Press acknowledges the financial support for its publishing
activities of the Government of Canada through the Book Publishing Industry
Development Program (BPIDP).

For Isaac and Flora,
the lights of my life.

Contents

List of Tables

Acknowledgments

This study began as my PhD dissertation some thirteen years ago. Accordingly, my first and chief acknowledgment must go to Bill Waiser, who offered brilliant supervision and who has served and continues to serve as a role model for me in how to balance one's professional and private lives. Helpful as well has been the University of Saskatchewan through various grants and scholarships when I was a student. My PhD committee offered valuable input, as did Moira Harris and Chris Kitzan, who proofread this when it was a dissertation, and the anonymous readers from the University of Toronto Press. Len Husband at UTP and Greg Kealey have been extremely supportive: they made this book possible. I would also like to express my appreciation to other UTP staff, including Frances Mundy. The University of Birmingham, my new academic home, deserves praise. In particular, I wish to acknowledge the help and support of my colleagues and friends Scott Lucas and Danielle Fuller, who have made me feel at home in the wilds of Birmingham. My gratitude goes as well to the National Archives of Canada for assistance in obtaining RCMP records and to those Mounties who shared their memories with me. Ceri Morgan read the manuscript and offered feedback, and I would like to thank her for making this a better book and, through her profound decency, me a better person.

Although my time in Saskatoon is now a part of the past, my friends from the period remain in my present. Thanks to all of them, including Robin, Tom, Dorinda, Warren, and Sheila. Extra special recognition goes to friends elsewhere, particularly Tony and Christabelle, for their friendship, help, and support. In addition, I would like to pay special tribute to Dave De Brou, my friend and former colleague from the

University of Saskatchewan, whose untimely death has left a void in so many lives.

Finally, I would like to thank my parents and family, including my late grandparents, for their unconditional love and support. Last, but not least, I wish to express my love for my children, Isaac and Flora, who make every day a wonderful one.

Preface

It was a tale of two birthdays.[1] One, the 125th anniversary of the creation of the North-West Mounted Police in 1998, received repeated fêting across Canada. The National Film Board commissioned a documentary look at the force's past and even the Canadian Broadcasting Corporation, described by the Royal Canadian Mounted Police in the 1960s as 'wooly [sic] and psuedo [sic] intellectual' contributed a special radio look.[2] The party even stretched into the following year, 125 years after the first Mounties trudged west in the 'Great March,' a nearly disastrous event for all involved. By 1999, thanks to time-inspired forgetfulness, it had even become an occurrence worthy of re-enactment. Fittingly, however, the new march experienced a measure of misfortune worthy of the original: a cabinet minister seeking a photo opportunity ended up on her backside courtesy of a camera-shy horse, as did a prominent journalist; they later had the company of some of the re-enactors, separated from their mounts courtesy of the car of an overeager local historian rushing to meet his heroes on one of their many stops in small-town Saskatchewan.

The second birthday went unnoticed. No slight irony emanated from the omission, for the latter event, in 2000, was the eightieth anniversary of the actual birth of the Royal Canadian Mounted Police. Such an oversight seems impossible. How could so many people have celebrated the birth of the RCMP, the world's most famous police force and a classic Canadian symbol, in the wrong year? Why did men and women on horses dominate the historical depiction of the RCMP when a more accurate rendering of the majority of the force's past would have involved intricate manoeuvers in automobiles? The answer is because selective commemoration suited a wide range of interests. For the current RCMP, the nineteenth century, at least the dominant perceptions of it, serves as a respite against the smudges of the twentieth and the twentieth-first: no Regina Riot, no Security Service, no 'dirty tricks,' no Brian Mulroney, no pepper spray, no Maher Arar. In turn, for many Canadians, the pre-1900 version of the Mounted Police offers a glimpse of a more comforting Canada where women, workers, and Aboriginals knew their place and there was no need to sign a petition opposing the wearing of turbans by Sikh-Canadian Mounties.

The link between the 'golden age' and the modern is the period between 1914 and 1939, when the nineteenth-century model of the Mounted Police became the twentieth-century edition; this development in Alberta and Saskatchewan, where the RCMP has dominated the policing story, is the focus of this book. The end result was not continuity with what came before but the transformation of an institution in response to a transformed nation. The challenges posed by industrialization, mass immigration, urbanization, and political radicalism emerged in full force by the First World War and never went away.

To handle these forces the state turned to the Mounties; it was a relationship based on mutual dependence: the state feared for its control over the nation and the Mounted Police worried about its very survival. Each met the other's needs between 1914 and 1939. Instead of riding off into oblivion the RCMP saved itself by riding to the rescue and ensuring the continuance of Anglo-Canadian hegemony. Only the celebratory candles remained to be blown out. No one noticed that there were too many.

Riding to the Rescue

1

Introduction: Policing History

Historical eras are like chapters in a book; they always have an end and a beginning. For the Royal Canadian Mounted Police (RCMP), an era initiated with the advent of war in 1914 began to spiral to a conclusion on the Montreal night of 26 July 1974, when a bomb that RCMP Constable Robert Samson was attempting to plant blew off the tips of four of his fingers. He initially claimed to have discovered the package, whereupon it had exploded. In reality, the Mountie, a member of the force's intelligence branch, most commonly known as the Security Service, had been planting the explosive when the blast occurred. Once Samson's story about the bomb crumbled, he began to talk freely about having done worse things for his employer. Soon exploits involving buggings, break-ins, and a barn burning occupied the front pages of Canadian newspapers. The people involved in these illicit activities were not criminals, at least not in the ordinary sense; they were police officers. Inquiries followed and eventually the Liberal government of Pierre Trudeau stripped the RCMP of most of its security/intelligence role; it returned to being primarily a regular police force, albeit the most famous one in the world.[1]

What follows is about how the RCMP became more than just a simple police force – not in a symbolic sense since it had always been different, but from a policing point of view. R.C. Macleod, the pre-eminent historian of the early Mounted Police, suggests that the First World War 'fundamentally altered' the nature of the Royal North-West Mounted Police (RNWMP). In the post-1914 era, the Mounted Police practised a dual role. Always a police force, it also became an intelligence service.[2]

The Mounted Police official story, which has lingered on for most

3

of the century, has dominated the way the police have been viewed, especially by the general public. Keith Walden describes the creation process of that tale:

> Because every human creation is inherently mythic, and every society agrees on some basic points about the nature of reality, the popular image of the Mounted Police may be viewed in terms of myth. When Britons, Americans, and English Canadians looked at the Mounted Police they collectively ignored certain aspects of the force, downplayed others, and emphasized those qualities and characteristics that to them seemed important. They thought they were describing a self-evident reality, but they were not. Instead they described what they wanted to see.[3]

The dominant public perception of the Mounted Police is very much a nineteenth-century creation. Essentially this script suggests that the force, undeniably quite powerful, did not abuse that power. Instead the heroic Mounties dispensed frontier law in a very public fashion from the backs of their horses as they policed the western frontier of Canada. These horsemen maintained a degree of professionalism and neutrality that won them the support of citizens on the Prairies and, in the process, offered a contrast with the imagined anarchy in the American West. There was both a practical and a symbolic aspect to this piece of Mountie history, the latter fuelled by popular culture, which has been well documented by both academic and popular historians and which remains as entrenched in the present as it was in the 1910s.

How the force was 'fundamentally altered' and emerged in its modern form after 1914 has received only recent attention. This book will examine the changes the Mounted Police underwent specifically in Alberta and Saskatchewan between 1914 and 1939. Although geographically narrow in scope, what occurred in essentially the force's home provinces is equally applicable to the other provinces in the same era. The approach adopted in this book allows for a more detailed take on a period in which the Mounties encountered their greatest threat and, in response, underwent their most dramatic change. To save themselves, the horsemen reinvented or transformed their purpose. They assumed security intelligence activities that initially overlapped with, and often overshadowed, regular policing duties. These two roles effectively turned the RCMP into a double-headed creature. First, there was the public Mounted Police with its daily policing in numerous communities. Then there was an invisible insti-

tution with a mandate to spy, infiltrate organizations, recruit informants, open mail, and act as 'agents provocateurs' – all the classic
characteristics of a secret police, an institution reviled in countries all
over the world.

There is also the broader question of what the police represent in
the wider society. Much of the history generated on the topic comes
from the United Kingdom. Whiggish history, such as Leon Rad-
zinowicz's *History of English Criminal Law*, dominated the first
interpretations of the creation of the professional police: politicians
formed police forces to quell disorder in the streets, and all classes of
people benefitted from such changes.[4] In his 1938 book, *The Police
Idea*, historian Charles Reith gave a succinct expression of this view:

> What is astonishing in the record is the patience and blindness
> displayed both by citizens and authority in England over a period of
> nearly two hundred years, during which they persistently rejected
> the proposed and obvious police remedy for their increasing fears
> and sufferings, in the belief that its adoption would endanger their
> liberties and create 'a super-State above the State,' or, in the phrase
> of the period, 'a power above the Parliament at Westminster.' Peel's
> single-handed correction of their error at last provided the solution
> of a national problem that had become intolerable.[5]

More complex interpretations of what the police represent would
eventually develop. The nature of this response resembles what historian William Baker has called

> the functionalist or pluralist perspective ... [which] in essence ...
> considers that police serve society as a whole and that police
> enforcement of the law and maintenance of order is, on the whole
> beneficial. This conceptual framework does not necessarily lead to
> an unsophisticated or uncritical examination of the police. The
> pluralist approach need not entail a belief that all social groups have
> an equal or just share of power or that social change will occur
> without conflict between competing groups.[6]

Many of the new interpretations, in a backlash against the earlier
Whiggish history, viewed the police as a political and exploitive tool
of the ruling capitalist class. From this perspective, even if the police
and the legal system they worked within treated everyone equally, this
simply maintained the status quo of inequality since, as Anatole
France once observed, 'the law in its majestic equality, forbids the

rich as well as the poor to sleep under bridges, to beg in the streets, and to steal bread.'[7] The police in capitalist societies became, then, enforcers of class injustice. Antonio Gramsci described this as a process whereby 'through "law" the State renders the ruling group "homogeneous," and tends to create a social conformism which is useful to the ruling group's line of development.'[8] Michel Foucault saw the police as part of a larger system of social control:

> Prison and police form a twin mechanism; together they assure in the whole field of illegalities the differentiation, isolation and use of delinquency. In the illegalities, the police-prison system segments a manipulable delinquency. This delinquency, with specificity, is a result of the system; but it also becomes a part and an instrument of it. So that one should speak of an ensemble whose three terms (police-prison-delinquency) support one another and form a circuit that is never interrupted. Police surveillance provides the prison with offenders, which the prison transforms into delinquents, the targets and auxiliaries of police supervisions, which regularly send back a certain number of them to prison.[9]

In critiquing traditional police history, Sidney L. Harring argues that too often 'research on the police has focused on concepts such as legality, professionalization, reform, political influence, crime control, police-community relations, and the like.'[10] Instead Harring argued that the American police in 'its modern form emerged from class struggle under industrial capitalism and that, in spite of reform movements and professionalization, we now have essentially the same police institution that evolved in the intense class conflicts of the 1870s, 1880s, and 1890s.'[11]

Like a pendulum swinging back and forth, challenges to this class-conflict based interpretation of policing soon arose, including those using the tools of the new social history. Among the revisionists were radical criminologists (self described 'left realists') who contended that the poor suffered from violence and crime, actions often committed by perpetrators from within their own classes, and on occasion the police afforded protection to these people.[12] To a certain extent, contends Clive Emsley, the appearance of a professional police force empowered the working class because it created the expectation that they too should be free of crime.[13] Writing in a Canadian context, Greg Marquis suggests that the relationship between the police and the working class had been characterized by 'ambiguity, not sheer domination.' 'If each city had adopted a uniformed police only after a riot, changing crime rate, or the need for a new kind of class-control agency,' points out one scholar about the American situation, 'many places would not today have a uniformed police.'[14]

Adding to the increasing complexity were attempts to view the police not simply as a tool of the state but as an independent entity in its own right. The best example of this is Robert Fogelson's ground-breaking study of American police forces, *Big-City Police*: 'Far from being mere administrative bodies that enforced the law, kept the peace, and served the public, the police departments were policy-making agencies that helped to decide which laws were enforced, whose peace was kept, and which public was served.'[15]

An equally significant development in the writing of police history occurred in the 1980s and 1990s with studies of 'state formation.' Some historians increasingly focused on the liberal-democratic state and the institutions used to maintain its hegemony, including the police. This preoccupation with issues of authority and order raised new issues. On the one hand, the development of professional police forces was not necessarily a good in itself – societies have always had alternative methods of ensuring order.[16] On the other hand, to label police forces and their operations as uniformly oppressive is to write history divorced from the contradictions of reality. To put this complexity in another way – this book is informed by the idea that the police, in this case the Mounted Police, have always served the interests of the state by maintaining the status quo. Occasionally, those interests coincide with groups other than the ruling classes, some of which supply members of the police, but the ultimate loyalty of the police remains with those at the top.

What about the specific historical literature on the Mounted Police? The trend of the scholarship resembles a similar pattern to historical writing outside the police world: a movement from the general, celebratory, and simplistic to critical studies of complexities, contra-dictions, and sophistication. There is one difference, however. The works in the former category could be listed in the dozens. One would only need the fingers of both hands to count the studies in the latter group. .

The value of the majority of the publications related to the Mounted Police is for their sheer entertainment value.[17] Much of the early work on the force was hagiographical in nature, fiction in the guise of history. Works such as A.L. Haydon's *Riders of the Plains* and R.G. MacBeth's *Policing the Plains* are packed with anecdotes of heroic young Englishmen confounding the criminals, earning the respect of Aboriginals, protecting the people, and doing it all with a stiff upper lip.[18] This sort of work dominated publications about the force into the 1970s and examples of the genre continue to appear.[19]

In a similar vein to these popular histories is another major segment of Mounted Police literature: memoirs and historical studies written by former members. The most notable of these works include books by former commissioners William Kelly, Charles Rivett-Carnac, C.W. Harvison, Assistant Commissioner Vernon Kemp, and less senior figures in the force.[20] Other less famous figures in the force have also contributed to this genre.[21] The only comprehensive history on the subject comes from William and Nora Kelly. Their *The Royal Canadian Mounted Police: A Century of History*, which appeared in 1973, the centenary of the Mounted Police, contained dated interpretations that flattered its title subject. Particularly grievous in this sense was their notion that the Winnipeg General Strike leaders planned to overthrow the government,[22] an argument that even the former official historian of the Mounted Police labelled as 'ignoring the scholarship of the last quarter century.'[23]

Then there was the actual work that the police did. In carrying out their duties the Mounties directed special treatment at several categories of people: members of certain ethnic groupings, organized labour, and radicals, primarily on the political left. For various reasons, individuals who belonged to, or were perceived to belong to, these groups were labelled as threats to the Canadian state and its institutions, including the national police force. Aboriginals, deemed by Anglo-Canada as a vanquished people in this era, were not viewed as a threat in the same way and largely escaped broader RCMP attention beyond normal policing except when communists showed a real or imagined interest in their cause.[24]

For those representing perceived threats, the RCMP spun a web of interconnections – ethnic minorities had to be monitored because they brought the alien seed of Bolshevism to Canada; they also threatened to undermine the Anglo-Canadian character of the nation, turning it into a mongrelized country. Certain kinds of crimes, usually ones connected with social deviance, were also associated with ethnic minorities; immorality, in turn, would have an impact on the 'white' population of Canada. Communists, a large number of whom happened to be of eastern European background, had to be watched because they inspired labour and ethnic unrest. Workers had to be spied upon because they were responsive to communist propaganda, and their members included ethnic minorities who were prone to violence and radicalism. Alone, these groups, while troublesome, did not appear to pose an overwhelming threat. As in other liberal-democratic nations, it was their many interconnections that made them a perceived danger to the state. Over sixty years, the web stretched outward from these groups to entangle students and academics, women's groups, gays and lesbians, and countless other organizations and individuals.

The nature of the RCMP's interaction with the groups at the centre of the web is explained by who the police were and the transformation they underwent. Too often historical work on police forces, particularly with the Mounted Police, concentrates on what the rank and file did, usually in anecdotal form, and not on who they were.[25] In reality, what police officers did was very much affected by their place of birth or origins, their social background, their male identity, and the values the force as an institution sought to instil in its members. In other words, gender, ethnicity, race,[26] and class, the four major components of social history, are as important to the story of the Mounted Police as the heroic arrests of smugglers or bank robbers. Mounties were white men in the sense of what whiteness meant in the first half of the twentieth century; that is, they were almost exclusively of Anglo-Celtic heritage.

Finally, to appreciate fully what members of the RCMP were and what they became, it is also necessary to understand the setting they performed in. Police forces do not evolve or operate in a vacuum, but instead function within boundaries imposed by society in general and politicians in particular. Both the Mounties and the changes they underwent between 1914 and 1939 need to be fully contextualized by placing them within the broader historical trends, especially since there is a universal aspect to police history.

What the Mounties did has generated discussion and debate. One contentious aspect within the historiography on the Mounted Police centres on the force's intelligence role. Critics contend that those who emphasize this type of work distort the historical portrait of the RCMP by downplaying or even ignoring the far more prevalent policing of crime that the force performed. In particular, R.C. Macleod has argued that the security operations were insignificant in both manpower and material records to the overall operations of the Mounted Police in the 1920s and 1930s, nor do they explain why the RCMP as an institution survived challenges to its existence. Instead, the more mundane, bureaucratic, and cost-effective function they fulfilled for the Canadian government by enforcing federal statutes and doing work on behalf of federal departments saved them.[27]

The idea of survival is apt but in a broader sense than envisioned by Macleod. The force eventually prospered because it managed to transform itself from a police force of the nineteenth century, equipped for dealing with the problems associated with Euro-Canadian settle-

ment on the western plains, into a modern police/security force ready
to handle the challenges to the state from an increasingly urbanized,
industrialized, and heterogeneous world. Provincial police bodies
existed to fight crime in Saskatchewan between 1917 and 1928, and in
Alberta between 1917 and 1932, and so ordinary crime fighting for
the RCMP was not as significant as some have contended. Police
forces normally operate under the gaze of citizens and under the
authority, at least in theory, of those who hold power. For these two
groups and for members of the police themselves, some aspects of
police work were simply more important than others. This statement
is true in any era. Today in Canada the arrest of a murderer receives
far more attention than the arrest of a burglar, yet petty thieving is
much more prevalent than homicide. In the 1920s and 1930s, certain
issues caught the attention of the public, the police, and the powerful
more than others. Left-wing radicalism, Bolshevism, the drug trade,
labour unrest, general disorder, and the challenges ethnic communities posed to Anglo-Celtic supremacy concerned both the Canadian
state and many citizens.

In the interwar period, it also needs to be said, there was no clear
distinction between intelligence work and regular criminal policing of
the type that the RCMP would experience after the Second World
War. Policemen performed both types of jobs on a regular basis. Nor
was this situation unique to Canada. Whether it was the fledgling
Federal Bureau of Investigation in the United States or the Public
Security Bureau in Shanghai, China, there was mixing of policing and
intelligence roles. What further linked the two roles is that each in
some way focused on deviations, be they physical or ideological,
from the norm as defined by the governing elite.[28]

The nature of the interwar Mounted Police connects to two important and interrelated questions that underlie this study. First, how did
the RCMP manage to survive this period? On the surface such a
question might seem surprising. Yet for a good portion of the Great
War and for several years afterwards the future of the RCMP was
anything but secure. The force had a persistent critic in the House of
Commons, labour member of Parliament J.S. Woodsworth, and a not
particularly friendly Liberal government in office for most of the
1920s. Prime Minister William Lyon Mackenzie King believed the
Mounties, especially the officer corps, to be the puppets of the hated
Conservatives. The Liberals as a party were also advocates of provincial rights, a principle that a federal police force ran against,
since under the British North America Act policing was a provincial
responsibility.

Secondly, why and how did the RCMP transform itself between 1914 and 1939? In 1914 the Mounted Police carried out duties similar to any other Canadian police force. By 1939 the RCMP's day-to-day activities had expanded beyond these traditional police functions to include intelligence gathering and other activities against communists, fascists, immigrants, workers, unions, students, academics, etc. Clearly the force had changed. The nature of that transformation answers the question of how the Mounted Police personnel survived challenges to their existence in the first two decades of the twentieth century.

Myths do not appear overnight; they take a considerable period of time to develop; they, however, can be shattered in the split second that it takes for a bomb to explode. The RCMP carried the reputation of being law-abiding, impartial, and benevolent. The roots of what destroyed this myth on that humid Montreal evening were planted, developed, and nurtured between 1914 and 1939 when the modern RCMP emerged.

2

The Architect, the Era, and the State

By October 1918, A.B. Perry, commissioner of the Royal North-West Mounted Police (RNWMP), product of a small-town Ontario United Empire Loyalist background, and a graduate of Royal Military College, was nearing the end of his calling. In a career that stretched back into the nineteenth century, the architect of the modern Mounted Police had first-hand experience of important events in his force's history. Having fought against the Métis in the 1885 Northwest Rebellion, he had slowly worked his way up through the ranks, achieving his final and highest position on 1 August 1900.[1]

Now in October 1918, with the bloodiest conflict in human history about to conclude, Perry was contemplating an uncertain future for the force, a reality for which the commissioner was partially to blame. A year earlier, in his haste to organize a police military unit for the war effort, he had encouraged the federal government to remove the RNWMP, the forerunner to the Royal Canadian Mounted Police (RCMP), from regular policing duties in Alberta and Saskatchewan. Consequently, his members continued regular policing duties only in northern Canada. Across the Prairies they belonged to a police force with nowhere to police. Instead, Mounties found themselves enforcing federal laws and statutes, providing assistance to federal departments, and performing other more secretive tasks. Ordinary citizens and provincial governments, meanwhile, realized that they could get by without the RNWMP. Could the RNWMP, however, survive without a guaranteed policing role? Would it continue as a marginalized institution, its members spending their days among Inuit and polar bears? Or, for that matter, would the federal government be satisfied with its security needs being fulfilled by the small Dominion Police,

Canada's security service up until the end of the First World War – a force so small that it often had to resort to hiring American detectives to collect information?[2]

The future of the Mounted Police at the close of the war was anything but assured as a series of crises, from societal to policy to political, created uncertainty. Perry, naturally, sought his force's survival. Recognizing its weakened position, in October 1918 he prepared a memorandum outlining three options for the RNWMP's future. Restricting his troops' duties to the Yukon and the Northwest Territories was the first suggestion. The commissioner wrote that this selection required no more than one hundred men and if followed the force might as well be disbanded. Perry's second option, based on the long military tradition of the Mounted Police, would have seen it amalgamated with the Canadian militia. He noted the militaristic characteristics of the Mounties, but concluded that with their reputation they would be far more valuable as a civilian body. The commissioner's preferred alternative was to see the RNWMP joined with other federal police forces to form 'a Canadian Constabulary.' The new force's duties would include intelligence gathering, the policing of Indian reserves, and the enforcement of federal laws and statutes. 'The chief advantages to be gained,' emphasized the veteran policeman, 'would be co-ordination, and increased efficiency as a result of careful selection of personnel and thorough training, uniformity in enforcement of federal laws and freedom from local influences.'[3]

A month later, in a second memorandum, Perry called specifically for the amalgamation of the RNWMP and the Dominion Police in order to provide for more effective policing. He suggested the new police force be 'subject to a rigid discipline and control ... [and] be armed and trained as a military body so that it can act effectively should it be required to do so.'[4] This emphasis on military values reflected Commissioner Perry's vision of the Mounties in an era that seemed to promise profound change.

The first stage of the reorganization occurred in December 1918 when the force became the federal police for all of Canada west of Port Arthur and Fort William. Then, in the aftermath of the Winnipeg General Strike, Prime Minister Robert Borden decided that the federal government needed a better system of national security. At a 5 August 1919 meeting, Borden asked Perry to submit options for a new national police force that would be responsible for homeland security. Amalgamation was the commissioner's answer, either as a single body or with the continued geographic split (Mounted Police in the west, the Dominion Police in the east), but under one boss. Perry preferred a complete merging of one force into the other. He pointed out the strengths of his side: the Mounties were disciplined, military-trained, armed, and, significantly in an era of labour disputes, non-unionized. He also drew particular attention, according to official RCMP historians, to 'the dual nature of the force ... Its members were peace officers who could be used instead of the military to maintain order in the streets. The Mounted Police also had experienced detectives and commissioned officers who had recognized social status in the community.' Finally, and perhaps most importantly, Perry emphasized his organization's history and tradition and positive national image. The commissioner's arguments and logic won Borden over.[5] On 1 February 1920 the Royal North-West Mounted Police and the much smaller Dominion Police merged to form the Royal Canadian Mounted Police. 'Merger' is actually inaccurate, since it suggests the joining together of two bodies: in fact, the Mounted Police completely absorbed its rival.

In writing these memos and constructing his arguments for the government, several things clearly swirled through Perry's mind – the force's history, the new challenges to Canadian society, and the nature of the relationship between various governments and the RNWMP. All three factors determined the course of the Mounted Police's transformation from the First World War on. By then, almost half a century had passed by since the North-West Mounted Police (NWMP) came into being in 1873. Sparked into action by the brutal massacre of a group of Cree in the Cypress Hills by whiskey traders, Prime Minister John A. Macdonald created a body that he had long believed represented the ideal tool for ensuring the orderly development of western Canada as opposed to the perceived lawlessness that seemed endemic in the American West. Originally Macdonald had considered employing westerners, specifically Métis, albeit as rank-and-file members and not as officers, in this new force. This plan ended with the Métis-initiated Red River Resistance. Instead, the personnel came largely from eastern Canada. The first glorious tale of adventure, the initial trek across the west in 1874, nearly ended in tragedy because it was poorly planned and organized.[6]

Clumsy beginnings aside, the nineteenth-century scarlet-clad force represented a fundamental break with a policing tradition in British North America that was based on the English system of the local constable and the common law. First appearing in the eleventh or twelfth century, constables were often known as tythingmen, borsholders, or headboroughs depending on the particular region of England in which they served. Their duties were first codified in 1285 under the Statute of Winchester, the only major English act on law enforcement until 1829.[7] The constable served at least three masters: himself, the Crown, and his fellow citizens. The final two competing loyalties were recognized in song by Surrey constable James Gyffon:

> The Justices will set us by the heels,
> If we do not as we should;
> Which if we perform, the townsmen will storm;
> Some of them hang's if they could.[8]

This form of policing first appeared in British North America in Quebec after the 1837–8 rebellions.[9]

The Mounted Police had completely different origins. Wanting a police force that could perform both military and civil roles in what amounted to Canadian colonial lands, John A. Macdonald modelled the men in scarlet after the Royal Irish Constabulary (RIC). The goal of the RIC's English masters was to control the Irish. In this respect the RIC was not a traditional police force, but a paramilitary one with the firepower to match and a home base in barracks. Still, it managed to perform the functions of a regular police force, while acting as a subtler tool than the military for dealing with turmoil in Ireland.[10]

Like the RIC, the Mounted Police policed its domain as an outsider. Serving as the police force in western and northern Canada, Mounties slowly strengthened their position as they balanced law and order with community policing needs. Prostitution was one area where the NWMP often looked the other way. On the other hand, when the men in scarlet elected to rigidly enforce liquor laws a huge civilian furore ensued forcing the police to back down. A more serious setback occurred in 1885 when the Métis soundly defeated a group of Mounties at Duck Lake and removed the force from the remainder of the rebellion.[11]

The force's future looked especially dim as the nineteenth century ended. Wilfrid Laurier and the Liberals, strong champions of provincial rights, captured power in 1896. The new government's responsibilities included overseeing the Mounted Police, a federal remnant of the Conservative era. And they had little sympathy for Mounted Policemen, now that western settlement, the original purpose behind the force's creation, seemed well underway. Then, in a scenario that would be echoed at the end of the First World War, an event arose that helped save the NWMP from extinction. Prospectors discovered gold in the Yukon and Mounties went to work policing the gold fields. Once again, they were seen to have brought law and order to a lawless frontier.[12] The importance of the NWMP was further demonstrated when it remained as the provincial police force for Alberta and Saskatchewan after the provinces' creation in 1905.

Slowly the fame and myth of the NWMP grew. Here, after all, was an outfit that had seemingly kept the frontier orderly and safe for settlers; memoirs, and works of biography and fiction, paralleled later by films, only reinforced this view. The Mounted Police gained even greater attention when some policemen, in keeping with the paramilitary nature of the force, fought as a unit in the Boer War. For this participation and thirty years of service, King Edward VII rewarded the entire force with the title 'Royal' in 1904.

Their service before and even into the First World War involved a wide variety of tasks, some representing familiar police work, others less so. Traditional police pursuits like investigating murderers and, in an important crime that reflected the agrarian nature of the west, cattle and horse rustling filled the former category. Upholding moral laws played a part in police work as well. Arrests were made for crimes such as seduction or abortion and even libel. Then there were the more varied tasks: regularly reporting on the quality of crops; visiting settlers in remote locations; enforcing a variety of provincial and federal ordinances and statutes, particularly the Indian Act, and arresting and transporting to asylums those deemed insane. It even served as a de facto prison branch for on average more than a thousand prisoners a year convicted of minor offences or awaiting trial.[13]

Although a degree of continuity remained, the Great War had an immediate impact on the Mounted Police. Prairie Canada was home to thousands of immigrants, including Germans and Austrians. With war, overnight they became 'enemy aliens.' Fearing the presence of a fifth column in western Canada, the government increased RNWMP ranks by 505 noncommissioned officers and constables shortly after the war began. Almost all of these new recruits were trained at Regina, headquarters of the Mounted Police, and also the location of a reserve unit capable of dealing with any major disturbance. Cumulatively, 93 per cent of the force's membership was stationed in Saskatchewan and Alberta in 1914.[14]

Until the end of 1916 the Mounted Police mixed regular policing duties with new war work, including the monitoring of enemy aliens in Alberta and Saskatchewan, the latter task mandated by an Order in Council passed by the federal government in October 1914. At the beginning of 1917, Alberta and Saskatchewan formed their own police forces, thereby freeing the Mounties from regular policing, except for the continued enforcement of federal statutes and other special duties. The decision reflected, in part, the simple fact that the Mounted Police was trying to do too much with too few resources. Commissioner Perry had written Borden in October 1916 to suggest that a more effective force was possible only if it was freed from regular policing duties in Alberta and Saskatchewan.[15] The senior Mountie also wanted his charges to make a direct contribution to the war effort with an overseas unit of their very own, instead of being relegated to more mundane work like enforcing new prohibition laws on the home front. What the commissioner had no desire to lose, however, was a monopoly on internal security. The Mounted Police continued to patrol the prairie section of the border with the United States while keeping a 'close supervision of enemy nationalities' and maintaining a special unit in Regina ready to be sent wherever mayhem might arise.[16] Perry had established priorities for Mountie attentions that would survive the war.

This was the history of the Mounted Police up to the time when Perry began to churn out memoranda in 1918 and 1919 on the future of the force. It was about to enter an era of uncertainty. The same was true of Canada. In effect, the First World War marked the collapse of the nineteenth century and the beginning of a completely different world. Sixty thousand Canadians would not be returning from France; they may not have recognized home anyway. That change actually began before the war, but the conflict intensified it. To create a role for the RNWMP in the postwar period, Perry had to be aware of the realities of the new Canada.

That new nation really began with the arrival into power of Wilfrid Laurier and the Liberals in 1896. Laurier, as has been frequently noted, declared that the twentieth century would be Canada's. Western Canada would play a key position in his dream. This hinterland region was to be the great breadbasket for the rest of the nation and the world. Immigrants were the key factor in constructing this new Canada. Under the influence of cabinet minister Clifford Sifton, massive immigration to Canada began, including the entrance of nontraditional immigrants such as 'men in sheepskin coats' – hardy peasants who knew how to make a farm work because it was in their blood and the blood of countless generations before them. Those Sifton deemed unsuited for life in western Canada – urban proletarians, African Americans, Asians, and southern Europeans – were discouraged from entering. While Britain and the United States continued to be the main sources for new Canadians, for the first time eastern and central

Europeans began to arrive in Canada in sizable numbers. The population of Canada as a whole increased by 64 per cent between 1901 and 1921.[17]

The newcomers arrived in a nation undergoing rapid change; they were part of the transformation, but it extended beyond them. The year 1921 was a significant one in that metamorphosis – for the first time, the Canadian population became half urban. This urban component included a growing industrial proletariat, a reflection of the increasing importance of industrialization and manufacturing to the economy of Canada. In the west the workers of the new factories, railways, and mines were often eastern and central Europeans who could not make a successful career at farming or who, despite Sifton's opposition, had been brought in by business interests as industrial labourers in the first place.[18]

Rapid change sparked friction. The presence of non-Anglo-Canadians, or 'foreigners' as they were derogatorily labelled, generated hostility from entrenched ethnic groups, particularly those of a British background. British Columbia became the centre of anti-Asian sentiment, largely fuelled by a belief that the targets of the hatred could not be assimilated.[19] For other newcomers, assimilation – or, in the rhetoric of the day, 'Canadianization' – was to be their fate. Even those more sympathetically inclined towards immigrants, such as social gospeller J.S. Woodsworth and author Ralph Connor, believed in the need for assimilation. Education became the key for building these new Canadians and anything perceived as an impediment to such important work met with widespread opposition. When the government allowed immigrant groups like Ukrainians to establish block settlements, the hackles of nativists rose out of the fear that such settlements discouraged assimilation.[20]

More than immigration was changing Canada. Organized labour was also on the rise: its numbers grew fivefold between 1900 and 1914. The growth of capitalism in the late nineteenth and early twentieth century had driven Canada's immigration policy as businessmen sought a cheap pool of labour. Workers increasingly saw their strength in unity and numbers. Slowly, in turn, the Canadian unions they belonged to became branches of larger American ones.[21] Those who belonged to unions, however, tended to be the skilled workers. The unskilled, including a large number of non-British labourers, were left to fend for themselves.

Industrial disputes often occurred, with many degenerating into violent clashes between strikers and the militia or police. Once the war began, labour peace quickly ensued in the initial excitement and patriotism of the conflict. This respite, however, lasted only mid-way through the war when a new spirit of resistance emerged, inspired in part by rampant inflation and the enormous loss of life which fuelled discontent on the part of Canadian workers. Conscription only made matters worse; they might have to go off and die in France while business leaders such as Joseph Flavelle grew financially fat off of supplying the war effort. The number of strikes in Canada, which had declined precipitously in the first two years of the war, rose rapidly in its last years.[22] As Commissioner Perry wrote his first memorandum on the future of the force in October 1918, the Winnipeg General Strike was only a few months away.

Even more disturbing to those in power than the growth of union-ism and labour strength was the concomitant appearance of radical-ism. Organized labour tended to support the traditional parties, but some workers, especially non-British ones, began to listen to appeals from more radical adherents, including some from the socialist parties that had appeared in Canada at the turn of the century. These parties frequently fought amongst themselves over issues of policy and doc-trine, diminishing their threat to the status quo of capitalism.[23] The turning point in the growth of radicalism, however, occurred outside Canada in 1917, when first the tsar was toppled in Russia in February, and then the Bolsheviks under Vladimir Lenin overturned the govern-ment of Aleksandr Kerenski in October creating the world's first communist state. The Soviet Union was a clear challenge to capital-ism in two ways: it represented an alternative to the capitalist status quo, and it demonstrated to workers around the world the potential strength of working-class people. Moreover, senior Bolsheviks, espe-cially Lenin, sought to promote world revolution.[24]

Commissioner Perry had more than Reds, radicals, strikers, and immigrants to consider in late 1918 as he drew up a blueprint for the RNWMP's future. His worries also included the audience for his list of proposed changes – the government of Canada. He had to reflect on the demands and needs of the Canadian state (state constituting more than the political face of government and including various levels of government as well as government departments).[25] Was it an arm's length association or one of a police force that did the bidding of the state without asking questions?

The belief in the independence of the police is very much a British concept and quite different from attitudes in the United States, which has had a long tradition of mixing policing and politics.[26] On the other side, some theorists view the police as merely a tool of the state – there to ensure the dominance of one class, one group, and one ideology, often, but not exclusively, in the form of capitalism.[27] With the Mounted Police, notions of police impartiality and separateness from government are not historically tenable. The federal government served as the Mounties' creator, appointed their commissioner, set their budgets, repeatedly received information from Mounted Police reports, and often issued orders to the force. The words of one scholar effectively capture this relationship: 'The civil police is a social organization created and sustained by political processes to enforce dominant conceptions of public order.'[28]

This does not mean, though, that the RCMP, particularly its rank-and-file members, has always been a pliant tool of the government. The relationship has been more complicated, since the RCMP enforces laws and carries out policies designed by the Canadian state, while exercising a great deal of power of its own in determining the nature of these laws and policies and how they were to be enforced.

Who or what determined the policy and direction of the Mounted Police between 1914 and 1939? Personality and politics were significant. The Mounties experienced excellent relations with Conservative governments, both provincially and federally, during the opening decades of the twentieth century. Individual commissioners factored into the success or failure of the relationship. Commissioner Perry enjoyed a better relationship with the Conservatives than with the Liberals, while J.H. MacBrien, who served from 1931 to 1938 after being handpicked by the R.B. Bennett government, was arguably the most influential commissioner in the history of the post-Perry RCMP.[29]

While the party in power and the commissioner in charge were important, these factors alone do not answer the question of who or what ultimately directed Mounted Police operations. Official Mounted Police historians, Carl Betke and S.W. Horrall, have contended that the notion of an arm's-length relationship between the RCMP and the government, especially on security matters, was an illusion:

> It looked almost as if the politicians did not wish to be too closely associated in the public eye with the work of the security service ... Actually, nothing could have been further from the truth. The Minister of Justice met frequently with the Commissioner to discuss the activities of the R.C.M.P. In addition, the cabinet was informed through weekly or monthly reports of its intelligence work ... What the politicians preferred, however, was that the force appear to define its own role in these matters. The R.C.M.P. was left to steer the ship of security itself, but the Government was looking over its shoulder to make sure it was going in the right direction.[30]

The authors suggest that the RCMP was not entirely happy with this association:

> First of all, the Mounted Police were by instinct, training and experience officers of the law. They were used to having their conduct and responsibilities carefully defined by a multitude of statutes, regulations, and legal traditions. Secondly, in keeping them at arm's length, the government made the R.C.M.P. the principal butt of criticism for those opposed to its intelligence activities ... In their silent or evasive response to such accusations, the Governments tended to shift on to the shoulders of the R.C.M.P. criticism for policies for which they were in the final analysis responsible.[31]

There is a great deal of merit in Betke and Horrall's interpretation, but the situation was still more complicated than they suggest. Yes, the government maintained an artificial degree of separation in order to create a deniability factor when RCMP operations went awry. Even a strong commissioner like MacBrien discovered this reality in the aftermath of the Regina Riot, which had been provoked by the RCMP. The Conservative government of R.B. Bennett, which had followed the advice of its police force, sought to apportion some of the blame for the fiasco onto the RCMP.[32]

As at Regina in 1935, the advice offered by the RCMP appears to have been generally listened to by governments in this era, and that includes the government of William Lyon Mackenzie King during the 1920s. When J.S. Woodsworth contended in the House of Commons in 1924 that the Mounted Police had spied upon meetings he had addressed as well as upon other gatherings of radicals and workers, Ernest Lapointe, the minister of justice, turned to the RCMP for some words in defence of its actions. Commissioner Cortlandt Starnes sent the minister a lengthy memo which provided the government with a non-denial denial of the labour politician's allegations. This memo would serve as the basis for government obfuscation over whether Mounted Policemen were engaged in domestic spying activities.[33]

Yes, then, the government served as the ultimate controller of RCMP operations. But – and this is an important but – the police exercised a great deal of control over which policies the government selected. When the force offered options to the government, they were often designed to ensure the government chose the one preferred by the RCMP, or, at least, by the commissioner. The ultimate example of this selective packaging of proposals was Perry determining the future of the force at the end of the First World War. In his 30 October

1918 memo to the comptroller, one that he would duplicate for Borden in August 1919, the commissioner set forth three options for the force, the final one being his preferred choice. Accordingly, he was careful to emphasize the weaknesses of the first two options before recommending the amalgamation of the RNWMP and the Dominion Police.[34] The government issued the orders, but the advice of its 'experts' influenced the commands.

The frequent communication between the upper echelons of the force and various levels of government demonstrated the close relationship. Quite regularly, and especially during crises, RCMP officers shared confidential information with several different federal departments, particularly the Department of National Defence, which had a significant domestic security role to play during the period in question, and politicians, not to mention their provincial equivalents. Sometimes this was done at the behest of the department or branch of government, or just as frequently on the RCMP's own initiative.[35]

On rare occasions the Mounted Police found itself caught between two opposing levels of government. Again, the On to Ottawa Trek serves as the best example of this relationship. The Saskatchewan Liberal government under James Gardiner vigorously opposed the halting of the Trekkers in Regina during June 1935. Nevertheless, this became the preferred option of the federal Conservative government and of the RCMP, even though in this area the police should have officially answered to the government of Saskatchewan. In an earlier telegram to his subordinate S.T. Wood, MacBrien instructed him to ask the provincial attorney general to arrange for the riot act to be read in Regina in the event of disorder with the arrival of the Trekkers. If the attorney general refused, MacBrien ordered Wood to 'READ RIOT ACT YOURSELF IN YOUR CAPACITY AS JUSTICE OF THE PEACE BEFORE COMMENCING POLICE ACTION.'[36]

Municipalities had even less say when it came to the operations of the RCMP. In the early 1930s, the leadership of the city of Saskatoon worried about the potential for disorder that the operation of a temporary relief camp within city boundaries represented. On 6 November 1932, the mayor of Saskatoon contacted the deputy attorney general of Saskatchewan to request that twenty Mounties, plus horses, be sent to his city to police a demonstration of the unemployed scheduled for the following day. Despite going through proper channels, the mayor never received his requested RCMP contingent because J.W. Spalding, the assistant commissioner commanding Saskatchewan, decided, after consulting with his colleague in charge of the Saskatoon detachment, that they were not required.[37] Such communication illustrates that, at least when dealing with less powerful governments, it was often Mounted Police personnel who decided their own orders. But the concept of the Mounties as a reserve force to be plugged in wherever disorder occurred demonstrates their importance as an entity within the Canadian state, a reality outside of any particular partisan political context.

How did the state view the RCMP's role, and what was that role? Once more, the visions of the Mounted Police presented during the First World War are significant. In December 1918 Perry telegraphed the commander of the Mounted Police's military unit in Europe to alert his junior officer to the government's plan to fully reestablish the RNWMP by increasing its strength to twelve hundred and maintaining it either as 'a federal police force for the whole of Canada or a permanent unit of the Canadian Militia.'[38] The federal government had passed an Order in Council four days earlier that specifically set out various functions for the force to perform, not only in 1918, but for decades to follow:

(a) The enforcement of Federal Laws. (b) The patrolling and protection of the International Boundary Line. (c) The enforcement of all Orders-in-Council passed under the War Measures Act for the protection of the Public Safety. (d) Generally to aid and assist the civil powers in the preservation of law and order whenever the Government of Canada may direct.[39]

The enforcement of federal laws and statutes would make up a key portion of the work performed by the Mounted Police during the 1920s. Aiding the Department of Health in enforcing the Opium and Narcotic Drug Act (ONDA), policing Indian reserves, and administering the Inland Revenue Act kept the force busy. The number of RCMP investigations related to federal statutes increased from 2068 in 1921 to 8353 in 1932, while investigations undertaken for other departments and not related to federal statutes grew even more significantly from 8500 in 1921 to 83,216 in 1932.[40] R.C. Macleod sees this role for the police, particularly the latter point, as part of the 'great expansion of the Canadian state in the early twentieth century,' and thus crucial to the RCMP finding a niche to ensure its survival.[41] There is some validity to this notion, which fits well with the concept of 'state formation,' as the state expanded into a number of new areas, and the RCMP proved more cost effective in an era of penury; to completely subscribe to the argument is to ignore the deeper meaning of the force in the context of both its needs and the needs of the Canadian state in this period.

The concept of the Mounted Police as a military body, for example, was significant to the function it performed on behalf of the Canadian state. Right from the beginning, Canada's national police force had strong militaristic tendencies – hence its later military action in South Africa and Europe. It was for this very reason that Commissioner Perry suggested in his October 1918 memo that one possible future for the RNWMP would have seen it become part of Canada's permanent militia; this option was the path not taken by the federal government, which wanted more subtlety from the Mounted Police. Making them solely a military body would have transformed the RCMP from a hammer into a sledgehammer during an era of great disorder in Canada.

Strikes, radicalism, and discontent were widespread in Canada in 1918 and 1919. What options did the government have for dealing with the turmoil? The traditional method for handling a strike or protest was to send in the local militia to quiet the situation. This was a particularly blunt option since, in the words of Allan Greer, 'there was not much soldiers could do with rioters other than shoot them.'[42] Between 1876 and 1914 the militia was called out forty-eight times in Canada, thirty-three of them to deal with strikes. From the end of the First World War to 1970, however, the military was used only four times, despite the fact that 'aid to the civil power remained a military responsibility.'[43] The reason why is quite simple: the RCMP came to serve this function in areas outside Quebec and Ontario. The militia and regular military had become the course of last resort. This was true of the Winnipeg General Strike, the Estevan Strike and Riot, the Saskatoon Relief Camp Riot, coal strikes in Alberta, and events surrounding the On to Ottawa Trek. In at least three of these examples, military units were readied in case the RCMP proved incapable of dealing with the perceived threats. Only in Winnipeg did soldiers take to the streets, and this was after the Mounted Police had already invoked lethal force to disperse demonstrators.[44]

To make the Mounted Police especially reliable, the government passed an Order in Council in October of 1918 prohibiting members of the Mounted Police from forming or joining a union. Words within the Order in Council left little doubt as to the reasoning behind this prohibition; the police were responsible for 'the maintenance of order in connection with strikes, lockouts or labour disturbances.'[45]

Governments change, however, and policies frequently shift with them. Thus, arose the second challenge to the Mounted Police's future. If the first represented a crisis of context through the uncertainty of war, the second was a problem of politics and even personality. The Liberals since Laurier had viewed the Mounties with less than enthusiasm and this scrutiny only increased under King's leadership of the government. He became convinced, encouraged in this belief by the Liberal premier of Saskatchewan, James Gardiner, that when it came to promotions among officers loyal Liberal Mounties were being punished for their beliefs in favour of those with Conservative inclinations; on occasion he even complained about this perceived discrimination.[46]

King's concern about the anti-Liberal nature of the RCMP seemed to translate into a curtailing of the responsibilities of the Mounties in the interwar period. R.C. Macleod notes that Prime Minister King informed the House of Commons in 1922 that the Mounted Police would not police strikes and other labour disturbances. Despite this assurance, King was as ambivalent as usual and in the end the desire for state security trumped personal pique. During the debate in the House, the prime minister said that according to its governing act, quelling labour disputes should not be a function of the force and was more suitable work for the militia.[47] But at the same time as its leader was promising to refrain from using the RCMP in a traditional militia role, the Liberal government briefly transferred the Mounted Police from the Department of Justice to the Department of National Defence, a move which made sense, Macleod admits, 'if the RCMP were to act primarily as a backup for forces in cases of civil unrest, a role previously performed by the militia.'[48] Additionally, in the same debate in the House, two Conservative members of Parliament articulated the new role for the Mounted Police in the interwar period. Party leader and former prime minister, Arthur Meighen, called for the RCMP, which he believed to be a more effective tool than the militia when it came to ensuring law and order, to be a 'mobile police reserve' with forces concentrated in strategic locations across the country. Another Conservative member of Parliament encouraged the federal government to leave the RCMP under the control of the Department of Justice. In doing so he hinted at the essential role the Mounted Police could play in place of the militia: 'We have had troubles in past strikes and that sort of thing, and although under the present Militia Act it is within the power of a municipality to call upon the militia to turn out for the preservation of law and order, that is the very last resort that should be adopted in this country.'[49]

Then there was the force's security role, a crucial component in its efforts at maintaining order and in its quest for survival. Throughout the 1920s and 1930s Mounties in Alberta and Saskatchewan, and elsewhere in Canada, collected information on a wide range of people and groups. Some scholars question the significance of this role since the security records form a small percentage of the RCMP's overall total, and the RCMP security personnel at headquarters in the 1930s were no more than a handful. While numerically accurate, this observation glosses over the fact that in this period the force's security operations stretched from headquarters down to each division through the Criminal Investigation Branch (CIB). It was not until the 1930s that a greater separation between regular policing and security work began and long after the Second World War smaller detachments across Canada continued to have a blurring between the security and policing roles.[50]

Two additional points should be made. For the state and the general public in this or any period not all police activities had equal value. Spying on communists and busting Chinese opium dealers and addicts carried far more currency with the state and with many citizens than enforcement of some of the more mundane federal statutes. The Mounted Police was an instrument of control in itself, something the provincial governments of Alberta and Saskatchewan were well aware of. Soon after the RCMP replaced the Saskatchewan Provincial Police in 1928, the government of Alberta, which had previously blanched at replacing its provincial police force, considered a similar move. Premier J.E. Brownlee wrote to the attorney general of his eastern neighbour to collect information on the experience. The Mounted Police's effectiveness at policing the Noxious Weeds Act or at catching shoplifters in small-town Saskatchewan did not interest the Alberta leader; he wanted to know about the willingness of the RCMP to deal with challenges to order, specifically from labour and the unemployed.[51] His Saskatchewan correspondent assured him that the 'Police have co-operated in every way with us and ... I am satisfied will do everything they can to help us.'[52] Equally, regular policing duties, while significant, in no way made the RCMP different from the various provincial bodies they replaced. If daily policing was the determining factor in the future of the Mounted Police, then Alberta and Saskatchewan would still have provincial police forces.

No, the Mounted Police survived because the state saw it as more than a regular police force. After 1919 the RCMP had a national presence, allowing for the coordination of some aspect of policing efforts, whether criminal or security. The men in scarlet could also play several roles: a unit involved in ordinary policing; a heavily armed militia capable of dealing with strikes and riots; and a secret service charged with gathering information on a wide range of individuals and groups. The RCMP represented flexibility in relation to any policing alternative. These various roles, which often coincided in Alberta and Saskatchewan between 1914 and 1939, first appeared, and were acknowledged and emphasized as such, during the First World War.[53] And these powers of the Mounted Police became increasingly focused on those deemed threats to the status quo of order and morality: immigrant and ethnic communities, workers, and radicals. The RCMP had a domestic war to both police and fight.

Commissioner Perry knew of these realities in 1918. He was aware of the challenges, both real and imagined, to the status quo posed by a wide range of groups; he had a very good idea of what the state expected from the Mounted Police; and he understood the nature of the force. Any successful police force, he concluded in his 3 December 1918 memo, had to depend on

1. Its organization.
2. Its personnel.
3. Its discipline.
4. Its training.
5. Its Esprit de Corps.[54]

He did not, however, spell out any specifics. What then was the nature of the training that Mountie recruits went through? Who were the recruits? What sort of values did the world's most famous police force instil in its rank and file and officers? Many people at the time thought they knew what it was like to be a Mounted Policeman. After all, one only had to pick up one of the numerous books written on the topic or attend a moving picture show to see what glamorous and exciting lives the scarlet-uniformed men on horseback led. The actual life of a Mountie in this period, not surprisingly, differed considerably.

3

Men in Scarlet

'What did you say your name was?'

'Kemp,' I replied.

'Where did you come from?'

'My home's right here [in Prince Albert, Saskatchewan]. But originally I'm from England. The family came over a couple of years ago.'

'Ye gods,' he cried to the others. 'Did you hear that? Another bloody Englishman. How many does that make now in the post? Apart from the OC [Officer Commanding], who's a French Canadian, I'm the only native-born, true-blue Canadian in the place. The force is getting lousy with these blokes from England.'[1]

Fifteen-year-old Vernon Kemp received a rough ride from a barracks mate after he joined the Mounted Police in Prince Albert in 1910. After all, what was an Englishman doing as a member of the ultimate Canadian symbol? Far from being unrepresentative, in reality, Kemp exemplified the dominant characteristics of the force in this period: he was an English-born male.

Commissioner Perry's memos of late 1918 dealt with the force's future in a broad sense. However, who really were the members of the Mounted Police that Perry's recommendations would affect? How did these ordinary men drawn from society as constructed at the time see their job, their employer, and the world around them? Examining who the men in scarlet were leads directly to a better comprehension of what they did. Moreover, to understand some of the most important characteristics of the Mounted Police in this era – their gender, ethnicities, and class – requires inspection. Too often in previous works about the Mounties, these factors have been ignored.

First, there was the ethnic component of their background. Ethnicity/race was, in the words of Catherine Hall, 'increasingly seen as a crucial dividing line between peoples' and there was a clear hierarchy, even within so-called constructs like 'white.'[2] The socially constructed notion of race influenced how Mounties perceived the society around them. Ever a changing concept, those with power in society equated race in this era, including what it meant be 'white,' with what later came to be understood as ethnicity.[3] Thus to Mounties and many others in Canada at the time, both Ukrainians and Chinese were racial groups, albeit not equal ones in the view of the dominant society that created and enforced the legal system.

Like Kemp, many policemen were English, a label, according to Hall, full of significance and symbolism:

> That national identity [English] was powerfully articulated by middle-class men in [the nineteenth century]: men who claimed to speak for the nation and on behalf of others ... The search for masculine independence, for a secure identity, was built on their assertion of their superiority over the decadent aristocracy, over dependent females, over children, servants and employers, over the peoples of the Empire, over all *others* who were not English, male and middle class.[4]

This ethnic background made the Mounties an ideal choice for the Canadian state when it sought a tool to deal with class, ethnic, and political challenges to the status quo in the interwar period. After seeing their very future questioned in the early 1920s, Mounted Police personnel quickly found a niche for themselves. The fact that the force, especially its officer corps – described by one ex-member as 'an elite, above the nitty-gritty of day-to-day law enforcement' – usually shared the values, world outlook, and ethnic and gender background of those who designed public policy in Canada only increased its chances of survival.[5]

What were the wider values of Anglo-Canadian society from which members of the political and economic elite were drawn? Examining its roots provides some answers to this question. Although the Great War had discredited in many quarters the imperialist form of Canadian nationalism identified by historian Carl Berger, large parts of Canadian society still embraced perceived Anglo values and characteristics.[6] Ethnocentrism was a prominent part of this identity in the latter half of the nineteenth century and the first few decades of the next. Generations of children connected to the little island nation demonstrated it in the gratitude of their daily prayers:

How happy is our lot
Who live on Britain's isle
Which is of heaven the favour'd spot,
Where countless blessings smile.[7]

Anglo-Canada reflected its dominant origins in every way, including prejudice towards those of different backgrounds. The Canadian educational system, heavily influenced by Britain, cultivated and reinforced these prejudices. Textbooks such as *History of England for Public Schools* inculcated Canadian schoolchildren with a sense of English nationalism and a pride and recognition of the fact that the English made up only a seventh of its empire's population:

Unless this fact is grasped clearly, it is impossible to appreciate the wonderful work being done in controlling and civilizing the millions of subject peoples, comprising hundreds of races, each with its own language, customs, and religion. Rarely, if ever, does Britain find it necessary to resort to force in governing her subject peoples. Even their prejudices are respected, their religion, their social customs, and local laws are seldom interfered with, unless for the purpose of preventing crime or abolishing brutal customs.[8]

Even reformers sympathetic to the plight of immigrants and ethnic minorities reflected the prevailing prejudices of Anglo-Canadian society.[9]

Whether born in Britain or Canada, the vast majority of Mounted Policemen were products of English-dominated societies. In 1914 Prime Minister Robert Borden, under questioning from the opposition, confirmed proudly in the House of Commons that the United Kingdom had supplied 79 per cent of the members of the Mounted Police. (see table 3.1). He added that of ninety-eight British recruits in 1913 '45 were old soldiers, a large proportion from the Guards and Cavalry. All promised to be very serviceable members of the force.' [10]

Not surprisingly, many, including some in the official opposition, wanted to know why Canadians lacked enthusiasm for their national police force. Two ready answers were poor wages and even worse working conditions, which discouraged Canadian men from joining, forcing the government to recruit actively in Britain. Sixty cents a day

Table 3.1. National origin of Mounties, 1914

Origin	Total	% of total
United Kingdom	490	79
Canada	76	12
Other British possessions	24	4
United States	10	2
Foreign Countries	17	3
Total	617	100

Source: Canada, House of Commons, Debates, 12 February 1914, 710

represented Vernon Kemp's initial wage upon joining in 1910. That daily amount for the bottom rung later rose to $.75 in 1912 and $1.25 in 1935 (approximately $17 in 2001 dollars).[11] For a considerable period of time this wage was below what an unskilled labourer could hope to attain, and unskilled labourers did not always have their jobs follow them home. Mounties, especially those in small towns and rural areas, found themselves literally on duty around the clock, having to deal with aspects of life, especially homicides and accidents, which no one else wanted to experience.

On the other hand, despite occasional bursts of excitement, banality reigned when it came to many of the duties of an ordinary Mountie in Alberta and Saskatchewan. The day-to-day life of most Mounted Policemen consisted of uneventful patrols, not criminal investigations. During the month of November 1919, for example, a constable at the Short Creek Detachment in Saskatchewan travelled 375 miles, or an average of 21 miles for each day he ventured out on his horse. In only one case did his journeys involve the investigation of a crime, the actual responsibility at the time of the Saskatchewan Provincial Police. Most of his excursions involved 'registering aliens,' 'general patrol,' and another activity categorized only as 'Re: Mail.'[12] Technology had crept in elsewhere at the same time. The North Portal Detachment in Saskatchewan used trains, an 'auto cycle,' and automobiles for transportation, allowing for a much wider area (934 miles) to be covered in a month.[13] The reality of police work translated into a little acknowledged statistic. In the first 120 years of the Mounted Police, the number one killer of those who died in the line of duty was not an escaped prisoner, a desperate bank robber, or an angry rioter. Instead, accidents claimed 62 per cent of those killed while on active duty, a figure twice as high as the number murdered on the job.[14]

Then there were the actual conditions many policemen worked under for their low wages. As late as October 1915, the six members of the Mounted Police detachment at Yorkton slept in a fifteen-by-twenty-foot room, situated directly above the guard room, which had no sanitary facilities for the prisoners and only one bathtub and four wash basins for the police and prisoners to share. Finally, after typhoid fever struck one Mountie, six constables petitioned Commissioner Perry for better facilities.[15] Such environments contributed to some seeking employment elsewhere (see table 3.2). In 1919, the last occasion when a detailed breakdown of discharges appeared, roughly one in four of those who opted to leave did so either by purchasing an early exit or by outright desertion (see table 3.3).

Whether in 1914 or 1919, the Mounties who deserted or purchased their freedom may have hesitated in complaining about poor conditions because of the force's harsh discipline, a further reflection of the militaristic nature of the RCMP. 'Desertions,' after all, are something soldiers do. Under section 30 of the *Rules and Regulations for the Government and Guidance of the Royal Canadian Mounted Police*, rank-and-file Mounties could face arrest for 'making any anonymous complaint to the government or the Commissioner; communicating without the Commissioner's authority, either directly or indirectly, to the public press any matter or thing touching the force.' The leadership of the force and the government also consistently blocked efforts at unionization throughout the twentieth century.[16]

The harsh life of a Mountie did not discourage all. Former British military men of the type Borden praised in the House of Commons found the emphasis on discipline and hierarchy especially appealing.[17] These same ex-soldiers, however, chose to enlist to fight for king and empire once the First World War began (60 per cent of volunteers from Canada by the end of 1915 were British born).[18] Many would never return from the killing fields of western Europe, but while Canadians replaced them, the values of the RCMP remained constant.

Even as Canadian content in the lower ranks of the RCMP increased throughout the 1920s and especially during the Depression, when alternative employment did not exist, a significant English presence remained. A new policeman discovered this reality upon joining in 1934: 'the four Commissioned Officers in 'Depot' were Englishmen. The chief Riding Sergeant-Major was born in England. The Corporal who was the riding instructor for my squad was an English man, former member of the famous British Cavalry regiment ... Our P.T. instructor was an Englishman ... Another drill instructor formerly of Gordon Highlanders stationed on N.W. Frontier

Table 3.2. Statistics related to Canada-wide non-commissioned officers and constables, 1914–1939

Year	Discharged	Engaged	Total members	% change from previous year
1914	262	767	1213	–
1915	630	286	869	–28.36
1916	354	225	740	–14.84
1917	434	297	603	–18.51
1918	310	876	886[a]	46.93
1919	564	1848	1540	73.81
1920	853	917	1608	4.42
1921	549	558	1610	0.12
1922	144	591	1167	–27.52
1923	261	188	1090	–6.60
1924	269	141	962	–11.74
1925	141	103	924	–3.95
1926	161	148	910	–1.52
1927	133	174	952	4.62
1928[b]	165	246	1033	8.51
1929	112	318	1145	10.84
1930	193	239	1189	3.84
1931	169	277	1292	8.66
1932[c]	197	1176	2257	74.69
1933[d]	415	571	2209	–2.13
1934	248	317	2263	2.44
1935	203	347	2410	6.50
1936	211	67	2261	–6.18
1937	187	212	2277	0.71
1938	234	239	2290	0.57
1939	1110	2274	2458	7.34

[a] This figure includes the 443 NCOs and constables who found themselves transferred to RNWMP 'B' Squadron (Cavalry), CEF, for service in Siberia.
[b] In 1928 the RCMP replaced the Saskatchewan Provincial Police.
[c] In 1932 the RCMP took over provincial policing functions in Alberta, Manitoba, New Brunswick, Nova Scotia, and Prince Edward Island.
[d] This year marks the beginning of annual reports that coincided with the end of the fiscal year (31 March). The first report covered eighteen months.
Source: RCMP Annual Reports.

in India – and on and on.'[19] Another who served in Saskatchewan in the 1930s simply noted that there were 'too damned many of them.'[20] Numbers culled from obituaries in the *R.C.M.P. Quarterly* of some of those who served in Alberta and Saskatchewan between 1914 and 1939 demonstrate that the English-born represented the single largest

Table 3.3. Mountie careers ended nation-wide, 1914, and 1919

Category	Total number in 1919	As % in 1919	As % in 1914
Time expired	45	7.98	4.96
Died	4	0.71	1.52
Purchased	92.	16.31	15.26
Deserted	45	7.98	10.30
Bad conduct	37	6.56	18.32
Inefficiency	25	4.43	6.20
Invalided	167	29.61	0
Pensioned	5	0.89	0.38
Spec. Csts. dismissed	69	12.23	42.74
Free discharge after rejoining on leave from CEF	69	12.23	0
Total	564	100	100

Source: RNWMP Annual Reports for 1919, 1914.

definable ethnic group among those not Canadian born (see table 3.4). It is also likely that a substantial number among the 'Canadian' category had some sort of connection to England. For instance, former commissioner C.W. Harvison was Ontario born. His father, however, left Britain at the age of four and although his 'memories of the Old Country were vague ... he retained a deep-rooted loyalty to England, the Crown, and the Flag.'[21]

Even more important than ethnicity in understanding the nature of the Mounted Policemen who persevered through military-style discipline, low wages, poor working conditions, and boredom, is gender. Whereas Mounties came from a variety of national backgrounds, albeit with Anglo-Celtic values in the dominant position, all members of the force were men. Gender analysis applied to male institutions is a more recent development in the historical profession. In *The Gender of Breadwinners*, historian Joy Parr dismisses the usual dichotomy of women as the product of gender and men of class. 'Men, like women,' she challenges, 'were gendered subjects.'[22]

Components of gender are also not rigid but frequently contradic-

Table 3.4. National origin of selected Alberta and Saskatchewan Mounties, 1914–1939[a]

National origin	Total	% of total
English	197	25
Irish	27	3
Scottish and Welsh	22	3
Other[b]	34	4
Canadian	517	65
Total	797	100

[a] Because of spotty reporting in the *R.C.M.P. Quarterly* and the destruction of manuscript records deemed historically insignificant, these numbers are not complete. Nevertheless, the sample size is large enough to indicate trends confirmed by other statistics and qualitative comments.
[b] Other includes the United States and other European nations.
Source: *R.C.M.P. Quarterly*.

tory, complex, and ever evolving.[23] In the case of masculinity, or, more accurately, masculinities, historian Gail Bederman distinguishes between manliness and masculinity. Manliness, more of a nineteenth-century notion, emphasized honour, self-control, and order. Masculinity, on the other hand, was displacing manliness as a primary middle-class male definition by the early twentieth century, or, in the phrase of R.W. Connell, was in the process of becoming a 'hegemonic masculinity.'[24] It stressed physicality, size, and violence. Masculine identity was constantly in flux, in particular in this era because increasingly middle-class men of a certain ethnic background believed themselves to be under threat from working-class men, a group closely associated with a more physical form of maleness.[25]

The early-twentieth-century men who wore the famous red serge reflected the broader middle-class currents of male identity and that identity was an important issue to the Canadian state between 1914 and 1939. Although not rigidly so, manliness remained more prevalent among the officers, authority figures perceived as calm and authoritative, while masculinity was primarily cultivated in the rank and file, the ones required to use brute force as part of the job.

Collectively, their class and the dominant Anglo-Celtic ethnicity meant that society had inculcated both officers and the rank and file with certain masculine values. Patriotism represented one such emphasis, although it was part of a larger group of values that contributed to the Victorian ideal of manliness: 'physical courage, chivalric ideals, virtuous fortitude, with additional connotations of military and patriotic virtues.'[26] In the later Victorian period, spartan stoicism was increasingly encouraged in the young. The belief, according to Bederman, was that 'by gaining the manly strength to control himself, a man gained the strength, as well as the duty, to protect and direct those weaker than himself.'[27] Part of the motivation behind the promotion of such values represented an effort at controlling working-class males.[28] Organizations, such as the Boy Scouts and the Boys' Brigade, sprang up in an effort to indoctrinate working-class boys with the values of their supposed superiors. The latter organization promoted 'the advancement of Christ's Kingdom among Boys and the promotion of habits of Obedience, Reverence, Discipline, Self-Respect and all that tends towards a true Christian Manliness.'[29]

The more popular and famous Boy Scouts (10,000 adherents in 1910 in English Canada) promoted similar values, albeit with the emphasis on Christianity replaced by a promotion of patriotism and militarism.[30] As Lord Baden-Powell's *Scouting for Boys* noted in 1908: 'Every boy ought to learn how to shoot and to obey orders, else he is no more good when war breaks out than an old woman.' Baden-Powell was also famous for the phrase 'BE A BRICK,' which encouraged scouts to accept the status quo and their lot within it:

If you are discontented with your place or with your neighbours or if you are a rotten brick, you are no good to the wall. You are rather a danger. If the bricks get quarreling among themselves the wall is liable to split and the whole house to fall.

Some bricks may be high up and others low down in the wall; but all must make the best of it and play in their place for the good of the whole. So it is among people; each of us has his place in the world, it is no use being discontented, it is no use hating our neighbours because they are higher up or lower down than themselves. We are all Britons, and it is our duty each to play in his place and help his neighbours. Then we shall remain strong and united, and then there will be no fear of the whole building – namely, our great Empire – falling down because of rotten bricks in the wall.[31]

The masculine Mountie exhibited the values of the society that produced an organization like the Boy Scouts.

As part of the transformation in 'white' male middle-class identity, the ideal male body shape changed. During the 1850s, a lean and wiry body was the middle-class ideal. By the turn of the century, however, there was an increasing emphasis on large, muscular bodies. It is no coincidence that this was an age when heavyweight boxing not only became the most popular form of pugilism, but also enjoyed increasing popularity outside the working class.[32] The RCMP celebrated the new ideal male body type. A thirty-five inch chest, the minimum requirement for a new recruit, was more highly valued in the Mounted Police of the early twentieth century than a high school education, the latter not a requirement until 1974.[33] Having a 'good physique' was the first thing that came to the mind of a former Mountie upon being asked the characteristics of a competent police officer.[34] Commissioner Perry reflected this approach to policing in the 1919 annual report when he lamented that many of those allowed in turned out to be 'unsuitable' mainly because of 'physical unfitness.' 'Examining surgeons do not recognize,' a clearly irritated Perry wrote, 'that the force has no place for weaklings.'[35] This observation reflected a turn-of-the-century discourse in which many in North America and Britain feared that the 'white race' was in decline. Two events confirmed and fuelled this apprehension. In 1903 a former military man alleged that the British Army rejected 60 per cent of volunteers because they had been found physically incapable, prompting talk of the deterioration of the 'manly British character.'[36] In the United States seven years later, the battering of that generation's 'Great White Hope' by Jack Johnson, an African-American boxer, ignited race riots and killings across the country as many so-called white men viewed the loss of the fight as a blow to their identity. The concern about racial decline sparked efforts and schemes to improve all aspects of white males.[37]

Commissioner Perry's remark additionally demonstrated the dominant-gendered construction of policing, specifically the emphasis on physicality. Policing had long been a profession that emphasized more physical masculine values as opposed to the Victorian emphasis on manliness. In his study of the early-twentieth-century Toronto police, historian Greg Marquis explored the masculine nature of that force: 'the atmosphere of the police station was akin to that of the military barracks where job socialization and the camaraderie of the all-male group interacted with working-class culture to produce an exaggerated masculinity.'[38] That 'police culture,' continued Marquis, was

> manifested in the maintenance of a bold front with the public, feats of physical courage, support of fellow workers, direct action and the use of colourful language ... The military background of many Toronto recruits no doubt enhanced this rough culture ... The image of the patrolmen as exercising restraint yet able to take care of

themselves in the rough and tumble of the beat, an image in keeping with the working-class concept of 'masculiness,' did much to maintain popular admiration for the department.[39]

These male characteristics and values were not simply applicable to the Toronto Police or the working classes; they were even truer of Mounted Policemen, many of whom actually lived in barracks in remote places and in all-male atmospheres.[40]

One practical factor encouraged Mounted Police personnel to embrace willingly the male identity constructed for them: their superiors employed these very values to judge their capability as a Mountie. For instance, the criteria used to evaluate noncommissioned and commissioned officers reflected both the older Victorian manly characteristics and the newer emphasis on physical power. The evaluation form contained a section entitled, 'Physical and Athletic Qualifications,' and assessed Mounties according to the following categories: 'Appearance,' 'Physique,' 'Strength,' 'Energy,' 'Endurance,' Horsemanship,' and 'Keenness on games.'[41] The reference to games reflected a Victorian English notion that athletics, especially team play, built character and promoted discipline, although athletics were the preserve of the upper classes and drill for the working classes. Baseball, it was also believed, served a similar role for many young Canadian and American males.[42] The RCMP must have hoped that those who played together, stayed together. When asked why he thought he would make a good Mounted Policeman, a retired RCMP member replied, 'I was athletic. I played football for Calgary and Winnipeg as a junior.' He also expressed admiration for a particular officer because the individual was an excellent athlete who frequently played rugby with the regular members.

This former Mountie's emphasis on athletics, however, additionally reveals the increasingly popular masculine characteristics of the age, especially among the rank and file who had to perform the police grunt work. He first came to the attention of Mounted Police recruiters when he played as a civilian on the RCMP softball team in Calgary. His physical size (six feet, four inches and two hundred pounds) and strength led an officer to ask him to enlist.[43] A fellow Mountie exemplified as well the physical characteristics of the era; in fact, a friend encouraged him to enlist after remarking, 'physically, [he] was ideally suited to be a Mounted Policeman.'[44] He, in addition, played professional football and was an accomplished boxer.[45]

Ultimately, the gendered values promoted in the Mounties would be reflected in their work. Physical size and strength came into play in policing strikes and riots between 1914 and 1939. Not surprisingly, the cultivation of masculine values, such as physicality, often led to the use of force – sometimes violence – in policing situations. In 1919 in Winnipeg, the Mounted Police rode over and shot protesters. At Estevan, Saskatchewan, in 1931 the RCMP lost control of a volatile situation and turned to violence; three miners died as a result.[46] Finally, the Regina Riot on Dominion Day 1935 is perhaps the best example of Mounted Police choices leading to violence.

Often the implied threat of violence, represented by physical size, served to ensure social conformity. In the 1930s the town of Melfort, Saskatchewan, acquired the reputation of being rough and lawless. The Mounted Police responded by sending into the town four of their physically biggest constables from Regina. Occasionally Mounties took matters (literally) into their own hands. In 1936 a policeman handled a local spousal abuser by challenging him to a boxing match and then pummelling him.[47]

The mixture of manly and masculine values, such as order, patriotism, militarism, and physicality, went hand-in-hand with being a Mounted Policeman and help explain why seemingly endless numbers of Britons and others from military backgrounds enlisted. In an era when the 'soldier-hero' was in vogue in parts of British society,[48] the RCMP as an institution full of 'tact, and courage, and an endless patience and persistence' could not fail to attract the keen.[49] Even the fabled Mountie uniform, Douglas Owram argues, carried with it a great deal of patriotic symbolism: 'The scarlet coat of the North West Mounted Police had been deliberately chosen in order to evoke the British tradition. Thus the myth of the police became in reality a part of the tradition of law in British society ... The man and the abstract concept merged into a symbol that few dared to challenge.'[50]

New recruits would need such confidence and dedication if they were to last as a member of the Mounted Police; theirs was a quasi-religious undertaking – the McDonald Commission would later describe the RCMP as having 'an ethos akin to that found in a monastery or religious order' – in a militaristic organization which would rule almost every aspect of their life and demand a monastic-like commitment in return, including, apparently, celibacy.[51] Until the 1970s, except under special circumstances, the RCMP accepted only single men whom it required to serve several years in the force before getting married. This rule forced some police officers either to marry in secret or to leave the force to wed.[52] Under the circumstances, it seems likely that Mounties frequented houses of 'ill-fame.' R.C. Macleod devotes a chapter in *The North-West Mounted Police and*

Law Enforcement to the policing of prostitution, arguing that the Mounties tolerated it because they were attuned to attitudes in the communities they policed.[53] Another potential reason for Mountie tolerance was that policemen regularly sought the services of prostitutes.

The prohibition on marriage plus the experience of other all-male environments and, indeed, the variety of sexual orientations among the wider populace, raises the possibility of alternatives to heterosexuality. In the 1880s a Mountie was discovered performing oral sex on another male. Even though it occurred before such an act was illegal, this did not prevent him from being drummed out of the force. The incident also indicated the reception for such an identity, with its accompanying negative stereotypes, especially in a hyper-masculinized institution like the Mounted Police.[54] Here is what Jack Fossum, a twenty-year veteran of the force who served during the 1930s, had to say (in his unintentionally ironically entitled autobiography *Mancatcher*) about a fellow barracks member:

> Next to [another Mountie was] Earl – a Cockney, an Imperial Army type whose every sentence was spiced with four letter words. He was in his mid-thirties, a powerful man with the build and walk of a gorilla. We suspected him of being a fag. He had a crush on Jeff for whom he'd buy sweets and little presents. Jeff, a lusty hetero, would often as not toss the presents back to him with a curt 'stick it!'

In the force's Lethbridge barracks all the washroom cubicle doors were removed specifically to inhibit acts of 'sexual perversion.'[55] More than the all-male environment of the barracks symbolized the force's militaristic nature. As Commissioner Perry observed in his 1918 memos on the future of his organization, militarism was a traditional characteristic of the force. Of course, the model for the Mounted Police had been the English-designed Royal Irish Constabulary, a paramilitary force which operated out of barracks. It was no coincidence that three of the four commissioners who served between 1914 and 1939 graduated from the Royal Military College (RMC); the lone exception during this period was Cortlandt Starnes who had served in the military before enlisting in the NWMP. In fact, the education ranking on Mountie evaluation forms offered two choices: university or RMC.[56] Personnel could be appointed directly to the officer corps of the Mounted Police simply by graduating from the RMC, as future commissioner Stuart Taylor Wood would do, or by being an officer in the Canadian militia. There was no requirement for an officer to have risen through the non-commissioned ranks of the Mounted Police or to have any policing experience.[57]

The connections between the militia and the Mounted Police went even further. The governor general had the 'power to prescribe the rank and seniority in the militia which Officers of the force shall hold, for the purpose of seniority and command, when they are serving with the Militia.'[58] The *Rules and Regulations of the Royal Canadian Mounted Police* even listed the honorary ranks in the militia held by officers of the force.[59]

Clearly many viewed being a military man as being conducive to working as a policeman. Certainly, the comptroller of the RNWMP in 1918 believed in this linkage when he sent a memo about recruiting to his superiors in the federal government. A.A. McLean's recommendation, written while the postwar disorder was underway and at a time when the RNWMP was having trouble finding new recruits, recommended that all former members returning from the war be reenlisted. If that recruiting approach failed then he advocated the signing up of any members of the Canadian Cavalry in the Canadian Expeditionary Force (CEF) 'who might be desirous of joining.'[60]

Military service also had symbolic importance in terms of male identity, according to Graham Dawson: 'Military virtues such as aggression, strength, courage and endurance have repeatedly been defined as the natural and inherent qualities of manhood, whose apogee is attainable only in battle. Celebrated as a hero in adventure stories telling of dangerous and daring exploits, the soldier has become a quintessential figure of masculinity.'[61] The recruitment campaign conducted in Ontario during the First World War directly equated being a real man with serving in the military; posters depicted those who avoided service as emasculated men.[62] The English construct of this type of military hero in this era did not exist in a vacuum. Instead, the cool and calm English male served as a contrast to the emotional path followed by 'Johnny Foreigner.'[63]

Some military experience does turn up in the backgrounds of those who served in the force in this period. Still, Mounties came from a wide variety of experiences and class backgrounds, something that differentiated the Mounted Police from urban police forces that tended to be more heavily drawn from the working classes.[64] A definitive statement cannot be made about the class background of those who joined, although the examples in table 3.5 suggest a general mixture of working class and lower middle class backgrounds. Regardless, the nature of the male values promoted in the force were middle-class even if many of its members were not.

Table 3.5. Previous occupations of selected Alberta and Saskatchewan Mounties

Mountie	Previous occupation	Highest RCMP position
Alfred Allen	British military	Staff sergeant
Alfred Ball	Teamster	Sergeant
T.C. Davies	Messenger	Sergeant major
Franz Droeske	Dominion Police	Corporal
Gerald Engel	Junior clerk	Assistant commissioner
Phillip Hobbs	Clerk	Inspector
G.L. Jennings	Military	Deputy commissioner
H.P. Keeler	London Metropolitan Police	Staff sergeant
Radivoy Koyich	Yugoslavian police	Special constable
A. Lawrence	Teamster	Constable
Johann Leopold	Farmer	Superintendent
W.A. MacBrayne	Soldier	Staff sergeant
Stirling McNeil	Auto worker	Superintendent
Michael Moriarity	Glasgow Police/London Metropolitan Police	Sergeant major
Walter Mortimer	Accountant	Superintendent
Arthur Moss	Coal miner/Sawmill worker	Sergeant
Jas. Ritchie	Book keeper	Superintendent
J.O. Scott	Edmonton Fire Dept.	Superintendent
I.C. Shank	Student	Superintendent
J.G. Shaw	Middlesbrough Constabulary	Constable
John Skelton	Soldier	Staff sergeant
R. Smyly	Bank clerk	Sergeant
R.R. Tait	Farmer	Superintendent
Ted Turner	Jeweller	Superintendent
S.L. Warrior	Bricklayer/warehouseman	Staff sergeant
Stan Wight	Seasonal CPR worker	Staff sergeant
G.S. Worsley	Military	Assistant commissioner

Source: Interviews, *R.C.M.P. Quarterly*, obituaries, and RCMP Personnel Records.

The linkage between various concepts of masculinity and the military led the Mounted Police to indoctrinate their recruits with militaristic values under harsh conditions. Former Commissioner William Kelly described the goal of recruit training, or 'boot camp,' as an opportunity to instil discipline in young Mounties. 'Boot camp' was not the most pleasant experience in many Mounted Policemen's careers. Harry Morren, who joined the force in 1911 and would serve for most of the Great War period, noted that the training depot of the Police in Regina, constructed in 1882, offered little in the way of comfort: 'Heating was a problem, mud was a problem, sleeping was a problem and ventilation was thirty years in the future.'[65]

The first weeks of a Mountie's career involved physical exercise, marching, riding, and rifle and revolver practice. Scientific criminal investigation and the practices associated with it only arrived in a meaningful way during Commissioner J.H. MacBrien's tenure in the 1930s.[66] The *Rules and Regulations of the Mounted Police* characterized training as a 'process which will place the recruit in a good position to become familiar with all the duties of a member of the force, give him the broad outlines of the knowledge required to carry out such duties, and to instil discipline.'[67] The emphasis was on the physical, not on the intellectual, a priority that would generate criticism of the Mounted Police for most of the twentieth century.[68] The product of this traditional approach was, according to Commissioner Charles Rivett-Carnac, a police officer who could 'be depended upon to obey orders intelligently and without comment, under all conditions.'[69]

There was a practical reason why policemen obeyed without question: it aided promotion.[70] The Mounted Police throughout this period was a hierarchical institution, shaped like a pyramid in that at each level towards the top there were fewer and fewer positions available. In 1920 officers made up 4 per cent of the force's total strength of 1,671.[71] Ten years later the percentage remained the same.[72] In practical terms this must have fuelled competition since members were fighting over ever diminishing returns but this widespread promotion seeking and backbiting also reflected a middle-class gender construct that viewed one's self-worth as being determined by career success.[73]

The ultimate significance of the RCMP as a male institution related not to who the Mounties were but to what they did; they served as an important deterrent to challenges to the hegemony of the state. Opposing them meant being at odds with an institution whose male members symbolized the best of Anglo-Canadian society and, because of the power of this ethnic group, the best of Canada. A Mounted Policeman and everything he represented became synonymous with law and authority. Accordingly, in a hierarchical and patriarchal Canada, the Mounted Police derived power not simply from its physical strength and firepower (although these were certainly significant); its authority also came from the fact that the

Mountie as socially constructed in this era represented a 'white' middle-class ideal.

In turn, the values of the RCMP influenced what it defined as the norm in Canadian society. The Mounted Police between 1914 and 1939 was very much a British institution, reflecting all of the popular middle-class, Anglo-Celtic definitions of male identity, including a belief in racial superiority. Gail Bederman describes the goal of this version of male construction during this era as an effort to demonstrate that 'civilized white men were the most manly ever evolved – firm of character; self-controlled; protectors of women and children.'[74] As an institution the RCMP believed in order, discipline, and hierarchy, and strove for a world which reflected these values. Various ethnic groups, communists, socialists, students, university faculty, labour activists, union leaders, strikers, and anyone else not content with their place in the brick wall of society found themselves under suspicion, either directly from uniformed Mounties, or more subtly through hordes of RCMP informants, secret agents, and undercover Mounties. Be a brick or beware!

4

Dealing with Undesirables

By the end of the First World War, many Canadians, including members of the Mounted Police, believed that the nation was desperately in need of an exorcism. Who were the demons that required expulsion? Many of them resembled the 'men in sheepskin coats' previously held up as ideal citizens for Canada. Immigrants from central and eastern Europe had become the 'other,' representing the opposite of everything the Mounted Police and Anglo-Canadian society stood for in relation to ethnicity and masculinity.[1] The imagined nature of this Canada deliberately excluded certain groups on the grounds that they undermined the Anglo-Celtic character of the country and, in turn, the country's greatness.[2]

The police shared this apprehension about the newcomers. Members of the force had no innate immunity from the prejudice that pervaded much of Canadian society – they were ordinary men who bore the values of the society that bore them. 'Without fear, favour, or affection' is part of the RCMP's founding creed and never was it less applicable to Canada's national police force than between 1914 and 1939. In their operations in Alberta and Saskatchewan, Mounties did favour certain ethnic groups over their neighbours; others they simply feared. The usual suspects included Ukrainians, Doukhobors, Chinese, Finns, and, during the First World War, Germans. In this period, certain crimes and types of radicalism became ethnic and racial crimes. In the minds of the scarlet-clad men, Germans became synonymous with deceit, Chinese with the immorality of the narcotics trade, and Ukrainians with the operation of illegal stills, political radicalism, and labour disturbances.

In the early 1920s, as an institution the Mounted Police sought survival after having surrendered their regular policing role in the last holdout provinces, Alberta and Saskatchewan. What better way to demonstrate their utility to both the state and the wider society than to perform tasks connected to immigrant and ethnic groups, which were deemed terribly important by the decision makers of Canada: spying on ethnic radicals and enemy aliens, busting Chinese dope peddlers, investigating the backgrounds of individuals seeking citizenship, gathering evidence on subversive activities, and finally rounding up those to be deported. While the force performed assigned tasks in an era when its future was very much up in the air, it was not simply a case of the police following or leading public opinion. Instead the RCMP's actions mediated and contributed to the public discourses of the period. Members of the Mounted Police, especially the officer corps, held the same beliefs about ethnic minorities as did others in Anglo-Canadian society; they, after all, were drawn from its ranks. And unlike so many others for whom immigrants and minorities symbolized an abstract, albeit a strongly disliked threat, Mounties had a direct opportunity to do something about how they felt.

Many of the groups targeted by the RCMP and the Canadian state in the early twentieth century had, in a sense, one man to thank for being in Canada in the first place. Federal cabinet minister, Clifford Sifton, determined the groups that made up the 'other' that existed in western Canada in the early twentieth century. Sifton's immigration plan had opened the door to tens of thousands of previously non-preferred peasants – central and eastern Europeans. In a few decades Anglo-Canadians in the west found their numbers reduced from an overwhelming majority of the population to barely over 50 per cent. These immigrants chiefly settled on farms in the west, often surrounded by citizens from similar backgrounds.[3] Much to Sifton's chagrin, business had its own concept of the ideal immigrant. Owners desired a cheap labour supply that would aid in, among other things, the building of railways, the cutting down of trees, and the extracting of minerals from the soil. Ironically, the arrival of eastern and central European navvies increased under Sifton's replacement, Frank Oliver, a man who specifically stated his opposition to the arrival of non-British immigrants.[4]

The changes to Canada's ethnic balance triggered a reaction. Widespread nativism, however, did not appear overnight, but had always lurked under the surface of the Canadian mythology of tolerance. Historian Howard Palmer defined nativism as a merging of nationalism and ethnic and racial prejudice to form an 'opposition to an internal minority on the grounds that it posed a threat to Canadian national life.'[5] He identified three strains of nativism as pertinent to western Canada: Anglo-Saxon, anti-Catholic, and antiradical.[6] 'Underlying all the different variations of nativism,' wrote Palmer, 'was a distrust of difference, a sense that minority groups which attempted to maintain separate identities diminished the national sense of identity and posed a challenge to prevailing ideals and assumptions.'[7] Anti-immigrant feeling, just as prevalent in the United States, was fuelled by stereotypes. Immigrants and minorities were viewed as criminals; they were immoral; they were dirty; they were mentally inferior; they reeked of garlic; they lacked the proper sexual restraint that characterized the superior Anglo-Canadian society.[8] Some even suggested that they were heathens. 'To Canadianize them, they have to be Christianized' advised one Methodist minister.[9]

Incidents of nativism, although certainly not unheard of before the war, increased as the conflagration dragged on. Canada had lost nearly 1 per cent of its population in the muck and mire of the trenches of western Europe, and many, including returning survivors, sought vengeance. Those minorities who were exempted from military service because of either their religious beliefs or lack of citizenship received special scorn; if they happened to be from one of Canada's enemies, then so much the worse for them. Some of these same groups found their farms prospering because of war conditions; others took advantage of the shortage of labour to secure higher wages than they might otherwise have earned. None of this success was lost on Anglo-Canadian society. 'These foreigners have us where the hair is short as regards wages,' complained activist Irene Parlby in a letter. '[Meanwhile] their people over there are mangling and killing off our men.'[10]

Certain ethnic minorities, specifically eastern and central Europeans, also found themselves labelled as radicals. The upsurge of radicalism at the end of the war, symbolized externally by the 1917 Bolshevik Revolution and internally by the 1919 Winnipeg General Strike, was officially linked to ethnicity – 'foreigners' equalled radicals.[11] Thousands suffered directly because of prejudice. Close to 8,000 people, including approximately 5,000 of Ukrainian background, found themselves interned in camps during the war. In 1917 the federal government disenfranchised enemy alien males naturalized after 1902 and banned foreign-language newspapers. Finally, some provincial governments, including Saskatchewan's, used the war as an opportunity to reduce or eliminate non-English education rights.[12]

Even the general response from those considered more sympathetic to the cause of immigrants was indirectly threatening. Labour activist J.S. Woodsworth, and some in the Liberal party, embraced a policy of assimilation or, in the parlance of the time, 'Canadianizing' newcomers. This approach was not about making newcomers equal with the Anglo-Canadian majority, but about encouraging social conformity and an acceptance of the status quo.[13] Some made no pretence about their dislike for those who differed from the Anglo-Canadian norm, issuing calls for repressive measures against the minority groups.[14] Bishop George Exton Lloyd, the Anglican bishop of Saskatchewan, felt confident enough in the mid-1920s to describe publicly citizens of eastern European background as 'dirty, ignorant, garlic-smelling, non-preferred continentals.'[15] Only two solutions to the problem existed for those sharing the rabid rhetoric of Lloyd: restricting immigration so as not to allow undesirables into the country in the first place and deporting those who had already infested the country.[16]

Many Mounted Policemen exhibited the wider nativist sentiments. Commissioner A.B. Perry set the tone in 1919 when he supported the vigilante actions of returning soldiers against enemy aliens in western Canada, while offering advice on how to deal with minorities:

During the war ... all foreigners received the most considerate treatment as long as they obeyed the laws of the country and pursued their ordinary avocations. The returned soldiers found them filling their jobs and enjoying prosperity. In Winnipeg, Calgary, Medicine Hat and other points, the resentment of the soldiers found expression in small disturbances provoked by the indiscreet acts and words of these people, who, as a body, have shown little appreciation of the just and fair treatment meted out to them by the people of this country. They have shown themselves ready to follow and support the extremists who play upon their ignorance and appeal to their national prejudices and sympathy for the central powers. Bolshevism finds a fertile field among them and is assiduously cultivated by the ardent agitator. The assimilation of our large alien population is of the greatest importance and it demands wise and sympathetic action and constant attention.[17]

In 1932 Commissioner J.H. MacBrien employed Perry's scapegoat tactics when he commented on the problem of radicals to an audience in Toronto: 'It is notable that 99% of these fellows are foreigners.' Like Perry, he also offered a solution to his defined problem: 'Many of them have not been here long ... If we were rid of them there would be no unemployment or unrest in Canada.'[18] Even the naturalized were not free of suspicion since citizenship did not automatically cure inherent defects of breeding. Assistant-Commissioner S.T. Wood warned in a 1935 letter to the attorney general of Saskatchewan that certain immigrants, both naturalized and unnaturalized, threatened the police and the state:

> Wholesale murder of the police forces of the country is part and parcel of the program of the Communists in the overthrow by force of the Constitution. This was done in Russia in 1917, and it should be borne in mind that the Communist Party of Canada derives the bulk of its support from the foreign elements in this country, irrespective of whether they are naturalized citizens or not.[19]

Part of Wood's sentiment may have been symptomatic of real fear. A 1932 RCMP report noted that central Europeans in attendance at a radical gathering expressed enthusiasm when the speaker made reference to 'digging graves for Police.'[20]

Similar attitudes existed throughout the Mounted Police in this era. In describing a Communist Party of Canada rally in rural Saskatchewan, a constable, as was common, commented on the ethnic makeup of the audience: 'Proportion of foreigners present was 95 percent. Anglo Saxons [made up the remaining] 5 percent. The foreigners in attendance were all farmers ... of a particularly ignorant type.'[21] In 1919 Sergeant Major William George Edgenton reported on allegations concerning the poor behaviour of some of his colleagues, specifically complaints of Mounties in Regina 'associating with undesirable characters such as coons, etc.'[22] Detective Cecil Hildyard, a native of Yorkshire, England, and a graduate of Eton and Oxford,[23] wrote that a 1922 meeting in Saskatoon 'was attended by approximately fifty people, mostly of a decent British type, only about ten foreigners.'[24] And, reflecting the anti-Semitism of the interwar period, a Mountie secret agent, himself of eastern European background, noted during the Estevan miners' strike of September 1931 that 'all Jews in Estevan and Bienfait are 100% behind the Communist movement.'[25]

Of course, many Anglo-Canadians participated in radical activity. How did Mounties square that reality with their stereotype of all radicals as 'foreigners'? Demonstrating constructions of whiteness in the period, to at least one Mountie, those of Anglo-Celtic background who chose to involve themselves in radical activity with eastern Europeans were race traitors. Superintendent P.W. Pennefather of 'K' Division in southern Alberta described such individuals as 'renegade whites,' 'white agitators,' and 'certain white men, or so-called white men [who] have the upper hand over the foreign elements.'[26]

In addition to directing their ethnic and racial attitudes outward, Mounted Policeman also applied the same attitudes to potential or actual members of the force. In 1919 Assistant Commissioner W.H. Routledge underlined the words 'Russian Jew' and wrote '<u>NO</u>' in the margin of a letter that offered the services of an individual of that background.[27] In another case, a senior Mountie advised 'F' Division on its choice to replace Special Constable J.L. Eberhardt, a Mountie of Czech background: 'Mr. M. Black appears to have qualifications by way of education and experience much superior to those of Eberhardt – further, as he is of Anglo-Saxon origin – his value as an interpreter would far exceed that of Eberhardt.'[28]

Those Mounties of non-British backgrounds who belonged to the police were almost exclusively secret agents or special constables. This segregation reflected both practicality (they were recruited to spy on people like themselves) and prejudice in that with their backgrounds they could never hope to be a real Mountie. As such, secret agents and special constables experienced even less job security and employment rights than regular Mounted Policemen. The case of Jacob M. Tatko, who spoke nine languages, 'mostly of the slavic countries,' exemplified the transient nature of someone in his position.[29] In 1916 he joined the Mounted Police in Alberta as an interpreter and Secret Agent 125 and served in that capacity until 1928 when the force discharged him. He later rejoined as a special constable, lasting until 1937 when the commissioner dismissed him because of incompetence. Due to the nature of his service, specifically his secret agent work, Tatko did not qualify for a pension. He went so far as to hire a lawyer in a futile effort to change his retirement fate.[30]

Occasionally the exploits of non-Anglo Canadian Mounties received popular praise. Bohemian-born John (Johann) Leopold, through his activities as an undercover Mountie active in the Regina branch of the Communist Party of Canada, became, arguably, the most famous Mountie of the interwar period. Not even a Canadian citizen when he joined the Mounted Police in 1918, something prohibited under its regulations, the new recruit also failed to meet minimum height requirements.[31] At the time, the Mounted Police badly needed his non-English language skills, so it ignored Leopold's national status. Even with his celebrated exploits, Leopold still found himself regularly challenged by the guards at police headquarters in Ottawa because he was, in the words of the official historians of the RCMP Security Service, 'foreign looking.'[32]

Still, even a regular member of the force could find himself under surveillance because of his ethnicity. Shortly after the start of the Second World War, members of the RCMP began to worry about the loyalty of Corporal Franz Droeske, a German-Canadian Mountie. At first the RCMP sought to station him in less sensitive positions so as to avoid public criticism. (He was assigned to traffic duty.) Even that, however, was not enough to allay suspicions amongst his colleagues or his commander, who had Droeske and another Mountie of German background put under surveillance.[33]

The roots of the Mounties' dislike and mistrust of 'foreigners,' as with other Anglo-Canadians, stretched back to before 1914, but the war gave licence to the enmity. Once the conflict commenced, 'enemy aliens,' specifically Germans, who had previously been considered model citizens, and Austrians, the latter category including Ukrainians because they hailed from territory under the domain of the Austro-Hungarian Empire, became the targets of their venom. These groups came from nations that Canada now warred against; some remained military reservists for their old countries. The Borden government, in response to public fears about the loyalty of enemy aliens, enacted an October 1914 Order in Council which required certain classes of aliens to register at government offices, report monthly, carry government-issued identification, and acquire special papers for travelling. During the early part of the war, the Mounted Policemen supervised registration centres on the Prairies providing them with regular contact with ethnic minorities. In Saskatchewan and Alberta, the police investigated 173,568 citizens of German and Austrian backgrounds during the war.[34] In Manitoba alone, between April and September 1919, 75,000 enemy aliens made monthly reports to the RNWMP.[35] Some aliens required additional investigation. Police reports often included references to enemy aliens being given 'the thirty-two questions,' a list of questions asked of those being checked. They pertained to religion, nationality, naturalization, and loyalty.[36]

After referring to the large number of enemy aliens the RNWMP had to worry about in his 1914 annual report,[37] Commissioner Perry offered a more reassuring note the following year when he commented that the decline in the strength of the Mounted Police and a smaller role in dealing with enemy aliens was due to a lack of problems from 'enemy nationalities.'[38] Rumours of enemy alien activity, including a report that German agents disguised as Swiss farmers intended to spread 'hoof and mouth' disease among western Canada's farm animals, proved unfounded.[39] Perry's junior officers in

Alberta and Saskatchewan reiterated the commissioner's opinion, although they often portrayed Germans and Ukrainians in a stereotypical and negative light. At the same time, they reaffirmed the need for a RNWMP presence – if deviousness was inherent in the character of Germans, backs could never be safely turned. Ukrainians, on the other hand, were viewed as 'ignorant' farm hands and thus prone to being misled by others, especially the 'cunning' Germans. Superintendent J.A. McGibbon, in charge of the Regina District, reflected this mentality: 'The Germans as a body are no doubt very bitter, and only for the fact that they are very closely watched and know that the first move they make will get them into trouble, would no doubt try and do something.'[40] Superintendent F.J. Horrigan, in charge of 'K' Division, which covered southern Alberta, expressed similar sentiments, even though most of the German and Austrian population in his district had been naturalized: 'The sympathies of most of these people are all with the enemy and they require a great deal of watching; but in cases where they have openly expressed their sympathies, they have been firmly dealt with by us, with the result that they have become more chary of expressing themselves in public, and we now hear but few complaints against them.'[41] Horrigan echoed these sentiments in an 18 May 1915 letter to Perry, depicting naturalization as a threat since it offered protection to outsiders and radicals:

> The people say that the time has now arrived for action to be taken in regard to alien enemies, and that they should not be allowed any liberty or license whatever in regard to the cruel war now going on. As I have informed you in previous reports (and my conviction deepens the more I investigate the matter) a great many naturalized subjects are really worse than those who are not naturalized. It also appears to me, from my investigations, that those who became naturalized did so for a special purpose, and are here for that purpose ... the only proper term for them is Galvanized Canadians.[42]

This notion of a 'fifth column' based on ethnicity would emerge again in the interwar period.

Perry, well aware of the docility of the enemy alien population, responded to these various sentiments with a recommendation of caution. He reminded his officers that they 'must act carefully and not be carried away by popular frenzy or press agitation. You will have done your duty if you administer the law without fear or favour.'[43] The lack of seditious activity on the part of aliens led to a reduction of the RNWMP role in policing them. In 1915, for example, the Mounted Police office for registering enemy aliens in Calgary was closed and the function taken over by the city police, although some registration by rural Mounted Police detachments continued for the conflict's duration.[44] The force also fired nearly all of its secret agents taken on at the start of hostilities to investigate 'alleged unrest among the foreign population ...' One of those dismissed had worked as a barber in Edmonton in a shop that the Mounted Police paid the rent for and equipped.[45]

With the elimination in 1917 of the Mounted Police as the provincial police forces in Alberta and Saskatchewan, and the creation of a RNWMP unit for overseas service, the policing of ethnic groups grew even less significant. Still, Perry felt it necessary to reassure worried governments and citizens that the force's continued presence in these two provinces would involve detectives and secret agents monitoring enemy aliens.[46] A harsher police-immigrant relationship, however, was already at hand by 1917, as discontent with the war continued to grow. An increase in radicalism and opposition to conscription led to renewed anti-alien sentiment. A staff sergeant at Vegreville, Alberta, for example, threatened an alien organizing a meeting of the socialist party with arrest and imprisonment. 'He left and I don't think he has stopped yet,' the proud Mountie relayed. The policeman did lament, however, that the poster advertising the meeting which he 'attached would be allowed to be printed and circulated amongst ignorant foreigners as it takes very little to cause trouble amongst them.'[47] This report prompted the sergeant's superior to write the commissioner to wonder if legislation could be enacted making it illegal for 'anyone under any pretense whatever, during the period of the war, to make speeches which do or are likely to cause unrest among the foreign and enemy alien population? I do not think that the present War Measures Act covers it.'[48]

Reports of alien unhappiness with conscription flooded in. In the Hague District of Saskatchewan a Mountie found 'contempt' on the part of Germans and Mennonites towards the signing of National Service Cards.[49] This account prompted another officer to conclude that '99% of the Alien Enemies are disloyal to the core and those of Alien enemy extraction are very little better.'[50] Not just enemy aliens found conscription problematic. Anti-conscription riots occurred in Quebec, for instance, while many Anglo-Canadian prairie farmers expressed anger after the government ended the exemption for their sons. In 1917 Perry instructed one of the spies hired back, Secret Agent 25 (W.H. Balsinger), to investigate the attitudes of minority and French-Canadian communities in Saskatchewan towards conscription. The agent, pretending to be a cattle dealer, went among various groups and reported that most, especially French Canadians, opposed conscription. Perry forwarded the report to Ottawa and recommended that it be given to Prime Minister Borden.[51]

The following year, Perry's future successor, Cortlandt Starnes, wrote to the commissioner to recommend a renewed RNWMP policing role in western Canada. Specifically, he argued, this change would allow for greater 'prestige and authority amongst the foreign element and general public ... and we would be in closer touch with everything that went on.' He also encouraged the resumption of RNWMP control of enemy alien registration and reporting since '[t]his is one of the greatest aids in following the labor situation' and providing the Mountie in charge of Crow's Nest Pass, a centre of coal mining and labour discontent, 'Magisterial powers ... to be used only in cases where Alien Enemies are concerned, or of emergency.'[52]

The growing radicalism and discontent in Canada as the armistice approached, combined with a peaking of anti-alien hostility, created a volatile situation. The tense environment worried both the Canadian government and the Mounted Police. Neither had any doubt about the link between ethnicity and political and labour radicalism. In October 1918 the president of the Privy Council, Newton Rowell, asked for Mountie feedback on a proposal to have the force resume control of the coal mining districts of Alberta and British Columbia. Both Perry and the commanding officer, whose district included several coal-mining areas, favoured the proposal. The Alberta Mountie stressed that the RNWMP should have complete legal control over the mines. To do otherwise, he argued, would 'put the force in a poor light' especially since, he claimed, 60 to 75 per cent of miners were 'of alien enemy nationality ... [many] living with their families in close proximity to the mines.'[53]

With the conclusion of the war, Germans and espionage became a secondary concern to the police. (Eventually they recaptured in part the high standing they occupied prior to the start of hostilities.) Ukrainians and the threat of radicalism replaced them on the police agenda. The latter had not escaped unscathed during the First World War: several thousand found themselves interned after being deemed enemies of Canada.[54] Now many of these 'foreigners' and enemy aliens embraced radicalism and their choice was different: Bolshevism. In February 1919 Commissioner Perry demonstrated the new fears of alien radicalism when he reported to the comptroller on a conversation he had with Secret Agent 50 (F.E. Reithdorf) on the

Socialist Party in Edmonton and its ties with 'the Bolsheviki element among the Aliens.' He did not use 'the word "enemy,"' the Commissioner added, 'because many of the most pronounced are not enemy aliens, but are Russians, Swedes, Ukrainians and Finns, with a sprinkling of all other nationalities.' Their goal, in the words of Perry, was

> to secure a revolution by force ... Close supervision will be maintained on the conditions in Edmonton. I do not think it advisable, as yet, to commence prosecutions, which might, or might not, be successful. I am attempting to obtain accurate and complete information on the whole subject in Western Canada. When this information has been secured, then it ought to be considered whether vigorous prosecutions should not take place everywhere about the same time.[55]

The commissioner had already dispatched memoranda in early 1919 directing his subordinates to begin conducting widespread intelligence operations against anyone or anything with a radical, specifically, Bolshevik tinge. Aliens embodied the inspiration for these operations:

> 3. Attention is also drawn to the various foreign settlements located throughout Manitoba, Saskatchewan, Alberta, and B.C. which are very susceptible to Bolshevism teachings and propaganda.
> 4. Officers Commanding will take steps to see that careful and constant supervision is maintained over these foreign settlements with a view to detecting the least indication of Bolshevism tendencies and doctrines.[56]

The federal government also presented the police with new powers during the Winnipeg General Strike in June 1919. In keeping with the popular thinking that foreigners were behind labour unrest, it amended section 41 of the Immigration Act to allow for increased powers of arrest and deportation of non-naturalized troublemakers. A month later, the government passed section 98 of the Criminal Code, which allowed for jail terms of up to twenty years for a wide range of seditious offences and left it up to the accused to prove his or her innocence. Older legislation proved equally useful in dealing with immigrants. One officer noted in a November 1919 report that several prosecutions of enemy aliens had occurred in southern Alberta under the 1914 Order in Council's requirement of alien registration.[57]

This anti-alien environment created the potential for police abuse above and beyond the abuse already inflicted on individuals targeted for deportation. One example of how the power of the Mounted Police over immigrants led to mistreatment occurred in 1919 when several Ukrainian farmers in the Kamsack area of Saskatchewan alleged that a particular Mounted Policeman had extorted money from them while conducting alien registration. Stephen Malczewski, a Polish-Canadian lawyer, publicized the farmers' complaints. The first response of the Mounted Police was to investigate Malczewski. Eventually the Mountie in question was charged with several offences. The presiding judge at his trial was the commander of the RNWMP's Southern Saskatchewan District, who had already written to the commissioner in the immediate aftermath of the allegations to assure him that they were groundless. Not surprisingly, he discounted the testimony of the Ukrainian farmers and convicted the Mounted Policeman on only one charge: accepting a $1 bribe, an offence the accused had already admitted.[58]

Since many equated certain ethnic backgrounds with radicalism, the campaign against foreigners/radicals gathered speed. The war, and the subsequent disorder, left little tolerance for those outside defined political and social norms. Mounties at all levels began making detailed reports on the activities of non-Anglo-Celtic Canadians who were either involved in radical activity or merely perceived to be. In 1920 the newly amalgamated RCMP began compiling summaries of the reports and sending them out to a select group of politicians and officials. The 'security bulletins,' as they became known, contained considerable information on the activities of particular ethnic groups.[59]

The police emphasis did not completely lack justification. Some eastern and central Europeans did embrace radical politics in Canada for a number of reasons. Ukrainians, Finns, and Jews represented 80 to 90 per cent of all members of the Communist Party of Canada in the late 1920s. In 1929 the number reached 95 per cent. In the 1930s the Communist Party made a concerted effort to attract native-born Canadians, while at the same time large numbers of Finns left because of doctrinal disputes within the Canadian party and the growing menace of Stalinism. Those of foreign birth, however, remained prominent at all levels of the party; the Communist-dominated Ukrainian Labour-Farmer Temple, for example, experienced a membership increase from 8,080 in 1932 to 15,000 in 1938.[60]

Ukrainians figured prominently in police reports in the immediate postwar years. In 1923 Superintendent G.L. Jennings, the head of Edmonton-centred 'G' Division in Alberta, warned Commissioner Starnes of 'the anti-Canadian sentiment of the Ukrainians. This ap-

pears to be getting more so as time goes on, and the younger generations, who are born in Canada, grow up with ideas instilled in them
from many years of association with this propaganda.'[61] Moreover, in
a period dominated by prejudice, there seemed to be good reason to
worry. A year earlier, a Mounted Policeman had prepared a report on
the political leanings of approximately 100,000 'Ukrainians' in Alberta (at a time when official numbers were half of that). He labelled
25 per cent as 'militant' members of the Communist Party, and
another 35 per cent as 'semi-militant,' while suggesting that only
10 per cent of Alberta's Ukrainian population were 'on the side of
authority.'[62]

While the RCMP viewed Ukrainians as the main ethnic group
involved in radical activity, others did not avoid police attention. The
Finnish community enjoyed a strong socialist wing, but the RCMP at
Red Deer, Alberta, found it difficult to report on the revolutionary
activities of local Finns, because they were 'a very clannish race' and
thus difficult to infiltrate. The Chinese in Edmonton in 1927 came
under similar police scrutiny when the Communist Party there made a
concerted effort to recruit members from within their community.[63]

The Doukhobors, a religious sect from Russia, garnered similar
attention in the 1930s after a factional split led to acts of violence on
the part of the Sons of Freedom, including the burning of schools and
grain elevators. This group of settlers proved especially frustrating to
the Mounted Police because of their unwillingness to conform to the
precepts of Anglo-Canadian society. In fact, in 1933 the inspector in
charge of the Yorkton subdivision that had the responsibility of actually policing the Doukhobors, repeatedly told his superior, S.T. Wood,
that detectives and secret agents should be removed from their community. 'Leave them alone,' he counselled in response to police
concerns, 'for as they were burning their own schools they had to pay
for their re-building.'[64]

It was also inevitable that this minority, outside the mainstream,
would be linked to political radicalism. In 1936 Wood reported that
'Communist elements' in Saskatchewan sought to take advantage of
the pacifist principles of the Doukhobors.[65] The RCMP linking of
Doukhobors with Bolsheviks had also occurred in 1929 when Superintendent W.P. Lindsay, in charge of southern Saskatchewan, warned
headquarters about what he considered to be the unsavoury Soviet
background of Sons of Freedom leader Peter Verigin.[66] Four years
later, another Saskatchewan Mountie observed that 'Veregin [*sic*] has
turned completely Bolshevistic ... advocating the use of revolvers,
Rifles and machine guns.'[67] Whatever the case, the Sons of Freedom

sect of the Doukhobors were especially reviled because, like many Ukrainians, they refused to be, in the words of Assistant Commissioner Walter Mortimer, 'assimilated [by] Canadian ideas,' and would not 'bring up their children as Canadian citizens.'[68]

More than politics marked groups of people for special attention from the Mounted Police. In an era of heightened prejudice, crime and immorality, so often associated by reformers with those outside of the Anglo majority, became of special concern to the Mounted Police and the state. Anglo-Canadian society often viewed the cultural practices of minorities as being intricately associated with immorality. This sparked reform campaigns, such as the temperance movement, the anti-white slave trade campaign, and the crackdown on illicit drugs.[69] In an era of strong prejudice, when the Mounties sought to entrench their position as Canada's national police force, concentrating resources on crime rightly or wrongly associated with certain minority groups was sure to win the RCMP support from the Anglo-Celtic population of Canada. During the 1923 debate on a motion to restrict the Mounted Police to the northern territories, George Black, a member of Parliament for the Yukon, rose from his chair in the House and told those listening that if the RCMP 'did nothing but the work they performed in enforcing the Opium and Narcotic Drug Act (ONDA) the country has been well repaid.' He then read from the section on narcotics enforcement in the RCMP's 1922 annual report. On the same occasion, Sir Lomer Gouin, the federal minister of justice and the politician in charge of the Mounted Police, stated that enforcing the ONDA was one of the vital duties performed by the force.[70]

As part of its ticket to survival, the Opium and Narcotic Drug Act represented the most significant component of the RCMP's moral reform work. The rising concern about narcotics mirrored both a fixation on drugs among members of the Canadian elite and an international trend. At the beginning of the twentieth century, drugs consumption was not perceived as a significant social problem. Members of the Mounted Police found narcotics more of a nuisance as they pursued their war against alcohol.[71] This pattern began to change in 1907 when anti-Chinese riots erupted in Vancouver. The catalyst for rendering drugs illegal was a familiar face to students of Canadian history, William Lyon Mackenzie King. Charged with investigating Chinese-Canadian compensation claims in the aftermath of the riots, King discovered two requests for recompense from the owners of opium dens. He came away believing in the necessity of drug criminalization since 'opium smoking was making headway, not only among white men and boys, but also among women and girls.'[72] This theme of drugs, specifically opium, as a racial threat would be repeated throughout the 1920s in an era of moral reform campaigns. The message was spread most famously by Emily Murphy, celebrated suffragist and anti-narcotics campaigner, who, as 'Janey Canuck' in her book *The Black Candle*, warned of the assault by narcotics upon the purity of the so-called white race.[73] Anglo-Canada's hostility towards the Chinese emanated from an emphasis on 'the unassimilable Asian' but also from a belief, reflected in Murphy's writings, that, in the words of Madge Pon, 'Chinese men posed a moral and sexual threat to white women.'[74] By the 1920s, one instrument for the expression of anti-Asian sentiment would be the RCMP.

King introduced the first legislation that specifically criminalized drugs in Canada before the First World War. It would remain virtually unchanged until the enactment of the Opium and Narcotic Drug Act in the 1920s. Again, opium, associated with Chinese Canadians, was separated from other 'white drugs' (a prevalent term at the time) such as cocaine, morphine, and heroin.[75] The law would be amended in 1921 and 1922 and consolidated in 1923.

Although other police forces would play a role in the anti-narcotics campaign, it would be up to the Mounted Police, with its national presence, to lead the fight. In many ways the work differed little from the campaigns against communism, and, in fact, rank-and-file Mounties in the interwar period policed both.[76] Each, frequently labelled as immoral, served as an external menace brought to Canada from abroad by large numbers of non-Canadians who, it was believed, sought to undermine the structures of society.

With drugs, soon-to-be Commissioner Cortlandt Starnes struck the proper moral note in his first annual report in 1922: 'The repulsive nature of the work of repression, entailing as it does contact with ... [the] dregs of humanity ... [leads] our men [to] greatly dislike it, and it is undertaken only in accordance with duty, and because of the knowledge that while unpleasant it is a service to humanity.'[77] The Department of Health had requested two years earlier that the RCMP officially enter the anti-illicit drugs campaign. The force and its federal partner in the war on drugs, the Opium and Narcotic Drug Branch of the Department of Health, had a strong influence on the expansion of anti-narcotic laws in the 1920s.[78] The anti-drug campaign was especially important to the Mounted Police in an era when its only presence in Saskatchewan and Alberta was as an organization charged with enforcing federal statutes and aiding other federal government departments; it was one more way of proving the force's value, and thereby ensuring its ultimate survival.

Drug work did not represent the most important investigation category numerically, especially in provinces such as Alberta and Saskatchewan with smaller Asian populations (see table 4.1). In turn, federal statute investigations paled in comparison to work done on behalf of other government departments, although undoubtedly some of the tasks performed for the Department of Health would have been drug related.[79] Numbers, however, do not impart the significance that this type of work had in the Canada of this era, especially its synchronicity with the battle against communism. The image of the ultimate symbol of middle-class Anglo-Celtic maleness, the Mounted Police, leading a moral crusade against hated and evil Asiatics had a powerful resonance in Anglo-Canadian society. As Starnes acknowledged, it was repulsive work, but someone had to set things right – even if it meant saving only a handful of 'white' victims.

Throughout the 1920s, the Mounted Police leadership emphasized the problem of drugs and the importance of the force in dealing with the issue. In the first annual report to contain a specific reference to such work, Commissioner Perry declared that the 'investigations have convinced me that the evil is greater than appears upon the surface, and that a serious national menace has arisen.' Later in the same report, he reiterated

the deep sense of the danger of the traffic. Our investigators have uncovered a volume of addiction which seriously threatens our national life, and apart from the aspect of public policy, numerous and most distressing and lamentable cases have come to our notice. The dreadful suffering endured by those addicted to the drugs, the ruin of lives which should be useful, do not constitute the whole of the evil, for the ills spread to their families. Children rob parents, husbands and fathers plunge their families into misery, wives ruin their husbands. In one case which came to our knowledge, a man discovered that his wife had been an addict for months, that she had disposed of much of his property and had sold his clothes to procure the poison. To show the personal degradation suffered by many of our fellow-citizens, a young white girl was recently discovered in a Chinese resort so destitute as to be all but naked, her body pitted with the marks of the hypodermic needle. These are but single instances which could be multiplied from our records.[80]

Like the wider society it policed, prejudice dominated the Mounties' anti-illicit drug discourse. The Opium and Narcotic Drug Act was the

Table 4.1. RCMP investigations under the Opium and Narcotic Drug Act (ONDA)

Year (Sept. to Sept.)	As % of total cases investigated under federal statutes in Canada	No. in Alberta	Alberta total as % of total ONDA investigations Canada-wide	No. in Saskatchewan	Saskatchewan total as % of total ONDA investigations Canada-wide
1921	29	201	25	139	15
1922	32	123	22	50	4
1923	29	99	19	91	5
1924	15	83	13	75	4
1925	24	64	18	64	5
1926	20	45	9	23	2
1927	14	47	13	32	3
1928	14	15	5	69	5
1929	15	25	9	101	6
1930	16	40	11	54	4
1931	17	48	10	42	3
1932	8	35	4	22	2
1934[a]	4	71	2	32	1
1935	4	103	4	48	3
1936	4	48	3	35	3
1937	4	31	2	53	3
1938	5	28	4	44	6
1939	4	35	5	49	7

[a]Covers eighteen-month period.
Source: RCMP Annual Reports.

Table 4.2. RCMP categorization of those arrested under the ONDA

Year	'Chinese'	'White'	'Colored'	'Japanese'
1924	158	117	14	0
1925	280	168	2	0
1926	187	175	9	0
1927	160	88	0	2
1928	107	77	3	2
1929	255	45	2	0
1930	190	59	3	2
1931	127	92	4	1
1932	110	80	3	2
1934[a]	184	104	8	0
1935	108	86	2	0
1936	47	74	0	3
1937	50	115	4	3
1938[b]	31	93	3	1

[a] Covers eighteen-month period.
[b] For unknown reasons, this category ended in 1938.
Source: RCMP Annual Reports.

only category in the yearly RCMP reports which listed the racial background of those arrested (see table 4.2). Those of Chinese background usually topped the list of arrests under the ONDA, which is not surprising considering they were the group besieged by the law. The equivalent of the ONDA for the Anglo-Canadian population would have been, according to criminologist Neil Boyd, a law targeting saloons.[81]

Behind much of the anti-drug rhetoric of prominent citizens such as Emily Murphy and Commissioner Perry was the perceived threat of drugs to the purity of Anglo-Canadian women. C.W. Harvison, a rank-and-file Mountie at the time, touched upon this fear in his memoirs:

> The Chinese opium smokers were, almost invariably, peaceful and docile. Many of them were older citizens who had had the habit for years and could not quite understand why, suddenly, a fuss was being made. The non-Oriental addicts were younger people, some of them teenagers. Most were males, but there was a smattering of women ... the majority, if left undisturbed, would increase the frequency of their visits, until before long they were firmly 'hooked' and they too moved on to the use of morphine.[82]

Emphasizing the effect of drugs on 'white' women also allowed the police to position itself in the patriarchal role of protectors of innocent and helpless women and children.[83]

The Mountie linkage between opium and Chinese-Canadians would continue into the 1930s. The *R.C.M.P. Quarterly* in 1935 carried a diagram that connected drugs with a racist Chinese stereotype. Another issue included an article, entitled 'The Criminal and His Face,' which commented on the effects of opium upon the user:

> In the confirmed white smoker of opium, changes in the face always take place. The skin becomes more adherent to the facial muscles, whose fat has been partly absorbed. It assumes a yellow, ivory-like colour, more pronounced about the cheek bones. These, because of the shrinkage of facial fat, appear accentuated. There is slowly developed Mongolian or Chinese expression that discloses to the informed the cause of such metamorphosis. The 'opium look' often gives an insight to an otherwise unsuspected habit.[84]

Finally, in a poem entitled 'R.C.M.P.,' reprinted from *Punch* and carried in the *R.C.M.P. Quarterly* in 1940, two lines made racist reference to the war on drugs: 'White-skin, redskin, half-breed, Chink, / Illicit dealers in drugs and drink.'[85]

The RCMP leadership freely offered advice to the politicians when it came to anti-drug legislation. The 1922 commissioner's report advocated tough measures to check 'the calamitous nature of the traffic.'[86] One of the instruments adopted by the Canadian Parliament was unique to the British legal system: those charged with crimes under the Opium and Narcotic Drug Act were considered guilty until proven innocent.[87] Legislation in the 1920s expanded the options available to the police in dealing with the drug trade. The results, however, were mixed. One of the most powerful tools, granted in 1922, was the right to search without a warrant, although initially this authority did not include private accommodation. This changed in 1929 when 'writs of assistance' were added to the ONDA ending the exemption of private dwellings from searches without warrants. The expansion of powers also included the authority to investigate doctors and druggists suspected of trafficking in narcotics by using surveillance and undercover purchases. The force directly influenced some of these amendments to the ONDA in 1929, including the criminalization of parts of drug paraphernalia and the power to confiscate vehicles employed by traffickers.[88] In 1923 the RCMP announced a policy change in the war on drugs with the emphasis now being placed on the kingpins of the drug trade, while the small operators would be left to provincial and municipal police forces. In part, this policy shift appears to have been an attempt to explain the declining number of cases being investigated.[89] RCMP records from 1923 and 1924 also demonstrate that, at least in Saskatchewan, less serious violators were still being charged. Examples included W.J. Morrison of Mossback, arrested for possessing 'tablets alleged to be half grain tablets of morphine sulphate'; Mack Hoy of Birch Hills, picked up for possession of an 'opium pipe'; Katie Hooper of Viceroy, arrested for possession of 'one small glass vial containing morphine'; Yu Lung Chuny of Swift Current, charged for possessing 'one tin of opium'; and Lu Bnos of Kindersley arrested for opium possession.[90] Many, if not most, of these people would have been among the estimated 9,500 drug addicts in Canada in the 1920s. Despite suggestions to the contrary, altruistic concern for the addicts did not inspire the Opium and Narcotic Drug Act and its enforcement. The federal minister of health conceded as much when he admitted in the House of Commons in 1923 that the government had done virtually nothing to support addiction treatment because it considered the matter a provincial responsibility.[91] As the treatment of the Chinese in Canada demonstrated, the government and the RCMP had other reasons for pursuing a war on drugs. It was an expedient way of getting them out of the country.

The Chinese were not the only ones to experience the linking of ethnicity with a particular crime. The RCMP crackdown against illegal alcohol production under the Excise Act, an extension of state control into the wider society, became associated with ethnic minorities, specifically groups from central and eastern Europe. The validity to that linkage was based not on the inherent criminality of certain groups, but rather, as in the case of the Chinese, cultural practices that deviated from the Anglo-Canadian norm and thus had to be criminalized.[92] In 1925 A.B. Allard, commander of the Southern Saskatchewan District, called for more manpower 'to stamp out this type of lawlessness,' which occurred 'particularly amongst the thickly foreign-populated settlements.'[93] Two years later, the report for the same district noted that foreigners continued to make alcohol 'for their own use, chiefly because it is cheaper than the Government liquor and also because they have acquired a taste for home-brew and now prefer it to the lawfully manufactured liquor.'[94]

Be they Chinese-Canadian drug merchants or eastern European-

Table 4.3. RCMP assistance to the Secretary of State (Naturalization)

Year	As % of all assistance to other depts. in Canada	AB	As % of help to other depts. in Alberta	SK	As % of help to other depts. in Saskatchewan
1921	—	852	71	903	57
1922	54	550	54	470	45
1923	49	327	34	361	33
1924	35	872	25	872	19
1925	36	825	25	1014	22
1926	39	1126	33	1115	22
1927	33	804	22	848	17
1928	42	698	34	846	37
1929	55	718	32	3103	55
1930	51	1132	45	1327	33
1931	63	1662	54	1965	48
1932	56	2733	25	3270	60
1934[a]	35	3044	14	3447	47

[a] Covers eighteen-month period.
Source: RCMP Annual Reports.

Canadian bootleggers, how could, from the perspective of the state, the purity of Anglo-Canadian women and the social and political stability of the nation be preserved in the face of these alien menaces? After stringent background checks, those capable of being naturalized, ran the dominant prescription, should be assimilated – the rest deported. Naturalization investigations were an important task for the RCMP to perform: the Mounties made themselves useful to the government while reassuring Anglo-Canadian society that 'undesirables' would not attain British citizenship, let alone remain in Canada.[95]

The federal government looked to the RCMP for the key task of investigating the backgrounds of potential citizens (see table 4.3), and forwarding the information to authorities who would make the final decision, a relationship commented on by Commissioner Perry in 1922:

No small labour is incurred in reporting for the Secretary of State upon applicants for naturalization. The policy has been adopted by that department, when aliens apply for the privilege of becoming British subjects and citizens of Canada, of procuring independent and disinterested examination of their character and conduct. In many cases applicants live in remote places, or in settlements exclusively inhabited by people of foreign birth or origin ... In a number of cases it was ascertained that the applicants were not suitable for citizenship.[96]

The Mountie in charge of southern Alberta would boast in his 1927 annual report of the number of times his men had escorted 'undesirables' to the border where they were handed over to immigration officials for deportation.[97]

For the state, the ability to be assimilated helped determine suitability for citizenship. By 1920 the newly formed RCMP, both sensing and reflecting the mood among the Anglo-Canadian majority, increasingly reported on the process of assimilation among Canada's non-British ethnic groups, especially any resistance to it on their part. Resistance to assimilation was often linked with radicalism, both in reality and in perception. Education, a key tool of absorption, became a centre of Mountie concentration. Ukrainians tended to be on the receiving end of this type of attention because of their reputation for radical politics and the fact that many seemed determined to preserve their ethnic identity. A weekly security bulletin in 1920 described a large meeting of Ukrainians at Red Water, Alberta, where 'speakers did not refer to the assimilation with the Canadian race or the fostering of Canadian ideas in the educating of their children, advocating only Ukrainian Nationalism.'[98] The refusal by Ukrainian school children in Drumheller to salute the flag and carry on other nationalist trappings also was noticed.[99]

Ukrainian schools, mainly those with supposed radical connections, but also the more benign variety, especially concerned the Mounted Police. A 1920 RCMP security bulletin made reference to a Ukrainian boarding school in Saskatoon, the Peter Mohyla Institute, affiliated with the University of Saskatchewan, and the establishment in Saskatchewan of a Ukrainian Greek Orthodox Theological Seminary. The report noted that the priest of the seminary had earlier been involved in a dispute with younger men who were keen on maintaining Ukrainian cultural traditions, such as schools, language, and the flag.[100]

In 1923 Commissioner Starnes wrote to Premier J.E. Brownlee to warn of the danger of Ukrainian schools in Alberta. He included two RCMP memoranda, one from 1921 and the other from 1922.[101] In his 30 December 1922 memo to Sir Lomer Gouin, the federal minister of justice, Starnes warned of schooling carried out during the students' free time and designed by communists to encourage revolutionary thought. One section was very explicit in advising of the danger of Ukrainian schools:

> The principal subjects to be taught are the Ukrainian language, folk-songs, and revolutionary songs and music. Every effort is made to induce the children to hate religion, patriotism, and the government and social and economic system of Canada, and to desire and expect revolution, with its accompanying horrors. Great use is made of concerts; the elders are encouraged to attend entertainments at which the children furnish the programme, most of the recitations, songs etc. having revolutionary tendencies. Sometimes the children act revolutionary plays. The evidence is that these are attractive to the parents. Great hostility is shown to the public schools, which are incessantly denounced as designed to darken the understandings of the children, to teach militarism and religions, and to bolster up capitalism. Bitterness is shown towards those Ukrainians who imbibe Canadian ideals.

In the memo Starnes also reported that other 'nationalities dabble in this activity from time to time, but not in so organized and systematic a manner as the Ukrainians.' Additionally, he warned that even the school cultural activities of some non-Bolshevist groups represented hostility toward 'Canadianization.' The commissioner, however, advised against outright repression, observing that such schools operated outside public school hours, thus not affecting attendance, which was governed by law.[102] Instead, demonstrating his support for the ultimate solution for those who refused to be assimilated or encouraged others to resist such a path, he advocated the deportation of the teachers who worked at the schools.[103]

Police references to Ukrainian schools continued in 1926. The Mounties expressed concern, for example, over an increase in enrolment that occurred after the arrival of a teacher in the Edmonton area who was 'unusually well educated' and had the respect of the Ukrainian community, so much so as to render him a 'dangerous man.'[104] (The RCMP would have a direct impact on this man's life in the 1930s when evidence they compiled led to his deportation.) The report compiler added that English was not taught; instead, students learned to despise the British North America Act and other national symbols and to view the 'Red flag as the God of the workers.'[105] Security bulletin number 334 from 2 September 1926 reported that some schools were teaching illiterate Ukrainians of all ages to read for the purpose of allowing them to absorb radical literature. Their goal, the report added, was to prepare 'the members thereof for a revolution, with the Soviet System of Government as their objective.'[106]

Attitudes had apparently not changed nine years later, when the *R.C.M.P. Quarterly* carried an article, 'Training Young Communists,' that made an explicit link between education, ethnicity, and radicalism. Ukrainian schools, alleged the article, were 'carried on in strict conformity with the general Communist scheme of education and propaganda,' where 'considerable time and attention is given to music and drama which constitute a principal feature of the curriculum.'[107] As this suggests, simply demonstrating a willingness to hold on to traditional cultural practices indicated to the police an unwillingness to assimilate and, thus, by implication, potential radicalism. In a 29 January 1920 security bulletin, reference was made to the cultural practices of Ukrainians in Edmonton:

> 12. Ukrainian Propaganda
> On 10th January in the Greek Catholic Home, Edmonton, the 'Samo-Obrazowania Society', formerly the Ukrainian Socialist Party, performed a play, 'The Thorny Wreath' ... of a revolutionary tendency. This is the fourth drama of this sort performed since November. Our informant (who is of Central European Nationality) described it as effective propaganda against religion and government. At ... the 'Shewchenko' meetings of the Ukrainian Greek Catholic Association at Edmonton 11th January a resolution was passed protesting against the assignment of Galicia to Poland ... The general trend of the meeting was described as adverse to the Canadianization of Ukrainian immigrants.[108]

Even the activities of an all-female Ukrainian mandolin orchestra touring western Canada found its way into a security bulletin. At each stop in the west, reports or, more accurately, concert reviews, would flood in from RCMP informants and secret agents. One noted that while 'O Canada' was sung at the beginning of the concert, it was skipped at the end.[109] An Edmonton-area Mountie undercover operative covered a Ukrainian concert in that city, despite not being able to speak the language. Proving that everyone is a critic, the spy still did not like what he or she heard:

> The whole sentiment of the Concert was anti-Canadian and revolutionary in the extreme, dangerous to the peace of the country in as much as it was inciting the workers to revolution.

One deplorable and striking feature of the whole affair was the number of small children that took part and entered wholeheartedly into the seditious programme, their enthusiasm only being excelled by that of the younger members of the audience, who cheered and applauded in the wildest manner, the Chairman having to ask them to modify their applause. Most of the children present are all Canadian born, and speak English with no trace of a foreign accent, but the appalling fact as demonstrated above, is that they are being trained as REVOLUTIONISTS ...

The Concert was brought to a conclusion by the Ukrainian Mixed Choir singing the 'RED FLAG,' the audience rising. The Theatre was filled to capacity, about eight hundred being present; over ninety percent of who were foreigners, mostly Ukrainians. The audience was orderly throughout, and paid the closest attention to all parts of the programme, but after certain red seditious songs, etc., applauded in the wildest manner, showing the spirit of the audience was revolutionary.[110]

Depending on their behaviour, Anglo-Canadians considered the assimilation of Ukrainians possible although not necessarily desirable. For other groups of people, it was a different story. On the Prairies Asians and African Americans headed the list of undesirables. The latter had already been actively discouraged from coming to the Prairies by Canadian immigration officials while the former, primarily as Chinese male labourers, had arrived despite 'head taxes' and other discriminatory measures.[111]

Besides encountering Chinese in their anti-drug work for the Department of Health, the Mounties met them again while carrying out the 1923 Chinese Immigration Act on behalf of the Department of Immigration and Colonization.[112] In southern Saskatchewan in 1924, this meant the registration of 1,125 Chinese and, according to Superintendent A.B. Allard, 'a great deal of careful work, each registration occupying approximately three-quarters of an hour. This was not the finish of it, as the certificates were returned to be handed back to the Chinamen, and also in several cases further information was asked for by the Chief Comptroller, when the Chinamen had to be interviewed again.'[113]

Assimilation did not apply to the Chinese in Canada. Nor did it apply to those unwilling to accept the status quo of Canadian society, either culturally, economically, or politically. For these groups deportation increasingly became the preferred option in the 1920s and

1930s. It was the ultimate tool for dealing with the unwanted Chinese, trouble-making radicals, and those unwilling to be assimilated. In that sense, the Opium and Narcotic Drug Act was designed not to imprison Canada's unassimilable Asians but to get rid of them. Under the ONDA the non-naturalized guilty could be deported, a point the officer commanding 'K' Division in southern Alberta understood perfectly when he noted in his contribution to the commissioner's annual report for 1925 that of the twenty-eight people convicted in his district under the ONDA, twenty-six were aliens.[114] The Mounted Police turned over the names of the Chinese convicted to the Chief Commissioner of Chinese Immigration, thus playing an important role in enforcing legislation that between 1923 and 1932 the Canadian state used to deport nearly 2 per cent of the Chinese population in Canada, who had collectively lived in the country for an average of seventeen years.[115]

Deportation had already become a weapon in the war against perceived radicals in 1919, as it would become in the twenty-first century in the 'war on terror.'[116] It excised the problem entirely, a reality the federal government recognized when on 6 June 1919, Parliament passed amendments to the Immigration Act that allowed for the detention and deportation, without trial, of everyone, except naturalized Canadians, who advocated the violent overthrow of the Canadian government.[117]

The RNWMP in Alberta and Saskatchewan enthusiastically enforced the new rules. At the same time as the changes, the government appointed several senior RNWMP officers as immigration officers to provide them with the necessary power to make arrests under the new amendments. A government official made it clear that it would not be difficult to appoint additional policemen in this capacity.[118]

The effect of the amendment to the Immigration Act was immediately obvious in southern Alberta's 'K' Division. The monthly reports Superintendent P.W. Pennefather filed began to detail operations against immigrants and members of ethnic minorities. The first reference to the new law being used appeared in July 1919:

On the 18th of the month we made our first arrest under the new Immigration Act, that of Romeo Albo charged under section 41 of the Act, with attempting to create public disorder by word or act. The Minister gave his sanction for the arrest and prosecution of this man, and much good work was done in securing evidence against him. Being a man of some education he was prone to writing letters for the public press, most of them of a very inflammatory nature, and these were heavy evidence against him. In addition to this we were able to produce witnesses of statements he had made. Altogether a most interesting case was brought to a most satisfactory conclusion by the order of the Board of Inquiry for his internment and deportation to Italy.[119]

Pennefather moved against another perceived troublemaker the following year. The police arrested Sanna Kannasto, a Finnish socialist, because of her political activities. Pennefather, himself an Irish immigrant, wanted her tried under section 98, but was instead ordered to turn her over to immigration authorities who held a Board of Inquiry, apparently in an effort to have her deported.[120]

Such powers gave the Mounted Police a great deal of control over the lives of immigrants. 'I am of the opinion,' penned Superintendent Pennefather in a passage that made an explicit link between radicalism, class, and ethnicity, 'that the majority of these agitators have a deadly fear of being sent back to the countries they came from. The worst agitators in my District came from the slums and that is where they should be sent back to.'[121] Commissioner Starnes reiterated this point in 1929, when he forwarded a police report to the Department of Immigration. Spelled out in the report was the police interpretation that the majority of immigrants 'are sympathetic towards Communism, but they are afraid to join ... [since] they may be deported.'[122]

Deportation became less important in the mid-1920s as the economy turned around. A revolution had not occurred. The Liberals, a party more sympathetic to immigrants and less favourably inclined to infringements on civil liberties, took power in 1921 and, except for a brief Conservative interregnum in 1925, held power for the rest of the decade. Still, much of Anglo-Canadian society was displeased with the 1925 Railways Agreement that once more opened Canada's doors to those considered undesirable. The Agreement allowed railway companies to conduct their own immigration policy; they desired a cheap supply of labour. Thousands of previously 'non-preferred' immigrants once more began to enter Canada. As for the RCMP, they continued to worry about those who were different. Certainly deportation remained a weapon of choice – Starnes's recommendations that Ukrainian teachers and Doukhobors be deported are evidence of that.[123] Eventually, the Conservatives under R.B. Bennett, a party that shared the police's way of thinking, gained power. The arrival of both the Tories and the Great Depression made deportation a popular option once again.

Some Mounties wanted to make it even easier to deport undesirables. In 1933 S.T. Wood, at the time in charge of Saskatchewan's 'F' Division, urgently recommended to Commissioner MacBrien that sections 40 and 41 of the Immigration Act be amended to simplify deportation. Wood specifically objected to the fact that naturalized Canadians of at least five years were exempt from deportation and that it was up to the state to prove that an individual was an active communist, not merely a member, before he or she could be deported. Wood wanted amended laws because 'deportation is the one effective weapon against foreign agitators and one of which they are in continual fear. Communist Party directives stress the necessity of protecting foreign agitators by assuming English names and by other means.'[124]

Commissioner MacBrien himself had publicly called for the removal of radicals of foreign birth in a 1932 speech. His reference to expulsion as a solution to Canada's internal problems was not a rhetorical flourish; he worked to ensure that it became common practice. On 13 October 1931, MacBrien met in Ottawa with Major-General Andrew McNaughton, chief of the General Staff, W.A. Gordon, the acting minister of justice, the minister of national defence, and the commissioner of immigration. The topic of discussion was deportation of unnaturalized communists. It was decided that a military barracks in eastern Canada would be given to the RCMP for the creation of an 'Emigration Station.'[125]

Candidates for the station were readily available. In 1931 a senior officer wrote to the commander of 'K' Division in southern Alberta to inquire how long a particularly troublesome Communist had been in Canada. 'If he has been here five years he cannot be deported,' the superintendent added.[126] A year later, the head of the Mounted Police detachment in Saskatoon wrote to his superior to report 'of the 750 single unemployed receiving relief from the City, not more than 20% are residents of Saskatoon, the remainder are transients, a great number of which are foreigners, many of them not yet having established Canadian domicile.' The clear message to his superior was that these unemployed men, who were beginning to challenge authority in the Saskatchewan city, were an exportable commodity.[127]

The RCMP viewed deportation as a preventive measure, as punishment, or both. A violent riot had occurred in Estevan, Saskatchewan, on 29 September 1931, two weeks before MacBrien met in Ottawa with other officials to discuss deportation. A local Mountie believed that non-British locals caused the violence: 'The rioters consisted largely of Foreigners as very few English speaking people took an aggressive part in the riot.' As a response he recommended 'discriminate deportation of the radical foreign element.'[128] Two months later,

Superintendent J.W. Spalding, commander of the Southern Saskatchewan District, expanded on this idea when he supplied the officer in
charge of the Estevan area with a list of names of possible communists
or at least men with '"Red" tendencies.' He asked that the names on the
list be 'investigated with a view to their possible deportation.'[129]

The force was intricately involved in deportation operations in
western Canada. Often it was evidence supplied by Mounted Policemen as to the radical tendencies of a particular individual which led to
his or her expulsion from Canada. John Sembay (Symbay), a Ukrainian involved in the Ukrainian Labour-Farmer Temple Association in
Edmonton and mentioned in security bulletins in the 1920s because of
his connection with Ukrainian schools, was ordered deported under
section 41 on 10 May 1932. The decision was based on the evidence
of RCMP Secret Agent 125 (Jacob Tatko), which specifically linked
Sembay with 'revolutionary utterances looking to the overthrow of
our economic and governmental structure in Canada by the use of
force or violence.' The final blow was testimony from Mountie Sergeant John Leopold, a famous infiltrator of the Canadian Communist
Party, that the ULFTA was connected with the Communist Party.[130]
Gottfried Zurcher, on the other hand, was found to have contravened
section 41 of the Immigration Act based on the evidence of RCMP
constables – although in this case they neglected to find out the man's
nationality. And a Finn faced deportation in 1933 because of the
evidence supplied by Leopold that the Finnish organization the man
belonged to was a branch of the Communist Party.[131]

These are a few examples of a regular tactic employed in the
continual RCMP war against undesirables. The deportation of radicals, however, paled in comparison to the number of people deported
in the 1930s because they had become unemployed or were on
relief.[132] The Mounted Police played a role here by arresting vagrants
and others who could then be deported because they had not been
naturalized and thus lacked the protection of citizenship. Regardless of
the reasons for removal, the common belief was that as people they
were expendable and that Canada was better off without them.

Deportation was the final chapter of the Mounted Police's post-
1914 interaction with members of several of Canada's ethnic groups.
The relationship began in the early days of the First World War as
Mounties went out among enemy aliens to check on their allegiance
to Canada. At the end of the war, enemy aliens became less important.
Instead the attention shifted to ethnic radicals, particularly Finns and
Ukrainians, who threatened revolution, or so the Canadian state feared.
The RCMP, in addition, focused on 'ethnic criminals,' especially the

Chinese, in their efforts to survive as an institution and protect Anglo-Canada. Naturalization investigations and reports on the failure of some immigrants to assimilate served a similar role. Finally, the Mounties helped remove undesirables from the land of the maple leaf and the beaver.

The attention ethnic groups received in this period had one other ramification for the Mounted Police. The need to produce reliable and detailed information on the activities of non-Anglo-Canadians meant a different approach for the men in scarlet. It required recruiting personnel from the groups that one wished to collect information on. It also meant the use of undercover operatives and detectives, something at odds with both Mountie history and perceived British tradition. During the First World War, and in its immediate aftermath, the force underwent a radical transformation. That unnoticed change kept public the crime-fighting role of the Mounted Police, but it added a secret intelligence-gathering function that would eventually grow into the RCMP Security Service. Some Mounties had shed their famous uniforms for more inconspicuous attire. The men in scarlet had become the men in secret.

5

Men in Secret

It was a time of disorder, of radicalism, and of revolution. The Romanov dynasty had been toppled and eventually eradicated with bullets in Russia. Germany seemed poised to fall beneath the wheels of the Red machine. South of the 49th parallel, the United States had been experiencing industrial and political turmoil. The government of Prime Minister Robert Borden was, not surprisingly, frightened. The prime minister, in France to attend the 1919 Paris Peace Conference, received a frantic telegram from his cabinet requesting that a British cruiser be sent to Vancouver harbour as a tool of intimidation for those contemplating revolution right across Canada.[1]

By the time of the Winnipeg General Strike in May 1919, the Canadian government thought it had an institutional understanding of what was behind the widespread unrest because the previous year it had employed an Ottawa lawyer, C.H. Cahan, to undertake an investigation. In September 1918 he reported that Germans, targeted for attention by the police attention during the war, no longer posed a threat to the state. Instead, 'Russians, Ukrainians and Finns, employed in the mines, factories and other industries' represented the real danger since they were 'thoroughly saturated with the Socialistic doctrines which have been proclaimed by the Bolsheviki faction of Russia.'[2] In truth, the bogeyman (the threat was gendered male) he created mixed ethnicity, class, and radicalism. The immediate response of the Borden government was to enact two Orders in Council that silenced foreign-language newspapers and eliminated several anarchist and socialist organizations.[3]

Cahan, however, spoke to an audience that included more than the federal government. Commissioner A.B. Perry heard his warning, and the veteran Mountie worked diligently to ensure his charges had the proper weapons to deal with the radical menace that so many believed threatened Canada. Under the direction of Newton Rowell, the federal cabinet minister with responsibility for the force, Perry prepared three memos in early 1919 that created a branch of the Mounted Police, which lasted for nearly sixty-five years. His words detailed both the construction of a secret service and the targets of its operations. For the first time Mounties began to police on a regular basis not just what people did but also what they said and thought.

In his first memo, dated 6 January 1919, Perry warned of the growth of left-wing radicalism in Canada, specifically the increase in the 'pernicious doctrines of Bolshevism.' He also identified the geographic centre of radicalism as being in western Canada, and those prone to accepting such doctrines as residing in 'foreign settlements.'[4] A second memo, prepared the same day, informed his subordinates of the key soldiers in the coming battle with radicals: 'One of the most important branches of our work will be that of the detective service and this service must receive your particular attention with the object in view of obtaining all possible information without in any way causing suspicion on the part of interested persons or associations.'[5]

Perry clarified these points in a 5 February 1919 memorandum for his junior officers that was designed to offer 'information and guidance in connection with Secret Service investigations re Bolshevism.' Specifically, he listed three 'classes' of individuals connected with labour and radicalism. First, there were the 'responsible leaders of organized labour' opposed to Bolshevism. Next came workers 'who express approval of Bolshevism in general, as they look upon it as the workers' Government in Russia without knowing or realizing what it really signifies and without knowing the crimes which are being committed in its name.' Finally, and most importantly, according to the commissioner, came the 'third class which is believed to constitute a very small minority,' these being the real radicals. In advancing these views, Perry reflected the strong linkage in the minds of many in Canada between ethnicity and radicalism: '[This third class are] principally of foreign birth, who have imbibed the real Bolshevist Doctrine of a class war, and they believe in revolution as a method to obtain their ends.'[6]

The commissioner offered prescriptions for dealing with the three classes. The first group had to be dealt with carefully 'so that proceedings ... not be taken against men who in spirit are thoroughly loyal to Canada.' The second class was to be battled with 'education and counter propaganda.' The focus of the police would be on the third, and, in their opinion, most dangerous, segment.[7]

In his initial memo (6 January 1919) Perry had set out the tactics for dealing with such radicals, specifically with the idea of subversion, a modern nebulous concept readily exploited by the state.[8]

> 6. ... The R.N.W.M. Police is now the sole Federal Police force in Western Canada, and it is therefore our duty to actively enquire into and take such steps as may be legally possible to prevent the efforts of misguided persons to subvert and undermine the settled Government of Canada.
> 7. Officers Commanding should therefore keep themselves thoroughly informed of what is going on in their Districts and energetically deal with all unlawful and pernicious propaganda ...[9]

Additional personnel would have to be recruited to perform the new work that Perry envisioned:

> 10. ... You will take steps to select some good trustworthy men whom you consider could be employed effectively as secret agents and submit their names records and qualifications for my approval.
> 11. Too much care cannot be exercised in making such selections upon whom a careful check should be kept with a view to removing the possibility of their purposely furnishing improper or incorrect information ....

Then the commissioner offered a legal strategy for pursuing suspected subversives:

> 13. It will therefore be necessary to resort to the Criminal Code, dealing with them as treasonable and seditious offences.
> 14. In the matter of public speeches and addresses – very careful attention is to be given to them, and where a treasonable or seditious speech is anticipated, it should be taken down by a shorthand writer and in a case of great importance, two shorthand writers should be employed acting independently.
> 15. Attention is also to be given to street speeches more or less prevalent in large centres.
> 16. It is especially pointed out that investigations and enquiries must be conducted in such manner as not in any way to arouse suspicion or cause antagonism on the part of such associations or organizations.[10]

Finally, the commissioner indicated that this new intelligence function was being performed on behalf of the federal government, for it was 'extremely desirous that such unrest should not be permitted to develop into a menace to good order and public safety.'[11] The task of the Mounted Police was to keep watch on those unhappy with the status quo, keep the government informed about their activities, and be prepared to act if so ordered by its political bosses.

Canada was certainly not unique in its approach to radicalism at the end of the First World War. The United States was in the midst of its own war against those deemed un-American. As in Canada, the primary targets were organizations on the political left, especially ones with foreign-sounding names and members. Nativism was widespread in American society as the war in Europe bled to a halt. In the interwar period, however, Bolshevism, associated with anarchism and various acts of terrorism committed across the country, replaced enemy aliens as the primary menace to America. A dark star was born in the United States in this era with the beginning of the career of J. Edgar Hoover, who eventually as head of the Federal Bureau of Investigation (FBI) became, arguably, the most powerful man in the United States.[12]

Britain, whose traditions Canada more closely mirrored, also experienced the development of a political police force in this era. Even though it had secret police operating in Ireland and India, Britain had always prided itself on its lack of such institutions at home, viewing them as an infringement on civil liberties and more characteristic of the way policing was practised on the continent.[13] But in the years prior to the Great War, Britain began to take on many of the trappings of a security state. These developments were a response to both external events (the possibility of war in Europe) and internal events (labour unrest between 1911 and 1914). Those on the political right often linked internal problems, such as the unhappiness of British workers, to foreign agitators because, according to Bernard Porter, 'the implication ... was that British workers would still be working happily if it were not for them.'[14] This philosophy, which chose to explain complex social events and movements through the participation of individual actors, was common among police forces in the United States and Canada as well.[15]

How did an institution of 'the national insecurity state' reach the point at the beginning of 1919 where the Mounted Police commissioner felt the necessity to dispatch memos detailing the creation of a security service?[16] Widespread use of detectives and secret agents represented a new phase for the Mounted Police and for Canada in general. At the beginning of the First World War, the Dominion

Police, in effect Canada's security service, largely handled intelligence gathering through the use of various measures including the appointment of American Pinkerton private detectives. The Mounted Police took over the intelligence gathering among 'enemy alien' settlements in western Canada after the start of the conflict, relying on agents recruited for that task. Many of them were subsequently dismissed when it became obvious that these settlements did not pose a major security risk.[17]

Times changed and attitudes hardened as the war dragged on. Turmoil began developing on the home front, and nativism increasingly thrived. To the state, especially in the aftermath of Cahan's report, there seemed an increasing need for Mounted Police intelligence gathering, especially among aliens in western Canada.[18] By 1919 Commissioner Perry was confirming the development of a Mounted Police security service. Within a few months, it would be busy. In the early years, little distinguished the regular police side from the security wing. Regular detectives of the Criminal Investigation Branch (CIB), such as C.T. Hildyard in Saskatoon, spent one day conducting narcotics investigations, while the next day they would be spying on a local meeting of the Communist Party or receiving the report of someone they had hired to do that job instead. Occasionally the two jobs blended even more closely as in 1923 when Hildyard wrote an article on the dangers of drugs for a labour newspaper run by an informant in his employ who supplied information about the activities of the recently formed Communist Party of Canada.[19]

What was the framework of the Mounted Police security operations that allowed it to monitor radicals in Alberta and Saskatchewan? Or, more simply, how did it operate? There were three types of personnel involved in intelligence gathering: regular members of the force, secret agents, and informants. The first category included the regular members of the Mounted Police, often detectives, who went undercover for various periods of time; on other occasions they directed the operations of subordinates. The best examples of such personnel from Alberta and Saskatchewan were T.E. Ryan, who did undercover work in the Regina area at the end of the First World War, and Frank Zaneth, active in the Drumheller area and Calgary in the immediate aftermath of the First World War.[20] The most famous undercover Mountie in the history of the force, however, was John (Johann) Leopold, who in the persona of Jack Esselwein, a Regina house painter, infiltrated the Communist Party in the 1920s. The use of regular members, especially in undercover work, was a difficult option for the force, especially since its identity was so closely connected with the famous scarlet uniform, as one undercover member discovered in 1915 when he received a fine for failing to salute a superior officer.[21] In addition, British tradition, which heavily influenced the Mounted Police, equated surveillance and espionage with underhandedness and skulduggery – not the sort of role for the noble Mountie. When it was revealed in the aftermath of the 1933 Saskatoon Relief Camp Riot that a Mounted Policeman had infiltrated the Saskatoon unemployed, the Regina *Leader-Post* criticized the police methods: 'It should be recognized that Canadian public opinion is strongly against what might be referred to as secret police. The tradition of the country is against it, as also is the British tradition.'[22]

Leopold's activities proved both useful and troublesome for the RCMP. The diminutive Mountie – at five foot four, well below the force's minimum height requirements of five foot eight – came from an untraditional background and spoke English with an accent. He did not conform to the Mountie image constructed at the time. Such characteristics, however, made him ideal for undercover work. Using his alternative identity, Leopold joined the One Big Union (OBU) in Regina in 1919 and became an official of the Workers' Party of Canada, the legal face of the Communist Party of Canada in 1921.[23] Yet these undercover activities by someone who was a regular member of the Mounties created certain problems. First, there was a question of legality. How far could Leopold go as his alter ego, Jack Esselwein, in an effort to discover subversion? This aspect worried his handlers, even as he burrowed deeper into the radical left in Regina. After all, these experiences were new for the Mounted Police, and even in the present, questions of entrapment continue to trouble police forces. In July 1921 Leopold's main contact in the force relayed a conversation with his spy to the head of the Southern Saskatchewan detachment of the RCMP. The topic of discussion was how active a role Leopold should play in the fledgling Communist Party, since he had been approached by a party official to organize a branch in Regina:

> Should he take an active part, presumably that of leader or organizer, he would be liable to most severe punishment when the final break comes, as it would be out of the question to uncover him and even if uncovered he would still be liable, as it would be impossible for him to carry on without doing criminal actions occasionally. On being questioned, he assured me that he would never in any way promote the Communist Party unless forced to do so by circumstances and that he would use every discretion in the matter.

He further informed me on being questioned that he was willing if necessary and if in the interests of the work, to go to gaol and serve any term which might be imposed upon him, rather than be uncovered, if of course, he was still carried in the strength of the force. No. 30 is prepared to go to any length the Service requires.[24]

The undercover Mountie's handler assured his superior that any activity on the part of Leopold would be to the detriment, not the benefit, of the Communists. In Regina Leopold had already destroyed party flyers, wasted funds, and sabotaged party meetings; the sergeant now sought approval for the infiltrator to continue and extend his activities.[25] The official blessing was not long in coming. Four days later, Commissioner Perry wrote that the 'opportunity offered of gaining access to Communist plans must not be allowed to escape us.' At the same time, he cautioned, 'It is undesirable that No. 30 should actually commit illegal acts himself, or should incite others to commit them.'[26]

In return, Leopold promised that if 'pressed to organize the Regina Branch of the Movement, I will do so with the least amount of effect as possible, and endeavour to get someone also to do the actual work or appear to do it. I will be on my guard against doing anything which could be brought home to me individually.'[27] And, of course, anything which might be traced back to the Mounted Police. There was, however, some question as to how passive a role the secretive Mountie played. Once Leopold's identity became public in 1931, two members of Parliament, J.S. Woodsworth and M.J. Coldwell, criticized Mounted Police security intelligence activity in the House of Commons. Woodsworth questioned the government in 1934 about whether the Mounted Police still had police officers spying on the legal activities of unions since Leopold, as part of his undercover identity, had been head of the Regina Trades and Labour Council in 1925. The member of Parliament also recalled a meeting of his own with Leopold at which the latter invited him home for dinner, an offer he kindly refused.[28] In 1937 Coldwell recalled his contact with Leopold in Regina and how hard the Mountie had worked on behalf of the Communist Party, even urging a Coldwell acquaintance to join the organization. The veteran of numerous political skirmishes, reflecting popular sentiments of the time, derided such work as 'unBritish.'[29]

Eventually the Mounted Police did question the effectiveness of Leopold. The Mountie increasingly revelled in his undercover role, especially the freedom he enjoyed as Jack Esselwein. He began to act in a manner outside the control of his Mounted Police superiors, many of whom were still uncomfortable with the nature of undercover activity in general and his work in particular. In 1926 Leopold, much to the surprise of senior Mounties, made a trip to Winnipeg. This unexpected sojourn prompted Commissioner Cortlandt Starnes to wonder if 'this man is getting somewhat disposed to work upon his own, with insufficient consultation and direction from his superiors.'[30] The undercover operative increasingly appeared to be cracking under the stress of his life of deception. In 1927 his superiors received a report of binge drinking on the part of their undercover Mountie. He also failed to make regular reports.[31] Finally, in 1928, the Communist Party of Canada discovered his true identity and expelled him from the party. Headquarters advised him to quietly accept the expulsion so as not to give 'the radicals any material for propaganda.'[32]

John Leopold, however, did not quietly disappear. Transferred to the Yukon and regular duty after his exposure, he reappeared in 1931 to testify in the trial of the 'Toronto Eight,' eight senior members of the Communist Party of Canada who had been arrested under section 98 of the Criminal Code. His personal behaviour also remained troublesome for the Mounted Police. First, there was a bout of venereal disease while in the Yukon. Other discipline problems in the early 1930s, including continued trouble with alcohol, led to a reduction in his rank.[33] When Leopold was involved in the botched attempt to arrest the leaders of the On to Ottawa Trek in 1935, a cartoon in the University of Saskatchewan student newspaper, *The Sheaf*, mocked him as a drunk. In early 1936 he was reprimanded for being intoxicated on duty, for possessing liquor on duty, and insubordination. The communists had great sport with Leopold's trouble. In fact, the only thing that kept him in the Mounted Police, where he remained until his death in 1958, was the fear of an even greater communist propaganda victory over his dismissal.[34]

Leopold was not the only Mountie operating undercover in Alberta and Saskatchewan at the end of the war. Frank Zaneth also had a lengthy undercover career; but unlike his more famous colleague, he managed to keep his record clean and spent the western Canadian part of his secret career in Alberta. Zaneth, Italian-American by birth and thus capable of blending in with those targeted by the Mounted Police for surveillance, joined the force in December 1917. Three months later the rookie police officer appeared before the commissioner in Regina. Perry informed the new Mountie of his designation as the first member of the fledgling security service (eight secret agents and six detectives in the entire force in December 1918) a few months before the commissioner codified the operations of the branch. Zaneth would report directly to the top Mountie. In September 1918 Perry sent

Zaneth, posing as an enemy alien named Harry Blask, to Drumheller to keep watch on disgruntled coal miners. The undercover Mountie infiltrated the labour and radical scene before having his real identity revealed when he was required to testify at the Winnipeg General Strike trials.[35] Having to expose a valuable operative like Zaneth irritated upper echelons of the RCMP. That experience helps explain the subsequent reluctance of the Mounted Police to encourage the prosecution of radicals. The better approach was to watch quietly and wait.

Several Mounties went undercover for short periods during their careers. Constable T.E. Ryan served in an undercover role in Saskatchewan. Ryan, a co-worker of Leopold, once aided his bedridden and very ill colleague in 1919 while the two were but mere rookies in the big league of spying. The young constable managed to infiltrate the local chapter of the One Big Union and filed several reports before the past enveloped his career.[36] Constable H.M. Wilson infiltrated the relief camp in Saskatoon just prior to the 1933 relief camp riot. 'I have,' he reported, 'firmly established myself as a radical.'[37] Constable Harold Philip Keeler, a former member of the London Metropolitan Police, joined the Communist Party in Alberta between October 1930 and May 1931 before once again donning the scarlet to testify against party members in court. Corporal R.C. Rathbone had undercover periods in his career, first in Winnipeg in 1922 and then in Edmonton in 1932, where he worked at a relief office and made regular reports on the unemployed.[38]

The second component of Mounted Police security operations in Alberta and Saskatchewan involved secret agents whose job it was to infiltrate targeted organizations.[39] The prime qualification to be a secret agent, reflecting the nature of the work or more accurately the targets of their work, was linguistic skill, hence the original recruitment of Leopold in this capacity. Secret agents, because of the distaste society felt about their work and the desire of the force to distance itself should an operation go awry, had even less job security than regular members.[40] In the nature and the low status of the work, the position had, in effect, been ethnicized. Specific guidelines for the use and handling of secret agents developed through trial and error as the bureaucracy of an intelligence agency slowly grew; after all, much of this was new to the Mounted Police, as 1919 instructions regarding the activities of agents in 'K' Division indicate:

Confirming the instructions given you today you will arrange to meet our Secret Agents at appointed place, and in this connection, so far as possible, it will be well not to have all together at one time. The matter in hand is more or less connected, still they can be given work to do that will avoid their doubling up on same, and in reports submitted. Corroboration of certain information, is of course, useful in many instances.

The important point [is] to have these men apply themselves in the obtaining of inside information from the Strikers, particularly the Red element, of moves they are likely to make, so that we will know in advance, and as early as possible, of any contemplated action on their part likely to cause serious trouble.[41]

The Mounted Police's experience with secret agents in Alberta and Saskatchewan was a mixed one. The employment of non-Anglo-Celts could on occasion unleash Mountie prejudice. In 1919 the commanding officer of 'K' Division derided the work of two of his secret agents and complained of the difficulty of training 'foreigners' for secret agent work. The nature of the work, as well, could lead to distrust. If a secret agent was willing to lie, cheat, and betray to collect information, how could such an individual be truly trusted? In Calgary in 1919, a detective informed his superiors that he did not have faith in one of the secret agents working under him; the Mountie feared that the agent might either be lazy, simply passing off Frank Zaneth's work as his own, or actually a double agent who was feeding the Mounted Police disinformation. Mervyn Black, recruited in Saskatchewan in the early 1930s as a secret agent, later occupied a desk job and exercised a great deal of power in handling agents. At the same time, his bosses received criticism from their superiors because they considered Black too much of a security risk to be handling sensitive operations.[42] One Mountie warned Commissioner MacBrien in 1934 that secret agents needed to be closely monitored: 'This cannot be properly judged from their reports coming into Headquarters. It is found that some secret agents have been taken on without very careful examination in regard to them and their work has been of little or no value.'[43]

Agents came from many different backgrounds. W.H. Balsinger, a French Canadian, was sent out among French-speaking communities in Saskatchewan in 1916 and 1917 to listen to opinions related to conscription. In 1916 Perry authorized the hiring of Joseph E. Ruepp, familiar with German, French, and Italian, as a secret agent in Edmonton, specifically to ensure that 'enquiries [into radical activity] may be promptly and speedily made and thus [the RNWMP would] not be dependent upon outside assistance,' an apparent reference to (and inherent criticism of) the use of American detectives by the Dominion Police.[44]

Not only did the use of secret agents remove the necessity of relying on individuals from outside agencies, but these agents additionally served as a far more effective tool for a police force that was increasingly concerned about the opinions and words of citizens. Bernard Porter's definition of a political police force is applicable to the Mounted Police: 'a body of men and women whose duty is to keep tabs on the political opinions, activities and intentions of the subjects of a state.'[45] Commissioner Perry had instructed in 1919 that 'arrangements must be made whereby detectives are able to supply their Officers Commanding with a complete report as to what transpires at every meeting of these [radical] organizations.'[46] Agents and informants served as additional sets of ears to hear what was said and as added witnesses to testify about activities or statements in court.[47] Often what they heard was in a language other than English. T.A. Wroughton, in charge of 'G' Division which covered part of Alberta, including Edmonton, lamented in July 1917 that none of his detectives understood German or 'Austrian.' He suggested that two agents who spoke the languages of sedition and radicalism be transferred for his use.[48]

Nineteen-nineteen became the key year for the use of Mounted Police secret agents in Alberta and Saskatchewan. In Alberta the men in scarlet targeted Edmonton and mining areas. Perry, however, informed the chairman of Alberta's Board of Police Commissioners that secret agents were operating in every part of Alberta.[49] 'G' Division's monthly report for January 1919 noted that an attempt was being made to recruit secret agents in an effort to gather inside information on J.A. Knight, a perceived local radical and head of Edmonton's Trades and Labour Council. Unfortunately, the report author added, finding qualified men was extremely difficult. In Edmonton William Walker, a returned soldier, seemed promising. His recruitment also suggests a police recognition that it was not only non-English-speaking radicals who might prove a threat.[50]

By August 1919, the head of 'K' Division, which included the mining districts of southern Alberta, even went so far as to complain about the volume of material flooding in from agents; he requested an additional stenographer to handle the correspondence.[51] That material would continue to pour in from secret agents throughout the interwar period. There can be no exact account of the actual amount or the number of agents employed in the field. The only such information available is for 1923–4, unquestionably a lull in the war against radicalism between the end of the First World War and the beginning of the Depression. During that period the Mounted Police budgeted $130 per month each for thirty agents at a total of $46,800 for the year. Twenty agents received a subsistence allowance and travelling expenses of $3 per diem or a total of $21,900 for the year. Six more agents were employed part time at $3,240 for the year (or $45 per agent per month). Detectives of the force and the CIB's stenographers received $28,060 for the year. The total of the secret service operations for the 1923–4 year amounted to approximately $100,000 out of the RCMP's total budget of $2,587,999.11, or 4 per cent.[52]

Records from 1933 indicate a wide variance in salaries for agents working for Saskatchewan's 'F' Division, which in 1932 had its boundaries adjusted to include all of the province (see table 5.1). This list does not include all of the agents operating in Saskatchewan in the 1930s. At least two others, Secret Agents 942 and 950, were active. In the fall of 1933 they spied in the MacKenzie constituency where a federal by-election was to occur, and where communist organizers sought support. During the subsequent winter they covered relief camps around Saskatoon. In 1935 Secret Agent 942 worked his hours in the mining districts of Estevan and Bienfait.[53] Where agents spied (mining districts, urban centres, relief camps) speaks to the sectors given security priority by the Mounted Police. The 1930s was a decade of record unemployment, and various levels of government viewed the victims of the economic calamity, the unemployed, as a direct threat to social peace.

In 1936 Secret Agent 942 remained employed, having been joined by Secret Agent 983. Former secret agent and now Special Constable Mervyn Black handled both of them. Carl Betke and S.W. Horrall, in their official history of the RCMP Security Service, cite 'F' Division as a particularly efficient operation when it came to intelligence gathering. They also point to the fact that Saskatchewan was the first province to receive the Mounted Police back as a provincial police force, thereby providing a much wider RCMP presence and thus greater opportunities for collecting information. Stuart Taylor Wood led 'F' Division for several years in the 1930s; the future commissioner had a better appreciation of the importance of intelligence gathering than many of his contemporaries.[54]

Records related to secret agents in Alberta are not as detailed as those for its eastern neighbour. One agent active in the province was Jacob M. Tatko, who served as Secret Agent 125 in Alberta between April 1921 and February 1932 (from 1928 he also served as a special constable). His top salary as a secret agent was $125 per month.[55] Roy Koyich infiltrated the Communist Party in the 1930s, at one point

Table 5.1. Salaries of RCMP secret agents in Saskatchewan
('F' Division), 1933

Agent	Salary
Secret Agent 849 (J.L. Eberhardt)	$4.00 per day
Secret Agent 871	$50.00 per month
Secret Agent 881	$3.50 per day
Secret Agent 895	$35.00 per month
Secret Agent 909	$2.50 per day
Secret Agent 923	$35.00 per month
Secret Agent 935 (Mervyn Black)	$80.00 per month

Source: RCMP, Personnel Records of J.L. Eberhardt, Report of S/Sgt. B.H.
James, 28 February 1933.

even working as party treasurer in Edmonton. His testimony during
the Second World War led to the internment of several individuals
under the Defence of Canada Regulations; once his identity was
exposed, Koyich became a special constable.[56]

The final human resource of the developing RCMP intelligence
wing was informants or, perhaps more accurately, part-time spies.
Mounties used informants on occasion to cover meetings or to supply information on a particular organization or individual. They
employed them because, even in plain clothes, policemen could be
recognized at meetings, especially in small centres – a reality acknowledged in a 1919 report from the Saskatoon detachment: 'No
member of this detachment attended this meeting [at which J.S.
Woodsworth spoke] as there were a number of foreigners present,
also it was deemed advisable to keep away as labour men have been
kept in close touch with and recognition was a thing to avoid, however the meeting was covered fully by previous arrangement.'[57] Often
the value of an informant depended on his or her position in relation to
the organization or individual he or she was being asked to supply
information about. In Saskatoon in the early 1920s, for example, the
local Mountie secured information from an individual named Mill
(possibly Walter Mill upon whom the Mounties also had a file), a local
organizer for the Trade Union Educational League and the Workers'
Party of Canada. In Edmonton in 1928 an informant was high enough
in the local party to be asked by prominent communist activist A.E.
Smith, head of the Canadian Labour Defence League (CLDL), about
the activities of the Edmonton branches; in turn, the informant queried Smith on his party work.[58]

Informants were usually paid a fee for their work. In a 1925 Saskatoon example, one informant received $5.00 for reports on two meetings. Now and then, Mountie handlers employed more than one source at a meeting;[59] the testimony in court of two witnesses carried more weight than one. Having two in attendance at gatherings also allowed the Mountie handler, such as one in Calgary who suspected his source of having relayed details on a meeting garnered from a newspaper account, to use each individual as a check on the veracity of the other.[60] 'Be constantly on [your] guard against being purposely misled by the informants,' Commissioner Perry warned detectives.[61] Occasionally, the Mounted Police had good reason to be suspicious of the information they received. In 1924 word came from an informant that an important communist, Malcolm Bruce, was carrying the 'plans of Lenine [sic] and Trotzky [sic] for the world revolution.'[62] At his first opportunity John Leopold searched Bruce's suitcase in Regina, finding only ordinary party documents.[63]

Taken together, these various Mountie suppliers of information generated tens of thousands of pages of records on organizations, events, and individuals. The main division in record keeping was between organizations and individuals. In the case of the latter, the process of developing personal history files (PHFs) began in 1919. These were detailed records on who the Mounties considered particularly troublesome or dangerous. Commissioner Perry had ordered that a file be kept 'for each leader or official of any [radical organization] ... and as the information is gathered from time to time regarding these men it should be placed on the individual's file. By this means a complete history of these men and their doings to date will be available at any time.'[64] The files usually began with a description of the individual, including a ranking of the person's success as an agitator. A picture often accompanied the reports along with any subsequent records. The decision to start a PHF was usually predicated on the involvement of the individual in any hint of radical activity. Chairing a 1920 labour meeting in Carievale, Saskatchewan, a small town in the southern part of the province, was all that it took for the Mounted Police to create a PHF for Reverend H.D. Ranns, a Methodist minister.[65]

Who and what were the Mounted Police collecting files on in Alberta and Saskatchewan and, more importantly, why? The targets can be broken down in the following ways. First came the radical left, the main and consistent target from the end of the First World War to the beginning of the next. Other individuals and organizations also contained in the category of 'left,' specifically those of a social democratic nature, occasionally drew police interest. Gathering information on these organizations occurred almost exclusively in the early 1920s when the Mounted Police security role was still in its infancy. The force, for example, collected files on William Irvine and J.S. Woodsworth, two labour members of Parliament. The other political groups which interacted with the RCMP in Alberta and Saskatchewan occupied the far right. In the 1920s this category was represented by the Ku Klux Klan (KKK); in the 1930s fascist and Nazi organizations carried the banner.

Some groups tarred with the label of radicalism received only brief attention before being dismissed. In their haste in the aftermath of the First World War to collect information on any group outside the mainstream, the Mounties reached for restraint and found an empty holster. In a series of raids across western Canada to collect evidence for the Winnipeg General Strike trials, for example, underlings were ordered to seize 'Anything of a Socialistic or Revolutionary character.'[66] Individual officers determined what constituted such definitions.

Besides demonstrating a lack of sophistication, such an approach created the potential for excess. In one case Mounted Policemen collected information on a Jehovah's Witness organization. A security bulletin for October 1920 reported on a meeting of the International Bible Student Association in Prince Albert and the fact that the main speaker had declared that a religious revolution was at hand.[67] Reports on Witnesses had turned up in 'K' Division the previous year, when the police charged several with possession of restricted literature. Superintendent Pennefather commented that 'only nominal fines were imposed as it was plain that these people were not propagandists, but simply religious fanatics.'[68] The selection of Witnesses for repression in the immediate aftermath of the First World War demonstrated that during periods of turmoil the net of the state was often cast wide. The Mounties sought radicals of all stripes, and a religious group which viewed the state as satanic seemed, at least initially, an ideal candidate for repression. This is a reality the Witnesses would experience again during the Second World War when they would be banned as a subversive organization and compared by the commissioner of the Mounted Police to 'poison toadstools.'[69]

One Mounted Police enemy, however, could not be rehabilitated, nor shown moderation under any circumstances. That villain was the revolutionary left, represented over the years by different organizations but chiefly by the Communist Party of Canada. The priority towards the radical left was evident in January 1919 when Commissioner Perry ordered Mounted Police detectives to investigate every organization in their district for the following things:

(A) The purpose and object of the organization
(B) If the organization is one which could possibly be influenced by Bolsheviki propaganda in order to gain its ends
(C) Has the organization Bolsheviki tendencies at the present time?
(D) Is it a Bolsheviki organization?[70]

Why did the RCMP become obsessed with the radical left – an obsession that on occasion bordered on outright hatred? First, Communists in Canada were intimately connected with the Bolsheviks in the Soviet Union, a party which advocated the worldwide overthrow of capitalism. The Soviets made efforts in many countries, including Canada, to promote revolution, providing both financial and ideological guidance through Communist International (COMINTERN). The fact that much of this revolutionary activity was conducted in secret only drew greater attention from the police.[71]

Another important factor that made the Communist Party threatening to so many was its 'foreign' component. Regardless of how small its membership was or how divided the party was, both realities that applied for a good portion of the interwar period, the fact that the group challenging the status quo appeared to be both controlled and populated by outsiders, especially those considered beneath the majority because of prevailing prejudices, made the threat of the CPC that much greater. Communists appeared to be both un-Canadian and un-British since the movement had no Anglo roots; from this perspective, it represented an alien growth on Canadian soil. Ivan Avakumovic described the two solitudes thusly: 'To a native Canadian a Communist was someone who spoke English with an accent, used jargon incomprehensible to most Canadians, read newspapers in what seemed to be exotic languages, and who lived in parts of the town that go-ahead Canadians were only too eager to leave.'[72] Drawn from the Anglo-Canadian community, Mounted Policemen shared such perceptions. Superintendent Jas. Ritchie reported in 1925 that while English Communists were not particularly active in the 'G' Division area of Alberta, foreigners were 'unceasing in their efforts at organizing the so-called proletariate [sic] against the great day of emancipation, and the downfall of the Capitalist system, when they will take the power of Government, etc. into their own hands.'[73]

More than ethnicity defined one as 'foreign.' Communists often embraced atheism, completely rejecting the trappings of Christianity. RCMP security bulletins constantly emphasized this fact with one from 1926 describing CPC funerals in Drumheller involving 'Communist priests' who replaced religious rituals with political ones. Members of the Ukrainian Labour-Farmer Temple Association, alleged the same report, did not attend religious services, prevented their children from being baptized, and participated in marriages based solely on law and not religion.[74] Also, in Drumheller a local Communist apparently made disparaging comments about the Union Jack and the king prompting a local Mountie to warn that 'he is attempting, with some degree of success, to copy the Boy Scout movement but with the reverse objective.'[75] A 1935 article in the *R.C.M.P. Quarterly* picked up on the communist threat to children. It described radicals teaching children 'to hate capitalism and its institutions. Religion, being, according to the Marxian theory, a stupefying drug – the opium of the people – is treated accordingly.'[76] 'It is in keeping with the teachings of Communism,' warned the author of another article in the same publication, 'that Patriotism and anything that makes for love of Country, should be subject to attack whenever possible; the idea, of course, being to weaken such a spirit against the day of revolution.'

Finally, the CPC seemed to make hay while times were tough, especially during the 1930s. Superintendent F.J. Mead observed in the *R.C.M.P. Quarterly* that

a member of the Communist Party must always adopt a militant attitude towards authority when acting as a leader of some delegation. His requests are usually put forward in the form of demands and this attitude ... has caused some surprise to local Town Councils and to others who have no understanding of Communist organization and propaganda. These persons, in many cases, imagine that they are dealing with unemployed or workmen on strike, with whom they are often in sympathy. They fail to realize that they are dealing with fanatical agitators who are using those who follow them to attain their own end.[77]

A Communist-led organization, the Workers Unity League (WUL), was active in organizing workers that other unions would not touch. The WUL was also not afraid to mix it up by encouraging strikes, including one involving furniture workers in Stratford, Ontario, that led to the Canadian military being sent in to maintain order. Even more worrisome to the Canadian state was communist activity among the unemployed. The federal government, terrified at the threat that single, homeless unemployed posed to order, had wholeheartedly endorsed a Canadian military plan to establish relief camps in remote areas to prevent the men from gathering in the cities. In fact, the camp system made the communist job easier by bringing large numbers of unemployed together in one place, and a not particularly happy place at that.[78] The Relief Camp Workers' Union eventually organized a general strike of camp members in British Columbia. Then, a communist activist, Arthur Evans, led the men 'On to Ottawa.' In the 1930s such communist organizational activity among desperate young men made them an even more inviting target for RCMP attention than in the previous decade. The fact that the Bennett government felt the same level of dislike for the CPC as the Mounties did only reinforced the focus of police attention.[79]

In Alberta and Saskatchewan, CPC activities were largely centred in non-Anglo-Celtic communities. The police attention that this work received had a tradition; it was in ethnic communities in Alberta and Saskatchewan that the Mounted Police first began surveillance operations in 1914.[80] By 1917, however, the police focus began to shift in the two provinces. Sedition became less about loyalty to enemy nations and more about left-wing radicalism. 'Bolshevism' and 'socialism' became the new buzz words as the whole world watched the dramatic events in Russia. In Alberta the ever watchful eyes of the scarlet-clad men were drawn to Edmonton and the surrounding area because of its large Ukrainian population. The state still considered Ukrainians to be dangerous, but they were now also believed to be potential recruits into radicalism.[81]

Those with obvious radical inclinations, whatever their nationality, became the first police targets. Joseph Clarke, an Edmonton socialist, publicly opposed the war. The Mounted Police quickly concentrated resources on him in an effort to collect enough information to have him charged with sedition.[82] Again, this was the beginning of a pattern which would continue over the next few decades. The horsemen, with a few exceptions, never moved directly to silence those on the radical left. Their job, at least in the way they approached it, was to accumulate evidence and then turn it over to their political masters who made the decision as to whether charges should be laid and, if possible, deportation pursued. Then, they would do the politicians' or bureaucrats' bidding. In Joseph Clarke's case, Secret Agent 50 was actually sent to meet him in an effort to trip him up. The agent advised that Clarke would eventually incriminate himself, opening the way for his prosecution. In preparation for this eventuality, the RNWMP sent two detectives and a stenographer to Clarke's next public speech in order to collect detailed evidence.[83] Again this pattern of collecting detailed transcripts of radical speeches would characterize Mountie-radical interactions in subsequent years. In this case, however, Clarke was too clever. The commanding officer for 'G' Division in Edmonton reported, probably with some disappointment, 'The whole gist of his tirades seem to be to influence the minds of the ignorant, foreign element ... [but such words] hardly come within the scope of sedition.'[84] Apparently the public felt less troubled by Clarke's activities; they later elected him mayor of Edmonton.[85]

In filing reports in Alberta and Saskatchewan, the police expressed concern about two things: the actual content of the speeches, specifically any mention of communism or seditious behaviour, and the impact the words were having on the audience. Frequent references to the extent of applause, the amount of currency dropped in the hat that was invariably passed around the rented hall, and whether the audience seemed pleased with a particular speech (pleasure apparently demonstrating potential support) appeared in reports. The composition of an audience was also significant to the RCMP. Comments related to the ethnic component of a crowd were recurrent, but so were other observations such as the apparent occupations of audience members or the presence of women and children.[86] At the end of the First World War, the concern was with returned soldiers and policemen in the audience, since one was beneficial to those seeking revolution and the other was what the Canadian state needed to put down revolutions.[87]

In writing on the situation in Edmonton and all of western Canada, Commissioner Perry offered a cautionary approach to observing and collecting information. He sought 'accurate and complete information on the whole subject in Western Canada. When this information has been secured, then it ought to be considered whether vigorous prosecutions should not take place everywhere about the same time.'[88] He and his successor, Cortlandt Starnes, recognized that the prosecution of radicals simply created martyrs while at the same time exposing Mounted Police intelligence operations, as had happened during the Winnipeg General Strike trials.[89] As Perry himself had noted, the Mountie approach was one of prevention: gather details and be ready for any major displays of protest or subversion.

Once the Mounties had collected information, they did on occasion seek prosecutions. In Saskatchewan in 1932 Superintendent R.R. Tait forwarded a copy of the communist paper, *The Worker*, to the deputy attorney general of Saskatchewan in an effort to get A.E. Smith charged with sedition for an article he had written. The provincial bureaucrat said the evidence was not strong enough. The RCMP in Alberta and Saskatchewan continued to target Smith, an important communist, whenever he appeared in the west. In 1934 S.T. Wood ordered two Mounties to closely cover Smith's speaking engagements in Saskatchewan so as to be able to testify in court to any seditious outbursts.[90]

In conducting investigations, the horsemen quickly recognized which areas of Alberta and Saskatchewan were fertile ground. The prime focus of the security forces in Alberta would be urban centres, especially Edmonton, and mining regions such as Drumheller and Crow's Nest Pass. In Saskatchewan the two main urban centres, Saskatoon and Regina, and the mining districts in the south-eastern part of the province received a large measure of police attention.

There was not always a consistent pattern to communist activity, and this obviously affected Mounted Police coverage; it certainly did not stop it, however. Inconsistency of activity or a complete lack of it could also mean that communists were not always easy to find. A policeman at a rural detachment in Kipling seemed bewildered when asked to report on communist preparations for the arrival of A.E. Smith in 1930: 'I beg to report that a care-ful [sic] watch has been kept at all times as to any sign of Cummunism [sic] at or around Kipling and in fact through all this detachment area, so far we have failed to find any trace of workers or members of the party above mentioned, with the exception of one.'[91] Kipling was not the only Saskatchewan detachment to have trouble finding communists in the 1930s.[92]

If communists could not be found, it was either the case that they did not exist or that they remained undiscovered because of Mountie incompetence or communist trickery. To Superintendent Allard in southern Saskatchewan, it was just a matter of digging a little deeper. While no communists inhabited his area, he confidently informed the commissioner, there were 'several persons who lean towards Communism and although they are not members or directly connected with the Communist Party of Canada they have on occasion identified themselves with the aims, objects and fundamental principles of the Party in question.'[93] To Superintendent Ritchie in Alberta, no activity simply confirmed that communists represented the ultimate 'opportunists.' 'Personally I think that good mottoes to adopt are "Be Prepared" and "Always Ready,"' he reported in his best Boy Scout tones.[94]

Where was the best place to find communists in rural areas of Alberta and Saskatchewan, two largely agrarian provinces? Besides areas populated by foreigners, farm organizations appeared the best place for Red spotting. In fact, communists did carry out organizational activity among farmers.[95] The RCMP in Alberta and Saskatchewan submitted numerous reports on radical activity among farmers and farm organizations. Leopold covered a 1926 meeting at which the Saskatchewan Grain Growers' Association amalgamated with the Farmers Union of Canada to give birth to the United Farmers of Canada. He covered the activities of agrarian utopian E.A. Partridge. The undercover Mountie filed an additional report on the 'left-wing' in attendance at the meeting, represented by the Progressive Farmers Education League.[96] A memo from the period, entitled 'Special Report on Communism amongst Saskatchewan Farmers,' reported on communist influence in the Farmers' Union of Canada:

The Communists exercise considerable influence within the organization, in fact constitute a dominating factor. Their propaganda has penetrated the Union to such an extent that there was, for instance, not one delegate at the Farmers' Union convention who did not know that there was such a thing as a Communist Party ... The Poor farmers, of the ignorant type more or less, predominate in the Farmers' Union, and if they show radical tendencies the result usually is that some of the moderate leaders swing in line with the sentiment in order to save their positions.[97]

Mounted Police reports, one of which employed red type to indicate 'extremist talk,'[98] on CPC involvement in agrarian organizations such as the Ukrainian Labour-Farmer Temple Association, the Farmers National Union, and the Farmers' Unity League, continued throughout the interwar period.[99] In 1935 a Mountie warned in the *R.C.M.P. Quarterly* that the 'Farmers' Unity League embraces what is known to the Party as the "poor farmer class" ... The Party carries on propaganda in agricultural districts through this league, which aims at disorganizing rural Municipal Governments as much as possible.'[100]

With the notable exception of the 1931 arrests in Ontario of eight CPC leaders, including Tim Buck, the force felt content to collect information on groups and individual Communist Party members, such as Buck, Becky Buhay, and Tom McEwen, often passing it on to government bodies simply to keep the political masters informed, but, on occasion, to elicit an opinion as to whether enough evidence had been collected to make charges stick. In 1932 the RCMP asked the attorney general of Alberta if a statement by communist Harvey Murphy, 'I don't worry about my tea & sandwiches, I get mine direct from Moscow,' served as grounds for a sedition charge; the answer was no.[101]

Rarely, however, did the RCMP take direct action against individual Communist Party members.[102] The experiences of activist Jeanne (Jean) Corbin exemplified what would have been labelled as an anticommunist witch-hunt in the 1950s.[103] The Mounties began a file on Corbin in 1925; in language demonstrating the patriarchal nature of policing and even the masculine construction of dissent, comments appear in Corbin's file on her appearance ('slovenly') and that while she frequently attended Young Communist League dances she never danced herself. More importantly to the police, the PHF listed her as 'a good agitator,' and in training to be a schoolteacher.[104] Several factors made Jean Corbin appear particularly dangerous. First, there was the obvious: she was a communist. But, she was also a woman involved in an activity, political radicalism in the public sphere, which was perceived as an untraditional female activity, a point that must have influenced the male Mounties. One had warned publicly that 'no sphere of society, thought fruitful, escapes the Party policy of subversion – even women and children are brought within its influence ... It is from these ranks the militant females are drawn who are so prominent at the time of disturbances in making demands from local authorities.'[105] Then, there was Corbin's occupation; of all of the careers for a radical to select, schoolteacher would have topped the Mountie list as most dangerous. She would have had access to developing young minds and hence an opportunity to indoctrinate children with her pernicious beliefs. 'Would' is the operative word here since the RCMP never gave her the chance. In September 1926 Commissioner Starnes asked the commander of 'G' Division if 'any hint [had] been given to the Educational authorities that she [Jean Corbin] is a dangerous person to be trusted with the teaching of Canadian children?'[106] At this point no 'hint' [had] been given; that silence, however, soon ended. Ritchie met with an Alberta Department of Education official who assured him that Corbin would not be allowed to teach in any schools in the province. Through a bureaucratic blunder, she did end up with a teaching job in Alberta; when the Department of Education realized its mistake, she was quickly dismissed.[107]

A similar fate befell another Albertan communist. Norwegian born, Jan Lakeman was only a part-time radical. His day job involved working for the Canadian National Railway in Edmonton. In 1926 Starnes wrote railway officials about Lakeman's extra-curricular activities. The communist activist was dismissed from his job the following year.[108]

Individual Mounted Policemen considered even dirtier tricks. In 1919 Constable T.E. Ryan advocated breaking into the house of a Regina radical, described by the Mountie as one well-versed in the teachings of the 'I.W.W. and Carl [sic] Marx.'[109] When dealing with communist Jack McDonald in Alberta, Superintendent J.W. Spalding instructed a subordinate to dig up McDonald's war record, apparently in the belief that something might be found to discredit the radical in the eyes of his audience. And, in the most ludicrous example of the tactics the force considered in its war against the left, a policeman proposed searching asylum records after one communist, in the heat of an internal party dispute, labelled his opponent as mentally disturbed.[110]

More than communists on the political left encountered surveillance in the 1920s. Two of the founding fathers of Canadian democratic socialism, J.S. Woodsworth and William Irvine, represented subversives in the eyes of the Mounties, including one who spied on a 1919 Woodsworth speech: 'There is no doubt that Woodsworth is an advocate and upholder of Bolshevism, and is incidentally proselytising for the O.B.U. and the sympathetic strikes at present in force. I consider this man an extremely dangerous character ...'[111] Woodsworth did not spark uniformity in police appraisals. T.E. Ryan, Leopold's undercover colleague, described a September 1919 talk by the politician as 'very poor' and too moderate for his audience.[112]

Even with a growing realization that Woodsworth did not fit into the radical left-wing revolutionary mode, extensive watch was kept on his activities in Alberta and Saskatchewan throughout the early 1920s. Whenever he spoke at gatherings in the provinces, his speeches would be covered and detailed reports filed on their content. An address to an economics class at the University of Saskatchewan in 1920 filled the heart of a Mounted Policeman with fear; he proceeded to interview students to discover if the labour activist's talk had negatively influenced impressionable young minds.[113] John Leopold met Woodsworth in Regina that year. The labour politician confided to No. 30, performing in the role of Jack Esselwein ('It is a good thing to have the addresses of reliable men here in Regina' he allegedly told the spy), that 'he is trailed by Detectives of the Mounted Police wherever he goes. He asked me whether there were any spies present at the Ukrainian Labour-Farmer Temples. I informed him that I noticed one City Detective and two City Constables. On this he said, I think I fooled them tonight, they surely didn't expect me there (Ukrainian Labour Temple).'[114]

William Irvine received similar treatment. His connection with labour churches helped ensure that they were spied upon as well.[115] In June 1919 the RNWMP Comptroller received a police warning that 'this man Irvine is a most dangerous Agitator and I trust it will be possible to deal with him under the amended Immigration Act,'[116] an indication that the English-born Irvine would be deported. In November of that year 'K' Division's Pennefather counselled the commissioner that should Irvine take over editorship of the *Farmer's Sun*, 'he will do his utmost to convert it into a strictly labour and possibly a Bolshevistic agitating journal.'[117] Such a comment again demonstrated the Mounted Police's institutional lack of sophistication at being able to distinguish between the form of radicalism represented by individuals like Irvine and his colleague Woodsworth and those farther to the left such as the CPC, an organization often at war with social democrats. But again, these events occurred in the immediate aftermath of the Winnipeg General Strike and before the fledgling Mounted Police security service had much experience. Seven years later, Irvine, now a labour MP, would be rehabilitated in the eyes of the Mounted Police to the point where Superintendent J. Ritchie, commander of 'G' Division in Alberta, wrote to the commissioner praising speeches by Irvine that did 'much to combat Communism.'[118]

Clearly by the mid-1920s, the Mounted Police was more discriminating when it came to targets for its intelligence operations. The final report on Woodsworth appeared in November 1925 and brought a quick response from Commissioner Starnes:

> With reference to [deleted] secret report of 16th November, regarding the meeting of 15th November, I am removing it from the file. I do not wish such reports to be made upon Mr. Woodsworth; he is a member of Parliament, his attitude is before the public and it is not for us to interfere with him. You will remember that some time ago he charged in the House that the police were watching him, and that our Minister stated that this was not the case. Please see that he is not the subject of reports of this nature.[119]

Further Mountie sensitivity about targets was evident in the response to a 1922 Leopold report. The Mounted Policeman informed his superiors back in Regina that, while covering the District Convention of the Workers' Party in Winnipeg, he overheard a conversation in which one of the participants described Henry Wise Wood, the president of the Farmers of Alberta and an important figure in the young Progressive Party, as a reliable ally of radicalism.[120] The initial response to Leopold's report came from the top man in Regina, A.B. Allard: 'Forwarded for your information [Leopold's March 30 report]. I think that Mr. Wood's actions should be kept under close observation; he is the President of the United Farmers of Alberta, living in Calgary.'[121] Allard had never been one to distinguish between groups challenging the status quo. In 1919 he had forwarded a report on the Progressives to Commissioner Perry with the comment, 'Although this is purely Political I consider it advisable to cover all meetings held by this party until their main object is definitely established.'[122] In Wood's case, however, Starnes would not hear of such action: 'Our practice is not to concern ourselves with persons or parties only concerned in reputable politics or normal labour movements.'[123]

Starnes's handling of political targets was moderate in comparison to other commissioners of the period. He cautioned the government, for example, against using charges of sedition in an effort to thwart the communists because of the publicity such an event would provide the CPC leadership. The arrests of the 'Toronto Eight' in 1931 and the publicity surrounding their trials and imprisonment proved him right.[124]

If communists did not have a monopoly on police attention, then the left itself also lacked a similar stranglehold. The right wing of the spectrum did come in for occasional scrutiny, although the haphazard nature of this attention is instructive in itself. Former Mounties and those close to the force have taken great pride in the Mounted Police's work against fascism prior to the Second World War. In *Without Fear, Favour or Affection*, Vernon Kemp boasted that before the war the RCMP 'had for years maintained a close supervision over Nazi activities in Canada and were well informed on developments.'[125] Former Commissioner C.W. Harvison remembered that in 1936 the Mounted Police had suddenly realized that Nazis and fascists in Canada posed more of a threat than communists. Betke and Horrall in their official history of the RCMP Security Service used 1928 as the date by which the Mounties were well aware of the activities of members of Canada's extreme right.[126] The most dramatic account of the RCMP's war against fascists in the 1930s, however, appeared in *Pursuit in the Wilderness*, the memoirs of Charles Rivett-Carnac. Rivett-Carnac, who served in Ottawa as intelligence officer from 1935 to 1939, left little doubt that the RCMP was on the ball when it came to dealing with the threat posed by Nazis and fascists: 'In 1935, the drums of the Nazis were already beating, their cadence muffled it is true, but nevertheless strong enough to give cause for apprehension. We in the Intelligence Branch began – as the months went on – to form an estimate of the danger to Canadian institutions if war should break out, and to ascertain the identity of possible enemy agents and potential saboteurs ...'[127]

These respective views represent historical revisionism. Rightwing organizations were simply not a priority for the Mounted Police until the end of the 1930s. In fact, the *R.C.M.P. Quarterly* in January 1937 carried an article entitled 'Peace, War, and Communism' by Colonel C.E. Edgett that portrayed communism as being part of a nineteenth-century Jewish conspiracy. The piece also favourably contrasted fascism with communism.[128]

In 1939 Rivett-Carnac, chronicler of the force's heroic battle with the far right, wrote a lengthy memo in response to a report by a civil servant that had dealt with the threat posed to Canada by Nazism, fascism, and communism. Rivett-Carnac argued that the threat from Nazis and fascists had been exaggerated and that communists were still the main threat.[129] Even in 1941, nearly two years after the Second World War had started, Commissioner S.T. Wood publicly argued that the biggest threat to Canada came not from the Nazi with whom the nation was at war, but from the 'radical' or 'Red' at home, who 'has the protection of citizenship, his foreign master is not officially an enemy and, unless he blunders into the open and provides proof of his guilt, he is much more difficult to suppress.'[130]

Accordingly, the RCMP work on the right in Saskatchewan and Alberta in the 1920s and 1930s was not particularly thorough. The right simply did not appear to pose the same level of threat to Anglo-Canadian hegemony as did the far left. It is also fair to say that rightwing organizations often espoused values similar to the official ideology of the force and ones much closer to those held by members of the Mounted Police, a trend seen with police forces elsewhere, particularly the Federal Bureau of Investigation and 'white' racists in the 1960s.[131]

The most active right-wing organization in Alberta and Saskatchewan in the 1920s was the Ku Klux Klan, with thousands of members in Saskatchewan. The RCMP did take an interest in the activities of the Klan in Saskatchewan as early as 1924. Files related to Klan activities in Prince Albert and Saskatoon appear in the RCMP Subject Files Register. In some cases references to the Klan in the RCMP security bulletins appear because left-wing radicals under surveillance made mention of the organization. In 1927 reports to Lucien Cannon, the acting minister of justice, described the spread of the

Klan from southern Saskatchewan to the north.[132] A Mountie officer reassured the King government in June 1927 that 'the agitation now in progress in Southern Saskatchewan probably is one of the dying flickers of this movement.' Although he based his judgment on the incompetence of some of the initial organizers, Superintendent Worsley's judgment was premature. The Klan did not disappear in 1927. In fact, with new organizers it grew in strength over the next three years to the point where 25,000 people belonged to the KKK, a membership comparable with other Saskatchewan organizations, such as the Grain Growers' Association.[133]

It appears that the RCMP virtually ignored the KKK after 1927. Even when the Klan first appeared in Moose Jaw in January 1927, the local Mountie was instructed not to investigate the organization since it was being covered from Regina. Virtually no information, however, appeared in Mountie records regarding the Klan. When Premier James Gardiner sought details on the KKK, he did so through private detectives and sources in other provinces. The absence of material may reflect a similar situation in Ontario, where the head of the Ontario Provincial Police (OPP) stated that the Klan would be left alone until it broke the law and then a crackdown would occur.[134]

There is a deeper reason, moreover, why the RCMP did not take a greater interest in the activities of the Klan. When it railed against foreigners from continental Europe and anyone who was not an Anglo-Canadian, the Klan represented the opinion of many in Saskatchewan even though not every person who held these views joined the KKK. Klan leaders skilfully tailored their message of traditional values, such as law and order, to pre-existing prejudices.[135] Many Mounted Policemen shared such nativist sentiments; even Commissioner Perry used his annual report in 1919 to call for an all-out government effort to assimilate enemy aliens and to defend vigilante attacks on such individuals.[136] The fact that citizens of similar backgrounds to those who belonged to the RCMP held KKK memberships and were not 'foreigners' and/or members of the Communist Party, meant that the KKK did not challenge Anglo-Canadian traditions and institutions to the same degree as did the CPC. In Saskatchewan two dozen Protestant ministers belonged to the Klan. Provincial Conservatives had memberships in the Klan and even forged alliances behind shut doors.[137] Fine upstanding citizens wore the hood. Mounted Policemen could understand and relate to Klan messages that mentioned patriotism and 'white' manhood, not fear them.

The Mounties' reaction to other right-wing groups demonstrated a similar delayed reaction. The RCMP did not investigate Nazi and fascist organizations in Saskatchewan in any systematic way until 1938, not earlier as some of the revisionist literature suggests. In September of that year, and twelve months before the beginning of the war, Vernon Kemp, now the officer in charge of 'F' Division's Saskatoon branch, sent a report on the activities of fascists and Nazis in his area. He made few observations because little work on these groups had been done:

> I have not been in a position so far to explore the machinations of these organizations, but I think some such investigation should be made. If we find ourselves with the serious problem of war conditions again prevalent, there is the likelihood, even remote, of a problem being on our hands to check-up on the activities of Nazi sympathisers here in Canada. Presumably this condition is not restricted to Saskatoon, but if we are able to [delete] explore the activities of these organizations, we should be able to determine if any subversive elements existed.[138]

Brief reports on the activity of Germans in Saskatchewan had been filed a year earlier but that appears to have been the extent of the coverage.[139]

One example of the Mounties' lack of interest in the right was its treatment of Alberta's Social Credit Party. A party that in the run-up to its election openly questioned the political and economic status quo might have been expected to garner some attention from the Mounted Police. In fact, one scholar has speculated that the Mounted Police might have spied on it. No evidence exists, however, to support this view. Nor would such activity have been consistent with Mounted Police operations in the 1930s. The force had refined its selection of targets by the 1930s, and became even more fixated on the Communist Party than it had been in the 1920s. In addition, Social Credit swept to power rather quickly and, as in the case of J.S. Woodsworth and Henry Wise Wood, the Mounted Police intelligence wing demonstrated an aversion to spying on democratically sanctioned groups or individuals. Besides, the party's leader, William Aberhart, was a God-fearing man, having made a name for himself through his Christian radio program. Finally, while the Social Credit Party wanted to tinker with capitalism, chiefly in the area of banking, its adherents readily accepted the status quo of the capitalist economy. One reference to the party does appear in 1938, but once again it was in the context of the activities of the CPC. The officer in charge of 'G' Division commented upon the strange behaviour of the Communist Party in his province, since it apparently had 'no desire to embarrass the Provincial Government, in the form of any violent or subversive demonstrations, due to the fact that the Communist Party is aligned with the Social Credit Party, temporarily at least.'[140] Although some have argued that the Social Credit phenomenon is better situated on the political left, that movement simply did not represent the challenge to the status quo of capitalism that the CPC did.

Ultimately what united all of these groups, left or right, was that the RCMP paid attention to them on the basis of the threat they posed to Anglo-Canadian social structures; the further to the left, the stronger the threat, both real and imagined. And the CPC, more than any other radical organization, did offer a challenge to the status quo. The threat was in the form of inspiring others, hence the Mounties' attention to the effect the words had on others: the young, immigrants, ethnic minorities, farmers, and employed and unemployed workers. Of these groups, it was communist work among the working classes that concerned Mounties the most. Agitation among workers and the unemployed created the potential for both rampant disorder and a tremendous challenge to the Canadian state. Arthur Evans, a frequent target of surveillance operations, warned, as he led young Canadians on a journey of protest to their nation's capital, that the streets of Canada would run red with blood. Blood would indeed be shed in the 1930s on the streets of Estevan and Saskatoon and Regina – blood of workers and of the men in scarlet.

6

Policing Workers

Agitators like James Bryson worried the Canadian state. His work
among the unemployed in southern Alberta in the 1930s brought him
to the attention of an RCMP informant. According to the latter,
Bryson had 'dull and fishy looking' eyes but it was his skill in what he
did that represented the real menace: he 'will cause [a] riot, if allowed
to carry on as he has a most insidious way of creating trouble' warned
the informant.[1] Individuals like Bryson seemed to threaten the Anglo-
Canadian societal status quo through their choice of who they worked
among: members of the working class – both the employed and
unemployed. A strong middle-class bias existed in Canada and in
other nations in the Western world that associated members of the
working class with criminality, immorality, and violence.[2] The fact
that so many of the working class seemed to be non-British only
reinforced negative stereotypes and encouraged a belief in their collective inferiority.

The state feared the disorder that large numbers of employed and
unemployed workers under the influence of agitators represented.
The British traditions of Canada emphasized the need for an ordered
society. There could be no justice without order. There could be no
peace without order. There could no Anglo-Canadian hegemony without order. Fortunately, the Mounted Police specialized in ensuring
order. Workers encompassed all of the various groups the Mounties
policed in this period, including radicals and ethnic minorities. Here
the police sought to preserve order in the face of strikes, protests,
hunger marches, and demonstrations. Ironically, it would be the RCMP
that on repeated occasions in the 1930s sparked what Rodney Stark
calls 'police riots' and in the process forever shattered the image of
Canada as a 'peaceable kingdom.'[3]

Agitation does not exist in a vacuum. If it did, no one would possibly care. Agitators find work in times of unhappiness. Therein lies the rub. Governments and their police forces believe that agitators stir up trouble where otherwise there would be none, or at least not to the same degree. The late Frank Donner labelled this 'the agitator-subversion thesis,' which denied 'the relevance of social and economic factors as the cause of unrest.'[4] In interwar Canada it would be a case (literally on some occasions) of shooting the messenger while ignoring the message.

Agitators and activists found plenty of work in Canada between 1914 and 1939. This period included both labour calm and widespread worker discontent in Canada; it also embraced the decade with the highest level of unemployment in Canadian history. Although both Alberta and Saskatchewan continued to be largely rural provinces, they still experienced labour discontent and high levels of unemployment. Both provinces had urban areas where workers lived and where the unemployed gathered. Each province also had a mining district with high levels of industrial disputes.[5]

Labour peace generally characterized the first few years of the Great War. By 1917, however, discontent grew and the rise of worker unhappiness led the federal government to seek scapegoats since the alternative was to accept some responsibility for conditions; it had a ready supply available. Enemy aliens headed the list with labour activists attaining a close second. Organizations such as the Industrial Workers of the World (IWW) had begun to make inroads in Canada, although never to the extent that the government feared.[6] In 1917 a Mountie investigated reports of IWW agitation amongst harvesters in the Vulcan area of Alberta. He interviewed the individual making the complaint who pointed at a group of men and called them IWWs. 'Industrial Workers of the World?' queried the policeman. 'No. I mean "I won't works,"' replied the complainant.[7] This remained an era of perceived menaces. The IWW menace, which after the war would be replaced by the One Big Union menace, and then in the 1920s and 1930s by the communist menace, supplied the Canadian government with a convenient source on which to place the blame for worker unhappiness.

From the perspective of the Canadian state, including the upper echelons of the RNWMP, the initial rise of worker discontent came at a particularly awkward time. Anything that detracted from the war effort was downright traitorous in the eyes of many. What better justification for spying on those active in unions and for cracking down on participants in strikes than to view such actions as unpatriotic. When nationwide labour problems occurred in 1919, shortly after the end of the war, the connotation of treasonlike activity continued, heightened by the threat of Soviet Bolshevism. For the force, the rules of dealing with worker unionism and strikes remained the same in peacetime as in war.

There was not much doubt of what role the state and senior members of the force intended for the newly created RCMP in the continuing effort to ensure institutional survival. The police were to be a subtler tool for dealing with disorder than the other alternative, the military or local militia, as more than just the Canadian government had realized. During a huge coal strike in Britain in 1910, Home Secretary Winston Churchill ordered a large contingent of police into the strike area in an attempt to avoid deploying the military. The equation was simple: military intervention equalled bloodshed. In Canada the use of the military for domestic disputes declined precipitously, and not accidentally, with the birth of the modern RCMP in 1920.[8] Other Canadian police forces also performed such a role although because of unionization, among other factors, they were not as reliable as the Mounted Police. In the United States a similar development occurred in the first half of the twentieth century. When it came to dealing with labour disputes state police forces replaced National Guard units so that by mid-century military units were only deployed in particularly serious disputes. Gerda Ray labels this evolution 'an important development in the changing role of the state in labor relations which has largely gone unstudied.'[9]

In Alberta and Saskatchewan Mounted Policemen served as backup to their colleagues in the provincial and city police forces in policing labour and other disturbances between 1917 and 1928 (Saskatchewan) and 1932 (Alberta). Once the provincial police forces disbanded, the RCMP played a secondary role only in major urban centres and even then it served as a paramilitary force ready at a moment's notice to ride to the rescue. The deputy attorney general of Saskatchewan informed the chief constable of Saskatoon, a seeker of Mountie assistance, of the reality of this status in 1933: 'The R.C.M. Police force is an auxilliary force and is available at all times in cases of emergency, and in such cases [it] is willing to co-operate with the police force of the said cities when requested to do so.'[10] In 1932 Superintendent J.W. Spalding had assured the attorney general of Saskatchewan that the RCMP in Saskatchewan stood ready to handle any outbreak of disorder:

For your confidential information, may advise that on consulting the Officer Commanding, 'Depot' Division he states he could in an emergency turn out 75 or 80 men, fully armed and equipped. We also have two machine guns, two riot guns throwing gas shells, a supply of hand gas grenades and necessary billies for the use of men on foot and suitable batons for mounted duty. We also have arrangements whereby a special train at Regina will be placed at our disposal and I judge that if an emergency arose we could leave here with forty or more men and if necessary horses as well, in two hours time, and I judge the time of a special train from Regina to Saskatoon would be in the neighbourhood of five hours. We are thus prepared to meet an emergency with men, horses and train, for rioting and trouble such as may be anticipated or develop at Saskatoon or elsewhere in the Province.[11]

The military would now be used only in situations that proved beyond the capabilities of the RCMP.[12]

The very name 'Mounted Police' is suggestive. After all, horses have no role in urban policing – except to entertain schoolchildren and for use in crowd control. As future commissioner S.T. Wood observed in the aftermath of the Regina Riot, mounted members were undeniably effective at dispersing protesters. Starting in the last two years of the First World War, a large reserve of Mounties remained in Regina on Perry's recommendation, specifically to be used to quell disturbances. With the return of the RCMP to regular policing duties in Alberta during the Depression, riot control became an increasingly important function of the RCMP. One Mountie recalled being transferred to Edmonton in 1932 solely for riot duty. Part of his work involved training the horses not to be frightened by angry, shouting crowds. Another Mounted Policeman remembered serving in a similar squad in southern Alberta and being sent wherever disorder seemed imminent during the 1930s.[13] In 1937 the federal government passed legislation creating an official RCMP Reserve force. One of the justifications for this body was to provide a pool of potential Mounties. The other, wrote Commissioner MacBrien in his annual report, was 'to have a "Reserve" strength upon which to draw in times of emergency.' Two hundred and eighty men were signed up; 40 per cent went to 'Depot' Division in Regina.[14]

The nature of training illustrates the role the state and senior Mounted Policemen envisioned for the rank and file. In his December 1918 memo calling for the amalgamation of the RNWMP and the Dominion Police, Commissioner A.B. Perry advised the government that this new outfit 'should be armed and trained as a military body so that it can act effectively should it be required to do so.'[15] Accordingly, senior officers emphasized military skills such as drilling and equitation, and Mounted Police recruits were, and still are, organized in troops.[16] Cliff Harvison, who signed up in 1919, remembered well one important aspect of his training:

> We started our 'riot' training ... Riot training is designed to accustom the horses to noise, shots, quickly moving figures, and obstacles on the ground. It achieves this purpose but only after several sessions of lessening bedlam. Dummies with bells attached were suspended from the ceiling of the riding school so that they hung just above ground level. Logs and strips of white cloth were placed at various angles on the tanbark. A squad of men, carrying shotguns, tin pans, drums and umbrellas, took up position in the centre of the menage. When a mounted troop entered the riding school, the doors were firmly closed, and the troop in single file was given the order to trot around the school.
> ... Just as the troop was getting into some semblance of order, the dummies started swinging, shotguns blasted off, tin cans clanged, and men rushed toward the horses raising and lowering umbrellas and waving white cloths ... Surprisingly, the horses became accustomed to the clatter and moving objects after a few sessions.[17]

Some specific examples illustrate the militaristic nature of the Mounted Police. The April 1919 report for 'G' Division (Edmonton and the surrounding area of Alberta), a period which included the Winnipeg General Strike, mentioned that a machine gun section had formed and was training with a Lewis machine gun. In 1931, two weeks after the Estevan Riot during which the RCMP shot and killed three miners, the government convened a special meeting in Ottawa. In attendance were the chief of the Canadian General Staff, A.G.L. McNaughton, and a former colleague, Commissioner J.H. MacBrien. Events in Estevan convinced MacBrien that his charges were ill equipped to deal with such large-scale protest; he also seemed to believe that violent clashes could become a regular occurrence. Accordingly, MacBrien requested that the Canadian Army immediately send 300 bayonets, 30,000 rounds of .303 ammunition, and bayonet and physical training instructors to Regina for two months of service.[18] He also asked that a military detention centre in Halifax be turned over to the force 'temporarily for other purposes,' a possible reference to the establishment of a deportation centre for police targets.[19]

After another major police–worker clash, this time in Regina in 1935, the RCMP senior command did not fundamentally question police tactics that had led to the violence, but rather sought to render the RCMP more effective at crushing disorder. S.T. Wood, the individual primarily responsible for the bloody riot, filed an extensive report on how to improve RCMP crowd-handling capabilities. His words read like an analysis after a military clash. Members he surveyed opted for a future of hardwood batons instead of leather ones and the report advocated acquiring an armoured car and riot guns, the latter including sawed-off shotguns and Thompson machine guns, capable of firing widely dispersed shot. Tear-gas grenades had been found to be ineffective in Regina because the rioters were not concentrated so he advised that grenades that shattered or exploded on contact would be more efficient since they 'would prohibit the return of these grenades into our own ranks.' He also reported on the success of steel helmets at preventing serious head injuries. Shields were another necessary acquisition. Finally, Wood noted that the use of a dummy machine gun had been a useful tool of intimidation and that others should be deployed in the future to achieve the 'desired effect.'[20]

All of these RCMP tactics and plans were developed in response to actual strikes and disturbances. But even peaceful labour activity came under scrutiny. In fact, Greg Kealey argues that responding to the 'labour revolt' was at the heart of the Mounted Police transformation between 1914 and 1939:

> The Canadian state found itself unprepared initially to deal with labour radicalism in the late years of the First World War, but the solutions it devised, building on the mechanisms of repression developed for other purposes early in the war and on the similar experience of other Allied countries, proved successful and durable. When similar crises arose later during the Great Depression and the Second World War, the state would turn again to measures initiated in the years 1914–20 and to the institution, such as the Royal Canadian Mounted Police.[21]

Some of the 'measures' for dealing with labour problems included surveillance and intelligence gathering. After all, labour disturbances indicated to the Mounted Police that agitators had stirred up trouble where none previously had existed, hence the need for vigilance even in a period of tranquility. Since the Mounted Police usually had a secondary role in the physical aspect of policing strikes in Alberta and

Saskatchewan between 1917 and 1928, they took a preventative approach. Part of that role involved spying on workers, labour unions, and labour activities.

Spying on workers is an old habit of governments and governmental agencies. In *The Making of the English Working Class*, E.P. Thompson described the propensity of such espionage operations to sow distrust among workers and radicals, since the identity of the informant or spy remained unknown. Then, there was the possibility of an individual serving as an agent provocateur. Thus, those who made the most radical suggestions generated the greatest suspicion about their trustworthiness, a conclusion that J.S. Woodsworth also reached: 'Again and again visiting in the mining camps in the west I have had labour people come to me and say: If there is any suggestion made in the way of provoking trouble be careful, because that suggestion comes from an agent of the government.'[22] The modern drive towards intelligence gathering against labour began in Britain during the First World War. In 1916 David Lloyd George, then minister of munitions, instructed the head of Special Branch to form an 'intelligence service on labour matters for the whole country.'[23] Nor was this kind of policing peculiar to Britain. Since the nineteenth century in the United States, police forces and private detective agencies had made a regular habit of performing surveillance activities against workers. In France, the police spied on workers as part of their regular policing duties prior to the twentieth century.[24]

In Canada, as elsewhere, part of the need for Mounted Police intelligence operations emanated from the belief that outsiders, even foreign powers, caused discontent within Canadian labour circles. Commissioner Perry had instructed his detectives in 1919 to keep special watch on labour organizations because 'it has been found that this class of organization is particularly susceptible to Bolsheviki teachings.'[25] A vigilant police force needed to keep the government aware of the extent of these outsiders' influence, a constant theme throughout the 1920s and 1930s. As early as 1919, a Mountie report from Maple Creek, Saskatchewan, described A.E. Smith, a future member of the Communist Party of Canada (CPC), as extremely dangerous and worthy of surveillance because of his habit of telling an audience 'that if they are hungry or want anything they see, go and take it, it is as much theirs as anyone else's, and this man being a very fluent speaker and holding a responsible position, his words will have a strong effect on a mob of uneducated people.'[26] Commissioner MacBrien displayed similar thinking in a 1934 letter to the mayor of Winnipeg: 'Through the selling of strikes and creating discontent in many lines of industry, the Communists are really doing more harm now than they did parading the streets.'[27]

Of course, spying on workers did not begin in the interwar period. By at least 1916, the Mounted Police in Alberta targeted workers and worker organizations, they did so during a coal mine strike when an officer advised that once the dispute had ended 'personal enemies may be found willing to inform on these men at a later day.'[28] Yet 1919 proved to be a peak year for strikes and an equally busy year for RCMP intelligence gathering. Alberta and Saskatchewan experienced sympathy strikes in the wake of the Winnipeg General Strike.[29] In Calgary a secret agent working for 'K' Division identified by Mark Leier as long-time labour activist Robert Gosden, wrote a lengthy report on how to deal with the nationwide labour disturbances:

> If a programme could be announced which would meet with the approval of the Conservative Labour element, aiming at the elimination of basic grievances and a satisfactory financial settlement to the Returned men, and simultaneously the wholesale deportation of the alien trouble makers, the decisive and concerted arrest of the leaders of the movement and a quick trial, with a sentence making their release or confinement dependent upon their future policy, this movement could be headed off with little or now [sic] violence, and the ground would be cleared for a more intelligent form of general industrial reconstruction.[30]

At the end of 1919, 'K' Division headquarters in Lethbridge reported that 'all [OBU] agitators are kept under close surveillance and many reports have been forwarded during the month on their various activities. Our Agents are gaining good information, generally.'[31]

There remained a constant drive to discover information on unions and labour activists, and not just during strikes. Again prevention fuelled the effort, since the common belief was that agitators, often Red ones, inspired labour discontent. In 1920 a Mountie reported that Arthur Evans, later to be famous as the leader of the On to Ottawa Trek, had convinced strikers to stay off the job in Drumheller.[32] This tactic led the commander of southern Alberta to advise the commissioner that if Evans could be removed through arrest and prosecution 'the morale of the rank and file of the O.B.U. would undoubtedly be shaken.'[33] By November 1920 the author of a weekly RCMP security bulletin reported that enough evidence had been collected to convict Evans on a charge of spreading false information.[34] A court later convicted the labour activist on an unrelated charge.

Other labour activists also drew Mountie attention. Communist Malcolm Bruce made a visit to Saskatoon in 1922 that happened to coincide with a strike by printers at the Saskatoon *Daily Star*. Headquarters was assured that Bruce had not actually caused the strike, only that he made the printers 'feel a little more hostile to the Employers.'[35] Stacks of files exist on various other communist and labour activists (7,000 individuals had RCMP files on them by 1929). Even if they lived outside of Saskatchewan and Alberta, descriptions of their sojourns to the provinces appeared in their files.

Individuals in Alberta and Saskatchewan who received extra police attention usually worked for radical organizations such as the OBU, IWW, Mine Workers Union of Canada (MWUC), and the Workers Unity League (WUL). Certain groups received more concentration than others depending on the particular time and external events. The IWW received attention during the First World War and then was largely ignored by the police, although as late as 1926 the RCMP reported that an IWW organizer had been appointed in the United States to work among harvesters in western Canada. RCMP security bulletins from 1920 carried regular updates on the OBU's progress in gaining new members and made reference to its failures, dissension within the ranks, and splits among the leaders. Despite this material, many Mountie detachments, especially those in rural areas, could discover no activity by this organization.[36]

Eventually a new menace came along to replace the IWW and OBU bogeymen. A RCMP report from Alberta in 1922 warned that the Workers' Party of Canada 'is working along the same lines and principles as the O.B.U. formerly did, but having learned a lesson by the fate of the O.B.U. are proceeding more skillfully and cautiously by educational methods, their ultimate aim however being the same, that is direct action and control of the Government and Country by force if necessary.'[37]

By the end of the 1920s, communists became actively involved in front organizations, including labour and eventually unemployed organizations. Joseph Stalin ordered a shift in 1928 when he called for workers to form their own revolutionary organizations rather than work within existing reformist ones. The 'united front' of communist and other leftist organizations was dead. The so-called 'united front from below,' really the CPC taking a unilateral approach, was in. Communists now labelled social democrats like J.S. Woodsworth as 'social fascists.'[38] They also took their war against capitalism to another level when they organized their own unions, including the Mine Workers Union of Canada. This activity made RCMP work among mining unions in Alberta and Saskatchewan even more important, especially since the mining sector had a history of labour disputes. Part of keeping watch on union activities involved intelligence gathering. The 1935 MWUC convention report, for example, was forwarded to headquarters by the commander of 'K' division. James Sloan, the union head, became a Mounted Police target because of his reputation as a radical. Headquarters ordered detachments in southern Alberta to monitor the activist's statements in the hope that he might incriminate himself.[39]

Although there is no evidence that in Canada the RCMP shared its intelligence with private companies, the Mounties did regularly keep departments of both the provincial and federal government informed about the activities of the employed and unemployed. For example, a confidential Criminal Investigation Branch (CIB) monthly report for 'K' Division sent to the deputy attorney general of Alberta in 1932 included unemployment figures for the previous month, a list of strikes currently underway, and a category entitled 'Activities of Radical or Revolutionary Organizations.'[40] On occasion, government agencies of various stripes requested Mountie reports on unions or individual workers. Often, the RCMP would send an uninvited report to a government minister or bureaucrat. The favourite destinations for such reports were the Departments of Labour and Justice at both the federal and provincial level.[41]

In 1924 J.S. Woodsworth raised in the House of Commons the issue of RCMP surveillance against organized labour. His query forced Minister of Justice Ernest Lapointe to admit that some Mounties had been at a labour meeting addressed by the politician. In a memo prepared for Lapointe, however, the RCMP argued that it was up to the force to keep the government informed of such happenings in communities. The memo contained the unequivocal assurance that the 'Royal Canadian Mounted Police scrupulously avoids interference with trade unions or legitimate labour organizations.' Later in the same document, though, the RCMP hinted at the nature of most of its work – simple intelligence gathering that left no trail to the local police station: 'It is to be observed that no interference is alleged. No prosecutions have been entered, no threats have been made, no pressure has been exerted on any persons as a result of such attendance.'[42]

While Woodsworth's complaint led to the apparent end of surveillance against him, RCMP spying against labour continued unabated. A sergeant in Prince Albert reported in 1925 that plain-clothes men had covered a local labour meeting; he also warned that once it was realized the Mounties were covering the meetings, 'it may have the effect of making labour men very much more careful in what information is passed on to us.'[43]

Due to the nature of the work, ordinary Mounties had the task of dealing with labour and political activists, workers, and the unemployed. For a regular cop, policing labour was not the world of absolutes that it was for his boss and the state. Workers who policed workers experienced a much more complex environment. There is a certain irony in this policing equation that is too often ignored by those seeking to castigate the RCMP – Mounties were workers too. 'Working men in uniform' was historian Greg Marquis's turn of phrase to describe the Toronto police;[44] it was also applicable to Mounties who worked long hours in poor conditions, for a low rate of pay, and without the job protection that belonging to a union might have offered. Unlike other workers who freed themselves from their job when they went home at night, a Mountie could literally be on duty around the clock. Nor did ordinary employees have a boss interfering with their social life the way a scarlet uniform wearer did, telling him when he could marry and where he could live and controlling his behaviour in public, including the amount of facial hair on display. While the uniform did confer a certain amount of social prestige on those who wore it, especially in small towns, it also meant long, hard hours dealing with aspects of life that the remainder of society had no wish to encounter. One Mountie, recalling his years in red serge in Saskatchewan while tears collected in his eyes, confessed that if he had it to do over again he would not: 'The force asked too much of me.'[45] The point remains, however, that while Mounties did not, indeed could not, identify with ethnic minorities or radicals, they could on occasion, rare though they might be, relate to workers. This reality created a more complex policing situation than existed when Mounties dealt with radicals and non-Anglo-Canadians.

Work represented many things to Mounties. For one, it meant being aware that the world, like the atmosphere they toiled in, was a hierarchical one. Police comments regarding class appear in reports, mainly in the 1910s and the 1920s. Sometimes the comments represented class snobbery, notions influenced by ethnicity. Workers of Anglo-Celtic heritage were considered a step above their foreign compatriots. In Alberta, when Constable Frank Zaneth referred to the 'honest working class,' and Inspector J.W. Spalding mentioned 'the better class of labour,' they did not have eastern and central Europeans in mind.[46] Similarly when an RCMP security bulletin in 1920 described One Big Union members in Saskatoon as being of 'an inferior class of labour,' there was little doubt as to their ethnic background.[47]

The architect of the new Mounted Police, Commissioner A.B. Perry.

The very British Mounted Police being inspected by the Prince of Wales (the future Edward VIII) in Regina, 1919.

The variety of RNWMP uniforms demonstrates the multiplicity of roles performed by its members.

A crowd parts for two Mounties in Yorkton, Saskatchewan, June 1907.

Masculine Mounties at play in Regina, 1933.

Mounted Police recruits on parade at the training depot in Regina, pre-1925.

Mounted Police barracks and drill parade, pre-1925.

1873

1933

Sixty Years of Progress
(with acknowledgment to the Vancouver Sun)

1873–1933: A transformed Mounted Police matches a transformed nation.

The Lighter Side

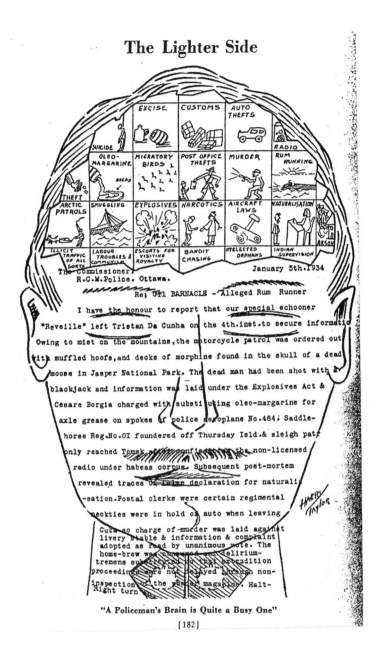

"A Policeman's Brain is Quite a Busy One"

[182]

A light-hearted but revealing look at the RCMP's many roles.

Mounties guard Trekkers in Regina on 3 July 1935, two days after the clash in the streets of the city.

That the more complex relationship Mounties had with workers is not discussed in much of the literature is hardly surprising.[48] The end result of RCMP contact with workers, specifically during the Depression, has been police-initiated violence, usually against a group of striking workers or protesting unemployed. With the force's return to regular policing in Alberta and Saskatchewan, it was once more the first line of defence against any form of disorder. Its leadership had no qualms about taking the side of the owners of capital or the state in any dispute and, if push came to shove, about ordering the use of violence. For those who actually had to deal with a strike or protest, however, such decisions were not as easily made.

In Alberta and Saskatchewan, mining districts were the centres of industrial disputes. Ensuring order became the primary police goal. Social peace frequently translated into the successful operation of the mines and that put the RCMP squarely on the side of the mine owners and against the interest of the miners. Taking sides in industrial disputes has led many to criticize the police as an instrument of class oppression. Sidney Harring, for example, in discussing the role of police in strikes in the United States, argues that the police had two choices when facing a dispute: side with the workers or side with the owners. By siding with the owners, Harring argued, the police became 'enforcers of class-biased law' and a 'class-biased institution.'[49]

What was the character of the Mountie role in policing strikes? William Baker suggests the nature of the work environment of a Mounted Policeman meant that he lacked sympathy for strikers. In contrast, R.C. Macleod portrays members of the Mounted Police prior to the First World War as 'honest brokers' in their handling of disputes. Others approached the question from more extreme positions.[50]

The actual Mounted Police record in policing strikes in Alberta and Saskatchewan was a mixed one. From 1917 to 1928 the men in scarlet served as an instrument of last resort. In Edmonton in 1923 the RCMP, backing up the Alberta Provincial Police (APP) and the Edmonton City Police, became involved in a violent clash that earned it the enmity of a great number of workers. The police had been protecting mine property, ironically owned by the provincial government, against trespass by the strikers.[51] In Drumheller in the same year, two members of the Alberta Provincial Police ran into difficulties with a group of 250 strikers. When the mine manager called upon the local RCMP contingent for assistance, he was told that 'it was none of their business [and] that the A.P.P. would have to look after their own affairs.'[52] The response of the mine owners was to ask the federal government to have the RCMP replace the APP, because, in the words of the commissioner of the APP, 'they [the owners] evidently want to show force and to intimidate the miners.'[53]

Even in 1919, the year of widespread labour unrest, evidence exists of a mixed Mounted Police reply to discontent and strikes. The usual response was to blame problems on outside agitators: 'There is no doubt in the minds of the general public that the strike has been engineered in the interests of some agitator, who were [sic] working hard to bring about a chaotic state of affairs, I presume in the hope of getting office in the general struggle. There is little doubt that the Unions were stampeded by cajoling and sophistry ...' A whole cast of characters fit the radical agitator description: socialists, anarchists, communists, IWWers, OBUers, or just plain foreigners.

Still, some of those who policed workers displayed a degree of subtlety that was absent in the higher ranks; they accepted, for example, that discontent was not entirely the fault of agitators. The 'G' Division writer of the previously quoted passage admitted that workers welcomed the siren call of agitators because of 'the high cost of living and the lack of employment in certain lines.'[54] A November 1920 security bulletin contained a warning that agitators would attempt to take advantage of already existing distress.[55] Corporal Charles Paris, in charge of the local detachment, remarked on a proposed coal miners' strike in Drumheller in 1919: 'I really believe that the majority of the people are sound, and from the most recent reports that I have rendered, it would seem that the men are not very anxious to strike.' He added that 'thoughtless and rash actions on the part of any operators (especially these, when are not over popular [sic]) can only tend to aggravate a situation, which if handled carefully will eventually right itself.'[56] C.T. Hildyard reported from Saskatoon in 1922 that farmers had little problem in hiring men for $35.00 a month, 'but the feeling is undoubtedly growing that this wage is completely insufficient, as after six months work, a man would only draw $210 which in case of his being out of work during the coming winter would force him on relief.' As if to reinforce the validity of his observation through a dose of class, Hildyard added, 'This opinion is held by many sound and respectable citizens.'[57]

There is no question that at times Mounties sympathized with workers, or at least managed to accept that two sides to disputes existed. The 1931 Estevan Coal Strike serves as a textbook example in Saskatchewan of the complex events that made up a labour dispute with a tragic ending. In this case, many of the officers 'on the ground' attempted to be balanced in their assessment of the reasons behind the strike and the course of action to be taken. In fact, some, despite their own ethnic and class prejudice, openly sympathized with the striking miners. Inevitably, however, in a hierarchical institution like the Mounted Police, the rank and file followed the orders of the senior officers, a group that strongly espoused the anti-communist rhetoric of the RCMP's political master, the Conservative government of Prime Minister R.B. Bennett. In doing so, the RCMP pleased no one. Three miners lay dead; police, other miners, and citizens were injured. Today, the dead lie buried in a cemetery on the outskirts of nearby Bienfait, Saskatchewan, under a common grave with a caption that reads, 'Murdered by R.C.M.P.'

The earth beneath Estevan, a small town in southeastern Saskatchewan, held an abundance of lignite. Without a union, in poor conditions, and for lower wages than their counterparts in Alberta and British Columbia, men toiled to extract the coal. When the Mine Workers Union of Canada attempted to fill the representational void, the mine owners refused to recognize the union, ostensibly because of its links with the Communist Party of Canada, prompting several hundred miners to walk off the job on 7 September 1931.[58]

Caught in the middle was the Mounted Police. Sergeant William Mulhall, a fifty-five-year-old native of Liverpool, England, and in charge of the local detachment, had no doubt as to where the fault for the coming strike resided:

> It would appear that a strike in this district would not be so disadvantageous to the mine owners as at first sight and it would seem that they are purposely avoiding a meeting with the miners. The most energetic personality in this is Mr. Moffat [sic], who is interested in the Western Collieries and apparently in favour of forcing a strike. Information from a reliable source is to the effect that this man is using his influence with the rest of the mine operators to prevent them meeting the miners and coming to a mutual agreement to avert a strike ... The number of miners in the Estevan district will be approximately one thousand of mixed nationalities, in favour of a strong foreign element. The majority of these miners are not in favour of communism, though they believe they have had unjust treatment and need a leader to guide them and air their grievances. If these had been adjusted the present situation would have been avoided.[59]

It was an incisive analysis of the situation. Even before the miners left the pits, the mine owners and managers began to call for an armed presence to deal with any potential strikers. Undoubtedly the owners planned on employing 'scab' workers and recognized the conflict this might cause. They expected the police to perform to their bidding. On 3 September 1931, eleven-year veteran Constable F.H. Steele met with a mine manager, who requested that at least five men, armed with shotguns, be stationed as guards around the Truax-Traer mine property. Steele could discover nothing to 'substantiate [the manager's] fears and it would appear that any outside interference would only tend to increase the ill-feeling against this company and thus cause trouble rather than further any amicable agreement.'[60] Despite scholarship to the contrary, the Mounties in Estevan did not meekly follow the company line. When, for example, Sergeant Mulhall encountered a group of striking miners on 11 September, he attempted to discover their grievances and even tried his hand at mediation.[61]

His superiors, however, envisioned a more sinister agenda behind the miners' strike, especially since the new union was linked with the Communist Party of Canada. A colleague advised Mulhall to place the union president and communist, James Sloan, and another organizer under surveillance. Reinforcements from Regina also arrived. A Mountie secret agent, John Eberhardt, received orders to proceed to Estevan and infiltrate the striking miners. Even with these transfers, Superintendent R.R. Tait, in charge of the southern Saskatchewan district of the Mounted Police, attempted to avoid any action, such as stationing Mounted Policemen at mine sites, which the striking miners might perceive as provocative. As the strike continued, tension grew. Mulhall believed that a particular mine manager, an American with experience in violent strikes in Pennsylvania, was responsible for the increasingly dangerous situation. The Mountie's continuing restraint in handling the strike angered several prominent Estevan citizens and led to the dispatching of an officer from Regina to investigate the complaints against his colleague; he found no validity to them.[62]

As Mulhall and other Mounties had recognized, the flash point to any violence would be the use of strikebreakers by the mine owners, something the newly arrived Detective/Staff-Sergeant Walter Mortimer communicated to headquarters.[63] A clash nearly occurred on 16 September when strikers surrounded a boarding house that held several strikebreakers. The Mounties, under Sergeant C. Richardson, arrived and restored order by informing the men that the police 'were neutral and were only there to keep the peace ... It was hard to explain to the striking miners, who were outside in the cold, that the men inside were not getting any more protection than they were themselves.'[64] Richardson, however, angered several on the side of management, when he told the boarding-house cook that it was up to her whether she should feed the strikebreakers. She refused and several of the men left. Intimidation of this type on the part of strikers compelled the major mines to dismiss the remaining replacement workers and shut down operations.[65]

These examples of Mounted Police intervention in the dispute did not satisfy the coal mine owners and managers. On the contrary, the owners openly expressed their discontent and frustration with the Mounted Police to the provincial authorities and in the media. Although the Saskatchewan government was concerned that a prolonged labour dispute might disrupt a valuable provincial industry, the provincial attorney general appears not to have issued orders to the Mounted Police; they kept him informed at every step and, in turn, he was content to let them do their job. Part of that job included following up on the complaints about policing voiced by the employers. The officer who did so defended Mulhall and added what he saw as the real causes of the strike, specifically miner grievances related to exploitation by company-run stores.[66]

In a 23 September message to the attorney general of Saskatchewan, Tait of the southern Saskatchewan District offered a detailed criticism of the mining companies. His letter also demonstrated the narrow path followed by the Mounted Police in their attempt to balance the interests of the miners and the owners:

> You will also note the reference made ... as to the attitude of the operators of the Taylorton Mine and Brick Plant, in which they express their opinion that the gathering of strikers at this point would constitute an unlawful assembly ...
>
> While technically speaking the gathering of the miners at the point in question might have been classed as unlawful assemblies their conduct was such as in my opinion did not warrant police intervention as at the time the situation was very critical and any indiscretion on the part of the police would undoubtedly have started a conflagration, the outcome of which would no doubt have resulted in loss of life and damage to property without in any measure relieving the situation.[67]

The complaints of the mining companies, however, did catch the attention of some at the highest level of the Royal Canadian Mounted Police. Commissioner MacBrien opined on the correctness of the force's role at Estevan by commenting on a response by an underling to the criticism of the mining companies.[68] Beside a defence of the police policy of not guarding mine property, MacBrien wrote: 'This seems peculiar. If the Operators wished to take in strike breakers they & their property should be given every protection unless there are some reasons for contrary action. It is not explained.'[69] While as a point of law MacBrien's comment was correct, it failed to take into consideration that rigid enforcement in a volatile situation increased the danger. Local Mounties at Estevan understood this reality. Although there is no evidence that the commissioner ordered a change in RCMP policy, the cumulative pressure from the police critics seemed to make the Mounties keener to protect property.

Eventually, the inevitable occurred in the town of Estevan. That day was Tuesday, 29 September 1931. The Mounted Police contingent, which had split into two units in order to protect mine property, found itself outnumbered in the town as the miners began a parade. A confrontation occurred between the miners and inexperienced Mounties (thirty-four out of the forty-three constables had under a year of police experience) and Estevan town police.[70] Earlier in the day, the town council had prohibited parades and the police sought to stop any such demonstrations. A fire truck, on the scene in case its water was needed to inhibit the demonstrators, became the centre of a confrontation. A miner leapt on to the truck and declared it captured; he was immediately shot dead. The police then fired indiscriminately into the now dispersing crowd, wounding strikers and citizens of Estevan alike; two other miners died from their wounds.

The Mounted Police admitted no responsibility for the mayhem, even to the point of claiming during subsequent investigations that shots fired from the miners' side had provoked the violence. Several police witnesses testified to having drawn their weapons only after being cornered, testimony contradicted by pictures taken during the riot showing their guns out much earlier. An old, broken military rifle was the ludicrous evidence presented to prove that the miners had fired first. In following this path a template was created for what would occur in 1935 with the Regina Riot. In each case, violence initiated by the Mounted Police was followed by the blame being placed on those subjected to the violence.[71]

Not all of the Mounted Policemen at Estevan escaped unscathed. Sergeant Mulhall, the Mountie most clearly sympathetic towards the miners and the individual charged with keeping the peace between the miners and the mining companies, became an internal scapegoat. His superior on the day of the violence criticized the Mountie's role during the riot, criticism that went on his service record.[72] Still, some officers continued to question the official line being spun by the mining companies and politicians:

> I have also investigated this Red Movement in this field and find that all Miners who are branded Red by the Mine Owners or Management, are men who are connected with the Union Movement and are on the various Pit Committees. It appears to me that the moment a man submits himself to be appointed on a Committee or some position in a Union, and has nerve enough to approach the Owners on behalf of the workers, he is immediately branded a Red. I have not yet interviewed the Owner or Manager of a mine in regard to the red element that has not given me the names of all of the men on the Pit Committee and the names of some Official of the Union ...[73]

Estevan demonstrated the complexities of policing a strike in the sense of not only having to balance the interests of two distinct parties but also of one's superiors. The goal of the local Mounted Police in this case had been to avoid violence, even though both the strikers and the mine owners seemed to be seeking a clash of some sort. Clearly, however, in the mind of Commissioner MacBrien, the most important role for the RCMP to play in Estevan was to protect the property of the mining companies, including any replacement workers that these outfits employed. The words of the top Mountie increased the pressure on the lower ranks, and ultimately what the local Mounties hoped to achieve – peace – was lost in the hail of bullets.

The small Saskatchewan town was not the only location where protest and the involvement of the RCMP would lead to violence. Two other clashes, both in Saskatchewan, involved a fundamental characteristic of the 1930s: large groups of unemployed workers. By 1931 the railways carried thousands of unemployed Canadians searching for work. Two years later the unemployment rate hit the highest level ever: 26.6 per cent. The Depression did not strike all areas of the country with equal fervour: Saskatchewan and Alberta suffered the worst economic devastation as the agricultural sector, the most significant part of their economies, collapsed.[74] The unemployed remained in the Depression's wake.

Various politicians attempted to deal with the human remnants of the economic devastation. After achieving office in 1930, the government of R.B. Bennett brought in $20 million in unemployment relief. Nothing, however, stemmed the rising unemployment levels and the declining economic growth. Quickly the target of the Bennett government became not unemployment but the unemployment, specifically those out of work who were single and homeless; they, authorities believed, represented a threat to social peace. The solution of the Bennett government in 1932 was to put into practice a proposal by Major-General Andrew McNaughton and establish military-run relief camps throughout Canada where unemployed men could be sent, in effect to keep them in quarantine far away from urban centres and potential agitators.[75] Ultimately this system and its widespread unpopularity among its inhabitants would drag in the RCMP. In 1935 Commissioner MacBrien noted in his annual report that his charges had dealt with a number of relief strikes that occurred in Drumheller, Edmonton, Calgary, and Lethbridge during the previous year. 'It has been necessary,' the commissioner added in military language, 'to maintain reserve strength at several strategic points during the past year and present conditions warrant its continued maintenance.'[76]

Part of the Mounted Police intelligence gathering operations after the First World War had always concentrated on the unemployed. Like their relationship with employed workers, the RCMP's interaction with the unemployed in Alberta and Saskatchewan had two parts: spying on those out of work and their organizations, and cracking down on their protests. In the same year as the CPC's birth, the RCMP began reporting in its security bulletins on the work of Communists among the unemployed. One section concluded with a reference to the recurrent theme of this era: 'The significant feature of these activities is that they are but the execution of plans conceived outside the country, and furnished to and imposed upon our agitators from abroad.'[77]

The police worried about the unemployed because of the nature of the agitators among them. As early as 1927 the RCMP in Alberta was reporting to the commissioner that the CPC had designated an individual to organize the unemployed.[78] Four years later, the force informed the Saskatchewan attorney general that 'certain Communistic Agitators are endeavouring to create trouble' among the unemployed in Saskatoon.[79] Individual activists became the focus of reports. James Bryson was one such individual. What was the solution to such a menace? Headquarters wondered if Bryson could be deported. Harvey Murphy, another communist active in Alberta, also received Mountie attention because of his work among the unemployed. His activities and those of others prompted the officer in charge of the Edmonton Criminal Investigation Branch to warn the commissioner in September 1932 that unemployed men and women were to be organized along a more militant basis over the upcoming winter.[80]

In Edmonton Mounties took their work to the large number of unemployed. A Mounted Policeman worked undercover in the local relief office, filing detailed reports, some of which ended up in the office of R.B. Bennett.[81] This kind of intelligence was gathered for preventive reasons. In November 1932, for example, the Mounted Police acquired a circular calling for a hunger march to Edmonton. The provincial attorney general received notification of the proposed protest, and that it was being organized by groups 'known to be affiliated with the C.P. of C.' The head of the force's 'G' Division in Alberta, recommended to the provincial government that the march be widely publicized, including a threat that anyone on relief participating would immediately be cut off and refused further assistance. He also indicated that the police would be rigidly enforcing the Railway Act prior to the date of the march to prevent marchers from reaching the capital of Alberta and participating in the march.[82]

Nevertheless, all of the planning, spying, and preventive measures did not stop violence between the RCMP and the unemployed in the 1930s. Two serious clashes occurred – one in Saskatoon in 1933 and the other in Regina two years later. The violence of 1933 involved a group of unemployed in a relief camp on the exhibition grounds of the city of Saskatoon. The vagaries of the relief system frequently led to those without work becoming vagrants in the hope of getting back on relief if they had been refused it or of getting higher payments in a wealthier municipality. Based on the British poor laws, local governments administered the relief or 'dole.' Cities, like Saskatoon, attracted transients because the potential for finding shelter and nourishment remained greater than in rural areas. A temporary relief camp had been established to accommodate the newcomers who journeyed into Saskatoon during the winter of 1931–2.[83] The fact that the camp, unlike most relief camps, sat within an urban centre concerned the RCMP. Walter Munday, commander of the Mountie detachment in Saskatoon, had informed the provincial government in November 1932 that of the men in the relief camp 'not more than 20% are residents of Saskatoon, the remainder are transients, a great number of which are foreigners, many of them not yet having established Canadian domicile.'[84] The situation in the city also led to problems of jurisdiction, since technically the city police held authority, but, perhaps fearing a confrontation, the city wanted the RCMP to take a more forceful role. Superintendent S.T. Wood advised the Saskatchewan government to separate the 'agitators' and arrest them on vagrancy charges. Already the Mounted Police had one of their own infiltrating the relief campers.[85] Munday warned the commissioner on 9 April

that the city seemed 'to act as a magnet drawing transients and undesirables from all parts of the Province and I am of the opinion that
serious disturbances will likely occur both at the camp and in the City
unless there is sufficient display of force to prevent them.' He added
that neither the city police nor the RCMP contingent were strong
enough to deal with the relief campers.[86] The next day, another senior
policeman advised the provincial cabinet that a reserve force needed
to be sent to the city in order to quell any serious disturbances. 'In my
opinion this troop will have to be used with great discretion,' he
concluded on both a cautionary and prescient note, 'and located well
away from the Relief Camp, to guard against surprise, and in order not
to precipitate a clash, particularly as the Communists object to our
presence in the Camp.'[87]

This important advice was ignored and Wood's recommendation
prevailed. Thirty-seven Mounted Policemen under the command of
Inspector James Sampson, newly arrived from Regina, invaded the
camp on the morning of 8 May, hoping to take its members by
surprise as they ate their breakfast. Instead, the men resisted the police
incursion. 'Stones began to fly,' wrote an eyewitness in the local
newspaper, 'and the officers, swinging their long cavalry batons, put
their horses to the gallop and started to scatter the crowd, chasing
them away from in front of the building, while their quarry scattered
and took shelter in the corners of various buildings and behind fences.
Wheeling their horses again and again, the policemen chased the
fugitives all over the grounds, striking right and left.'[88] As the riot
progressed Sampson fell from his horse and later died from injuries
sustained after his head collided with a pole. Twenty-three were
convicted of various charges, but no one ever faced prosecution for
Sampson's death. Despite the violence and mayhem that ensued after
the intervention of the police, Wood expressed satisfaction with the
operation, lamenting only that it was being treated more seriously
than need be because of the death of Sampson.[89]

Wood's reflections are important for one particular reason. He
would be in command in Regina in June 1935 when two thousand
determined Trekkers rolled into town on the top of rail cars. The
assistant-commissioner had learned nothing from Saskatoon, and the
same mistakes would be repeated in Regina with even more tragic
results.

The roots of that led the men to Regina lay in the military-run
relief-camp system, which quickly became unpopular with the men,
in part because of the twenty cents a day they received for often back-
breaking labour. Another reason for the animosity was the simple

realization that the camps were not designed to benefit the men; they were merely an excuse to remove the unemployed from urban centres. The camps offered easy work for communist activists including organizers for the Relief Camp Workers' Union who helped organize the men into a coherent force. Protests and strikes began in the camps and gradually grew in frequency. The discontent culminated in a provincewide relief camp strike in British Columbia in April 1935. Many of the strikers ended up in Vancouver. By the end of May, the strike appeared to be near an end. A sudden proposal to travel to Ottawa restored the energy of the strikers. The journey, which quickly became known as the On to Ottawa Trek, brought the Trekkers into conflict with the RCMP in the heart of Saskatchewan's capital.[90]

On 12 June orders came from Ottawa to halt the Trekkers in Regina. Various theories exist as to why Regina became the Trekkers' final destination. The city housed the government of Premier James Gardiner, a partisan Liberal and an enemy of the Bennett Conservatives. Winnipeg, a well-known centre of radicalism, was the next major stop after Regina. Major support for the movement could be expected in the Manitoban capital.[91]

Even more significantly, Regina held a large contingent of Mounted Policemen capable of enforcing the government's will, something consistent with the government's approach to perceived disorder in this period. Wood instructed his men on how to deal with the approaching group of protesters. He advised a cautious approach because '[a]t the moment there is considerable public support for these strikers as the public do not realize the motive and revolutionary tactics behind the movement.' The top Mountie in Regina worried that because of the popularity of the Trekkers the force would receive adverse publicity should mayhem occur. Still, Wood did not doubt the ultimate outcome of the RCMP's interaction with the Trekkers. He advised the officers under his command to carefully study a Mounted Police pamphlet entitled 'Demonstrations, Unlawful Assemblies, Riots, Etc.,' especially the section on coordinating dismounted and mounted men, and relay the important parts to their charges.[92]

Once the Trekkers arrived in the capital of Saskatchewan, their eastward progress ended permanently. The police did not permit any mass movement by rail or even by car – several who tried the latter method found themselves under arrest. Eight Trek leaders did travel to Ottawa to meet with the prime minister on 20 June. The meeting degenerated into a shouting match as Bennett, under advice from his police force, tried to trot out the criminal records of various Trek leaders. The leaders returned to Regina, but it was quickly clear they were going nowhere. By the end of June, only the date that the Trek would be disbanded remained to be decided.

The next day was 1 July 1935, or Dominion Day, a national holiday; it was also to be a time of violent conflict. In a detailed report to MacBrien after the riot, Wood described the steps that led to his decision to try to arrest the Trek leaders:

> Following the arrival of Sergt. Leopold here on the 1st instant with correspondence and documents from the east and other material from Vancouver ... [passage deleted under the Access to Information Act] Barristers, at once set to work to compile evidence against the leaders which would justify issuing a warrant for their arrest under section 98, in accordance with your instructions. After intensive work, it was decided at 4:00 P.M. ... to issue warrants for the arrest of Evans, Black, [names deleted under Access]. It was considered that the arrest of these leaders would quickly liquidate that movement ...
>
> Our first plan failed when it was discovered that the leaders did not congregate at Unity Center prior to going on the Market Square for the mass meeting; therefore, the alternate plan had to be put in operation. D/Insp. Mortimer blew his whistle at 8:17 P.M. The arrest of the two leaders, Evans and Black, first and second in command of the strikers, was effected as they jumped down from the speaker's platform and they were safely conducted to the Town Station in the police moving van, but only after there had been an attack on the escorts by strikers throwing rocks and other missiles.[93]

Wood seemed determined not to let the Trek leaders escape unpunished. The decision to arrest them, coupled with the location for the arrests – a crowded public square in the aftermath of a rally – made the result predictable. The Mountie-triggered violence that ensued led to the death of a Regina City policeman and dozens of injuries to Trekkers, Mounties, and ordinary citizens.[94]

In the aftermath of the clash, headquarters in Ottawa required an explanation for the debacle. Wood pointed to a breakdown in RCMP intelligence as one mitigating factor. For at least part of the Trekkers' journey a Mounted Policeman rode along disguised as one of them. One Mountie was instructed to join in Calgary, but he apparently did not make the journey. Mervyn Black ordered another to join up with the Trekkers in Moose Jaw. He lasted in their ranks until 18 June when after being identified he was ordered out.[95] The RCMP then became reliant on an undercover Canadian Pacific Railway policeman for information; Wood fingered this junior figure as being responsible for the decision to make the arrests on 1 July.[96]

Wood's search for a scapegoat served as a deflection from the reality that the RCMP, and he in particular, had indeed been responsible for the riot. He had ordered the arrest of the Trek leaders at a time when they were negotiating with the provincial government to disband the entire enterprise – the On to Ottawa Trek was on the verge of an unsuccessful but peaceful conclusion. The senior Mountie in Regina claimed to have had no knowledge that the Trekkers were negotiating with the provincial government. Yet the whole police operation seemed rushed, as if the policemen feared the Trek would successfully disband and its leaders escape from their grasp. Wood admitted on 2 July that the plans to arrest the Trek leaders were 'made hurriedly,' but somehow also 'carefully considered.'[97]

The outcome the officer in command at Regina envisioned when the Trekkers first arrived in his city did not include the men willingly giving up their protest journey after peaceful negotiations. The strategy became to prevent the men from leaving without being punished or even humiliated. In one attempt at negotiation, the RCMP tried to get the men to leave Saskatchewan's capital for a temporary camp near Craven, Saskatchewan. The Trek leadership rightly viewed the offer with suspicion. Wood's plan to end the Trek was to lure the men outside the city 'where they would be minus their supporters and where we could have dealt with them in a determined and satisfactory manner which would have compelled their 10 mile walk back to Regina, by which time they would have been in a frame of mind to accept any terms we might offer.'[98] He recognized the next day that the Trekkers would not voluntarily agree to go to this camp. Instead, the Mounted Police readied for what its commander saw as an inevitable outcome to the presence of the unemployed men:

> It is not expected that there will be many voluntary registrations tomorrow and that sooner or later there will be a demonstration in front of [deleted under Access to Information Act] office which will bring about Police action. The situation is suitable for our purposes in that it is opposite the Armouries and there is a large open space in all directions surrounding the building where we could use mounted men to advantage. Following any such clash between the police and the strikers, I anticipate there will be a movement then toward voluntary registration and dispersion.[99]

Six days later, Wood would get his violence, which, as he predicted, led to the dispersion of the Trekkers.

MacBrien seemed unconvinced by his junior officer's explanations as to why violence had occurred. When in one report Wood mentioned, 'You will recall that your instructions by telephone and telegram to me were to arrest the late leaders of this movement with as little delay as possible,' the commissioner underlined the last six words and wrote '[a]t an opportune time.'[100]

Wood directed a deliberate and largely successful campaign to deflect criticism away from the RCMP after the riot. He became, in the parlance of the modern political world, a 'spin doctor.' First, the senior police officer claimed that not a single member of the Mounted Police had fired a weapon. When the matter made it to the floor of the House of Commons, the senior policeman finally admitted that his men had indeed fired the bullets that had wounded the Trekkers.[101] The provincial government subsequently appointed an inquiry, the Regina Riot Inquiry Commission (RRIC), to investigate the causes of the riot. The RCMP, which initially ordered its members not to cooperate with the provincial body, sought to manage the outcome.[102] Wood informed the commissioner in January 1936 that he was 'well satisfied with the course of the investigation to date, and believe we have effectively established in the minds of the Commissioners and the public that this trek was a revolutionary movement, organized and directed by the Communist Party.' Initially, the force found it difficult to link the CPC with the Trek but this changed, the Mountie added, when he, himself, testified to the commission and took the opportunity to stress the communist connections to the leadership of the Trek.[103]

Responsibility for what occurred at Regina was a powerful issue. At times during the commission, it did not look as if the RCMP would escape unscathed. Even the force's biggest supporter, the Bennett government, appeared ready to blame the RCMP for the sake of political expediency. The counsel for the Bennett government, now out of office after the fall 1935 federal election, informed Wood on 1 February 1936 that all of the evidence entered so far indicated that 'the responsibility of issuing of instructions ... rested on ... [MacBrien] and the force generally.' Wood argued that, in fact, the commissioner received his instructions from the government of the day, but the counsel reiterated that no such evidence had been introduced. Saskatchewan Attorney General T.C. Davis rode to the rescue for the horsemen when he promised to make it clear to the RRIC that the Mounted Police received its orders from the Bennett government. All of these measures were designed to avoid, Wood stated, any 'blame being laid on the force for the instructions issued or, for that matter, anything in connection with the On-to-Ottawa march or the riot in Regina.'[104]

MacBrien, who had already spoken with Wood on the telephone regarding this matter, immediately had drawn up a draft memo, entitled 'Re: Responsibility' and sent it off to his subordinate in Regina. In preparing the memo, the commissioner consulted both his immediate superior, the new federal Minister of Justice Ernest Lapointe, and T.C. Davis. MacBrien, a former military man, stated that he enjoyed 'the authority of the Minister in control of the force, the Honourable Hugh Guthrie, for all orders sent you respecting the illegal travelling on trains by the "On-to-Ottawa" trekkers and their prevention from proceeding east of Regina.'[105] Thus ran the old general's argument: the politicians, accountable to the public, are ultimately responsible for the actions of their minions. Undoubtedly he was particularly sensitive on this issue because, like the good soldier that he was, MacBrien followed orders. The same issue had arisen three-and-a-half years earlier in the aftermath of the policing of the strike and riot in Estevan. Then three levels of government and the RCMP had bickered over what body was ultimately responsible for the actions of, and, even more importantly in the penurious 1930s, the expenses incurred by, the Mounted Police. In the aftermath of this battle, MacBrien consulted with the federal minister of justice to ensure 'that in future when extra men are required ... it will be necessary to make this request in writing and accept responsibility for the expense.'[106]

What happened in Regina in June 1935, as the RCMP sought to control a major demonstration of dissatisfaction with the government, displayed the complicated relationship between the RCMP and the government. To fully appreciate where responsibility lay for the broken lives, bones, and windows in Regina, it is important to know what sort of advice and options the RCMP offered the Bennett Conservatives. With the situation between the government and the Trekkers at a standstill in the middle of June 1935, Guthrie, the minister of justice, naturally approached the Mounted Police for advice on how to deal with the stalemate in Regina; he received a detailed memo on 20 June from MacBrien in which the commissioner specified the strategy for the government to take in dealing with its problem. It included the recruiting of more Mounties, the blocking of any further train travel east, the preparing of military units to deal with any outbreaks of disorder in Winnipeg, and the dispersal of the Trekkers and the arrest of their leaders if they made any attempt to continue their journey. Finally, he encouraged the government to portray the Trekkers' demands as illegitimate, play up the presence of communists among the Trek leadership, and make public Trek leader Arthur Evans's criminal record, a copy of which he helpfully included with the memo. Now Bennett and Guthrie became the good soldiers. The federal government followed the general's advice, which directly led to a breakdown in the talks between the two parties. Concluding his memo, MacBrien 'recommended that a general announcement should be made of the Government's determination to stop this illegal movement by all means at its disposal, and that the Provincial Governments and public generally be asked to assist with a view to controlling what may develop into a most dangerous situation.'[107] The federal government performed to the police script. After all, the police held the expertise in such matters. The strategy of the experts, however, failed, and the Trekkers paid the physical price for that failure. The Bennett government paid the political cost as it was ousted from office later that year. As for the RCMP and its leadership, MacBrien died three years later still in the position of commissioner; Stuart Taylor Wood succeeded him.

In the aftermath of the On to Ottawa Trek and other similar protests, the RCMP became even more interested in the activities of the unemployed. In 1938 merely the rumour of a new On to Ottawa Trek gave birth to a large pile of files on the activities of the unemployed. In that same year government offices were also sent orders from the Mounted Police on how to handle sit-down protests after a group of unemployed men occupied the post office in Vancouver and were then violently removed by Mounted Policemen. In Saskatchewan a lance corporal rode the rails disguised as a vagrant. Quizzing twenty fellow travellers failed to reveal any plans for a new trek. Instead the men headed for Regina in the hope of finding harvest work.[108] The events of September 1939 would take care of the unemployment problem.

S.T. Wood's emphasis on communist involvement in the Trek as a way of besmirching the movement best characterized the relationship between the RCMP and both unemployed and employed workers in the interwar period. He knew that many in Canada, including men in his own force, had genuine sympathy for workers, especially those who had the misfortune to find themselves without employment. Occasionally class snobbery fuelled by ethnic bigotry led to negative portrayals of workers in reports filed by Mounties. But if there had not been societal sympathy for this group, then there would have been no need to find scapegoats to blame for outbursts of worker unhappiness.

A paternalistic equation formed in the minds of many Mounties and those in the various government departments that received police reports. Workers were essentially good, and if they were just left alone to do their jobs, most, despite the occasional grumble, would have been content to punch the time clock and put in their hours. The menace, however, came from the outside. Agitators, chiefly of the 'Red' variety, and often as not 'foreigners,' promoted trouble where trouble did not exist. In playing both this perceived and actual role, these agitators gave the RCMP in Alberta and Saskatchewan a job to do. Mounties were policing soldiers with a mission to maintain order that had been given to them from on high and which would ensure a long institutional future; they used whatever means necessary to get the job done.

7

Conclusion: 1914–1939,
Transformation Complete

Upon the outbreak of war, the responsibilities and duties of the Royal Canadian Mounted Police were greatly multiplied; prompt action was necessary to arrest certain known enemies ... The Force also had to assume new responsibility ... over thousands of actual and potential enemy aliens to prevent them from any overt acts, and also to attempt to take care of any other citizens who might be used consciously or otherwise as tools for treachery.[1]

As these words of Commissioner S.T. Wood reflected, 10 September 1939 represented an important day for both Canadians and the Royal Canadian Mounted Police: their government had just put them at war with Nazi Germany. For Mounted Policemen, hostilities meant work to do. Under the Defence of Canada Regulations, which the force had helped to draft, a large number of Canadians had suddenly become enemies of the state.[2] The task of rounding up these legislated enemies would fall to the men in scarlet, and they performed the task with relish. Pat Lenihan remembered the zeal well. A long-time communist and opponent of Canada's participation in the Second World War, he made the police hit list. Just before the birth of his daughter in June 1940, the RCMP appeared and took him away; no problems of jurisdiction; no questions asked; nothing. Lenihan's new home was an internment camp at Kananaskis.[3] The RCMP was Canada's national police and security force all wrapped up into one and it had no challengers to that position.

Contrast Lenihan's treatment with that of Nels Bakkene of Ranfurly, Alberta, in the First World War. Bakkene wrote a letter criticizing the war to a friend in Europe that the post office intercepted and passed on to Percy Sherwood, the commissioner of the Dominion Police. In turn, Canada's highest ranking security officer at the time forwarded the report to the Royal North-West Mounted Police comptroller, who gave it to the commissioner, who sent it out to the appropriate division with an accompanying order to investigate. The investigating Mountie simply attempted to scare the man straight. That was the situation in 1917.[4] Twenty-two years later, Mounted Policemen would decide for themselves whom to ignore, whom to frighten, and whom to arrest.

A different environment prevailed in the previous war – the Mounted Police battled a rival for the affections of the state. The Dominion Police had handled security prior to hostilities and did the same in all of Canada except Alberta and Saskatchewan for almost the entire war. The force started the war as an ordinary police force, with its primary focus on Alberta and Saskatchewan. It lost even that aspect of ordinariness in 1917 when Alberta and Saskatchewan, with the support of Commissioner A.B. Perry, created their own police forces. Only in Canada's north did the Mounted Police continue regular policing duties. Operations in the south consisted of the enforcement of federal laws, assistance to federal departments, and security work. The force's numbers dwindled in the aftermath of the war as many questioned the need for such an institution. Certainly the government of William Lyon Mackenzie King felt no particular warmth towards an outfit brought into the world by Conservatives, and which appeared as a federal blot on provincial autonomy. The number of men in scarlet continued to decline. The move of the RCMP to the Department of National Defence in 1922, coupled with the resignation of Perry, the dominant figure in the Mounted Police for over two decades, offered strong indications that both an era and an institution were at an end.

Yet the RCMP survived its battles with the Dominion Police and politicians. For much of the interwar period the force strengthened itself on the Canadian landscape. What ended was the period of the old Mounted Police dealing solely with ordinary problems of the frontier. Canada was changing. Traditional Anglo-Canadian middle-class hegemony seemed under assault by new ethnic groups who refused to assimilate, and by workers and left-wing radicals who challenged the status quo of liberal-democratic Canada. The disorder at the end of the First World War only emphasized the changes occurring in Canada. At the same time, events like the Winnipeg General Strike triggered a tremendous backlash as Anglo-Canadian society responded to its challengers. The era of reaction emerged.

How did the RCMP respond to this Canada of the interwar period? As its history in Alberta and Saskatchewan demonstrates, the Mounted

Police underwent a metamorphosis. In part, this transformation, which began midway through the First World War, involved the force emphasizing its usefulness to the Canadian state by performing new and important work. In a country whose founding constitution emphasizes the principles of 'peace, order, and good government,' maintaining the middle value was a key task of the Mounted Police. Those in power in Canada at the end of the First World War profoundly feared the disorder represented by the Winnipeg General Strike and accompanying labour disturbances. This anxiety also extended to the activities of political radicals and non-traditional ethnic communities. In fact, the activities of radicals, workers, and members of ethnic communities were often interconnected both in reality and in the minds of the Canadian elite. In the case of the Communist Party of Canada (CPC), it really did not matter how many members it had or how legitimate a threat it was to the state; it became a target because of the nature of its constituency (ethnic minorities, members of the working class) and the values they espoused (anti-capitalist, anti-British, anti-Christian). The CPC was a symbolic challenge to everything that made Anglo-Canada great.[5]

Hence the state's need for an organization like the RCMP for dealing with its fears. The force was a national, quasi-military organization, free of the unionization that made other police forces less dependable, capable of meeting protest head on. Police officers on horses served as an effective method of crowd control, and, if necessary, the RCMP could supply even heavier firepower. Mounties did machine gun and bayonet training in the interwar period, not in preparation for external wars, but to curtail domestic ones.

The RCMP's transformation included the creation of a national network of secret agents and informants, who gathered countless pages of information on individuals and organizations. The perception by a Mounted Policeman that an individual was a radical was sufficient reason to create a file under the person's name or the name of the group to which he or she belonged. Either a regular member or a secret agent or informant infiltrated particularly troublesome organizations, exclusively on the political left. John Leopold, an active member of the force, advanced several rungs up the Communist Party of Canada ladder. From the party's birth, Mounties knew Communist plans as intimately as the party's members.

Usually the RCMP monitored and collected information with prevention being the key. During two periods of disorder, however, the labour disputes of 1919 and the growing anger of the unemployed of the early 1930s, the RCMP led crackdowns. In 1939, with the outbreak of war, the force continued the job as it compiled a list of suspects and then rounded them up.

The force in this era also performed a bureaucratic role for the state through the enforcement of federal statutes and the providing of assistance to federal departments.[6] Collectively, these measures represented the process of state formation whereby the state, with the help of the police, increasingly extended its tentacles into everyday life. Not all of these activities carried equal weight – certain tasks held much greater symbolism, even if statistically they lacked the significance of others. RCMP operations related to maintaining the moral, political, and economic status quo could not be mistaken for having been anything but fundamentally important to ensuring Anglo-Canadian hegemony.

Regardless of the nature of the roles, the sheer variety of them rendered Mounted Policemen extremely valuable to the Canadian state. That worth increased as the 1920s went on, making the force indispensable. One point in favour of the RCMP's resurgence in the 1920s was the simple fact that no other agency existed which was capable of performing such a variety of tasks, especially the security role. The Dominion Police already had grass growing over its grave. Turning intelligence gathering over to each provincial police force would have created a logistics nightmare, effectively ending any national strategy for dealing with radicalism and other perceived threats like narcotics.

Part of the value to the state came from the preventive role the RCMP played. Two examples, anti-communist and anti-drug activities, are indicative of this performance. In both cases the Mounties sought to prevent the spread of an infection, be it communism or drug addiction. In the case of the former, reports regularly detailed the response of an audience to a communist speech, or the success of a particular radical. This sort of information was of interest to Mountie superiors and their superiors' superiors, all the way to the top. Why the desire to know the volume of the applause that greeted a speech or the number of coins that fell into a collection plate? Because the respective responses demonstrated whether communism was dormant or infectious. The real concern was not with those making the speech; they were already infected. Even the positive response of an audience to communist rhetoric could be rationalized by noting that the group was primarily foreign (read central and eastern European). These people exhaled radicalism, according to the nativist mentality of the day, and thus were incapable of being cured. No, the real concern was over the impact of the message on the most vulnerable of society:

youth, women, some foreigners, principally those closest on the hier-archy to the British ideal, and elements of the working class. All needed to be protected from the Red plague. Michiel Horn's descrip-tion of the anti-communist campaign in Toronto is apt: 'It was re-garded almost as a measure of public health.'[7]

Drugs represented a similar threat. Again, the concern was not with the traffickers or the majority of the addicts. The Chinese, considered synonymous with narcotics in the minds of Anglo-Canadian society and members of the RCMP, were already labelled unassimilable and thus beyond hope of cure. They could best be handled through quar-antine in the form of deportation. Once more, the emphasis was on preventing the menace of drugs, primarily perceived as opium and inherently linked to the Chinese, from spreading to Anglo-Canadian society. They endangered middle-class Anglo women by threatening their purity through racial defilement. The 'cult of domesticity' from the period held women up as purity personified. Women were the foundation of the family, of the home, of society, and of the race. Emily Murphy, prominent Canadian feminist, police magistrate, and anti-drugs crusader, specifically described the dangers of drugs as being the defilement of women;[8] women required special protection in this instance. Riding to the rescue of these damsels in distress were the Anglo-Canadian Mounties.

With both drugs and left-wing radicalism, prevention was the name of the Mounted Police venture. Commissioner Perry established the rules in 1919 when in a memo he reiterated that detailed and accurate reports were crucial because 'the only information which is of any value in connection with Bolshevism is the reliable and first hand information of *what is going to happen before it occurs* in sufficient time to permit arrangements being made to offset any intended disturbance.'[9]

Mounted Policemen and the various tasks they performed also proved of value to the provinces of Alberta and Saskatchewan, even more so once they replaced the members of the Saskatchewan Provin-cial Police and the Alberta Provincial Police. Saskatchewan was the first to discover this benefit in 1928. Now, the Mounties, in addition to all of their other roles, had a regular policing job to play on the Prairies. This new role was often similar to what they did for the federal government. Maintaining order during strikes was especially important in Alberta and Saskatchewan, two provinces with a mining sector that had experienced a great deal of conflict and devastation courtesy of the Great Depression. It is no coincidence that the three most violent clashes of the 1930s (Estevan, 1931; Saskatoon, 1933;

and Regina, 1935) all involved cities in Saskatchewan, and all involved the Mounted Police. In Estevan it was a case of maintaining order, which in the end turned into protecting the property of mine owners at all costs. In Saskatoon the RCMP removed individuals who local officials believed threatened civic order. At Regina a botched Mountie effort to arrest the leaders of the On to Ottawa Trek, even as the movement was preparing to disband, sparked a huge riot. In all three cases, the RCMP lacked the subtlety and skill needed to avoid violence. An emphasis on military training and military values, the recruitment of former military personnel, and the creation of an 'other' among minorities, radicals, and workers left the RCMP little better equipped to handle protests than the militia would have been. Hence an institutional resort to violence was made almost inevitable because as Clive Emsley and Richard Bessel note about the wider issue of police violence, 'If policemen are encouraged as a group to view agitators and disturbers of the peace as political subversives, as members of a dangerous class or as inferiors, possibly because of their ethnic origins, then it scarcely needs a "rotten apple to trigger disorder."'[10] This, of course, assumes that the outbreak of violence was an unintended consequence. One could make an equal case that in following this path the RCMP did not fail the state; the protests and disorder were curtailed. Mounted Policemen, however, failed themselves since they violated their mythic image as neutral peacemakers.

Symbolism also meant that not every police task was created equal. Working to help deport non-British minorities, or at least to keep their activities in check, carried great symbolism with the majority of the Anglo-Celtic population in western Canada that found itself in the grip of nativist sentiment in the 1920s. Many people inherently linked criminality and radicalism with immigrants and ethnic communities, often equating differing cultural practices with racial characteristics. In turn, Mounties had no immunity from the wider society that produced them. Thus, comments from them, including various commissioners, linked radicalism, discontent with the status quo, criminality, and even depravity with immigrants and ethnic minorities. For Commissioner Perry, the solution, reflecting the tenor of the times, was assimilation. Commissioner Starnes in the 1920s saw discriminate deportation as an efficient tool for fixing the leaky faucet of radicalism.[11] In 1931 Commissioner MacBrien recommended widespread deportation as the solution to problems of radicalism and unemployment.[12] 'Send them back where they came from' was the rallying cry of many nativists and many Mounties.

But if these roles had been all that the Mounted Police had performed for the state then they still may not have left the force in the dominant position it occupied at the beginning of the Second World War. The background of members carried almost an equal weight. The force recruited ordinary men who mirrored the dominant elements in Canadian society including subscribing to Anglo-Celtic, middle-class values. It was no coincidence that the first Mounties' veterans organization, created at the end of the First World War, had promotion of British imperialism as one of its goals. Many policemen shared the nativist values that were popular in the 1920s and 1930s.[13] Those that reached the upper echelons of the RCMP most clearly reflected the ethos of the force and of the powerful in society (friends in high places also helped on occasion). In a hierarchical, militaristic institution, one did not advance by being an iconoclast; one progressed by following orders and by espousing the beliefs of one's superiors, or at least by keeping one's mouth firmly shut. Good soldiers like S.T. Wood went to the top; bad soldiers like William Mulhall in Estevan – who made powerful enemies by asking questions – saw their careers stall. A policeman serving with the RCMP in the 1930s saw first hand the danger of being a Mountie and expressing queries about broader societal issues. On a particularly nondescript day in 1937 he wondered out loud to a colleague why there were so many unemployed. 'You must be a Communist,' was the immediate reply. The questioner quickly realized 'even an unsubstantiated rumour of being a Communist sympathizer, if it reached the ears of the governing hierarchy might wreck my career, so from that day on, I avoided asking why we had unemployment or passing opinions on matters which might have political implications.'[14] Those who advanced beyond the noncommissioned ranks also reflected the culture of the RCMP: it was a male identity that mixed Anglo-Celtic middle- and upper-class values with the working-class physicality of police life. The Mounted Police reflected both the new trend in western societies at the time, which increasingly saw the middle-class male identity linked to physicality and violence as opposed to the older ideal that emphasized rigid control and discipline. Ethnicity was another important characteristic. Put simply, the Mountie represented the ideal Anglo-Canadian middle-class male image of early twentieth-century Canada.

The power of the force went deeper than its members; it represented the Canadian desire for order and control. It mixed security powers and nationwide policing, which other police forces such as the Federal Bureau of Investigation enjoyed, and still managed to be the local police force in countless communities across Canada. The combination of these three factors made RCMP personnel unique and powerful. That power made them, in essence, above the law. In its final report, the McDonald Commission, formed to investigate illegal activities on the part of the RCMP Security Service in the 1970s, discussed the mixing of regular policing and security work: 'A security service will inevitably be involved in actions that may contravene the spirit if not the letter of the law, and with clandestine and other activities which may sometimes seem to infringe on individuals' rights.' The report noted in the next sentence, however, that 'these are not appropriate police functions.'[15] These inappropriate police functions that derailed the Security Service in the 1980s emerged between 1914 and 1939. The opening of mail by the Mounted Police, for example, began during the First World War.[16] By the end of the war detailed files were being kept on individuals considered troublesome to the state. The police attempted to influence the careers of such people because of their radical activity. Illegal activities were suggested and, in at least one case, carried out.

Because the force grew in a time of disorder, it found itself in a particularly powerful position. In many ways, the First World War never ended for Mounted Policemen. They policed labour, minority groups, and radicals during the war; in the immediate aftermath of the conflict, widespread disorder that was associated with these three groups occurred. Thus the state directed Mounted Police members to, in effect, continue their wartime role. Then in the 1920s two greater menaces, communism and drugs, appeared. Again RCMP personnel performed a mixture of police and security intelligence work. Similar labour continued in the 1930s when the activities of tens of thousands of unemployed seemed to threaten both the status quo and social order. The 1930s ended with Canada again at war and the RCMP with additional security concerns involving radicals of the far left and right, although the state viewed the former as particularly troublesome because they were too different. Commissioner Wood informed the Canadian public in 1941 that Nazis were not the biggest threat to Canada. Rather, the 'Red' at home with 'the protection of citizenship' was the biggest challenge to the freedom of Canada. He then launched into a shopping list of the problems communists caused, a list that could just as easily have come off Commissioner Perry's desk in 1919:

1. Affiliations with labour bodies and a pretence of being the only champion of the 'working class' constitute its main line of attack ...
2. The Communists, always quick to take advantage of human misery in any form, found the unemployed and underpaid easy

tools for the spread of their doctrines of hate. The criminal and weakminded classes were even more enticed by their promises of gain.

3. Youth by nature is radical and therefore receptive to subversive propaganda promising social and economic reforms.

...

7. The Defence of Canada Regulations have all along been the point of attack by these enemies of democracy. So long as these stand there is little chance of getting on with the Revolution. So they are subjected to continuous attack on the grounds that they are unconstitutional, forbidding freedom of speech, press and assembly – the very foundation stones of democracy. The Communists, of course, are only interested in the 'rights' of democracy as a means of destroying democracy, but the gullible public is easily mislead.[17]

When on a muggy Ottawa night in September 1945 Igor Gouzenko smuggled top secret documents out of the Soviet Embassy revealing the existence of a communist spy ring, the RCMP had additional confirmation that its emphasis had been correct. Hailed by some as the symbolic first shot in the Cold War, Gouzenko's revelations helped trigger anti-communist 'witch hunts.'[18] For the security branch of the RCMP, now a separate entity within the force and heir of its secretive nature, it was business as usual; only the scale of operations changed after the Second World War. The rest of the duties were the same – surveillance and intelligence gathering related to the far left in Canada. Anti-communist searches were old hat to the RCMP. Mounties were free to continue their decades-long battle with their favourite enemy, communists.

From the mid-1940s and through the 1950s that is exactly what they did. In the 1960s the rules of the game changed somewhat. First, the operations of the RCMP Security Service came under far greater scrutiny in an era of heightened concern over infringements on civil liberties. The 'New Left' came into being and the RCMP found it difficult to shift its focus from the Communist Party of Canada that was by now all but completely irrelevant. Quebec nationalism also emerged as a new challenge in the 1960s. By the end of the 1960s and into the 1970s, the federal government pressured the RCMP Security Service into shifting resources to deal with the separatist threat. The tactics that 'the men in shadows' used against Quebec nationalists, while not completely different from those used against communists in earlier eras, proved the undoing of the RCMP Security Service.

Members of the force demonstrated an inability to distinguish between the Front de libération du Québec (FLQ), which employed terrorist tactics, and the Parti Québécois (PQ), which sought independence through the ballot box. Mounties broke into PQ headquarters and made off with membership lists. A barn was burned. Mail was opened illegally. A phony communiqué was issued calling upon FLQ members to resume a campaign of violence after Pierre Vallières, the intellectual father of the movement, had renounced violence.[19] Throughout this period the security branch of the RCMP did what its predecessors had done: it collected information about Canadians. By the 1970s the RCMP database on subversion contained files on over 800,000 citizens.[20]

All things, however, come to an end. In a sense, being the 'good soldier,' which had helped save the RCMP in a previous time, proved damaging. Cliff Harvison, who began his career in the 1920s and then served as commissioner of the force from 1960 to 1963, wrote in his memoirs that critics who saw or pretended to see 'the dangers of a "police state" in almost every action of law-enforcement bodies' had it all wrong. 'Surely that danger arises,' he wrote, 'only when the police disregard or refuse to follow the enactments of Government.'[21] The Trudeau government was at war with separatists just as the Bennett government had once fought communists. Mounties served as the government's front line soldiers, and they fought dirty. For a turn they also became casualties of the hostilities when in 1984 the government, based on recommendations of the McDonald Commission, largely, but not completely, stripped the force of its intelligence role developed so long ago.[22] Such a future, however, could not have been foreseen by Mounted Policemen in the halcyon days of September 1939. Then, they clearly knew who their enemies were and what was to be done with them. During the previous twenty-five years the RCMP had faced trials and tribulations and had been transformed. The force and its vision had triumphed.

Notes

Preface

1 Steve Hewitt, 'Re-Inventing the Mounties,' in Michèle Kaltemback, ed., *Le Canada face ses nouveaux défis/Canada Revisited* (Toulouse, France, 2005), 247–56.

2 William Cobban, *Mountie: Canada's Mightiest Myth* (Ottawa, 1998); National Archives of Canada (NA), Record Group (RG) 146, vol. 65, file 97-A-00044, Frank Underhill, pt. 2, Canadian Broadcasting Corporation, Communist Activities Within, 27 November 1963.

1. Introduction

1 Jeff Sallot, *Nobody Said No: The Real Story about How the Mounties Always Get Their Man* (Toronto, 1979), 94–5. For a more recent study of the Mountie myth, see Michael Dawson, *The Mountie: From Dime Novel to Disney* (Toronto, 1998).

2 R.C. Macleod, *The North West Mounted Police, 1873–1919* (Ottawa, 1978), 18.

3 Keith Walden, *Visions of Order: The Canadian Mounties in Symbol and Myth* (Toronto, 1982), 11.

4 See, for example, David Philips, 'A "New Engine of Power and Authority": The Institutionalization of Law-Enforcement in England 1780–1830,' in V.A.C. Gatrell, Bruce Lenman, and Geoffrey Parker, eds., *Crime and the Law: The Social History of Crime in Western Europe since 1500* (London, 1980), 157.

5 Charles Reith, *The Police Idea: Its History and Evolution in England in the Eighteenth Century and After* (London, 1938), v.

6 William M. Baker, 'The Miners and the Mounties: The Royal North

West Mounted Police and the 1906 Lethbridge Strike,' *Labour/ Le Travail* 27 (spring 1991), 62–3.

7 Anatole France, *Le Lys Rouge* (Paris, 1894), as quoted in Robert Reiner, *The Politics of the Police*, 2nd ed. (Toronto, 1992), 3. One of the first serious works to argue the class nature of authority was Douglas Hay, Peter Linebaugh, John G. Rule, E.P. Thompson, and Cal Winslow, *Albion's Fatal Tree: Crime and Society in Eighteenth-Century England* (New York, 1975).

8 Antonio Gramsci, *Selections from the Prison Notebooks of Antonio Gramsci* (London, 1971), 195.

9 Michel Foucault, *Discipline and Punish: The Birth of the Prison* (London, 1977), 282.

10 Sidney L. Harring, *Policing a Class Society: The Experience of American Societies, 1865–1915* (New Brunswick, NJ, 1983), 4.

11 Ibid., 3.

12 Paul Rock, 'Foreword: The Criminology That Came in out of the Cold,' in John Lowman and Brian D. MacLean, eds., *Realist Criminology: Crime Control and Policing in the 1990s* (Toronto, 1992), ix, x.

13 Clive Emsley, *The English Police: A Political and Social History* (London, 1991), 75.

14 Greg Marquis, 'The History of Policing in the Maritime Provinces: Themes and Prospects,' *Urban History Review* 29, no. 2 (1990), 94; Eric Monkkonen, *Police in Urban America, 1860–1920* (Cambridge, 1981), 57, as quoted in Reiner, *The Politics of the Police*, 46.

15 Robert M. Fogelson, *Big-City Police* (Cambridge, MA, 1977), 111.

16 Allan Greer and Ian Radforth, Introduction, in Allan Greer and Ian Radforth, eds., *Colonial Leviathan: State Formation in Mid-Nineteenth-Century Canada* (Toronto, 1992), 9; Bryan D. Palmer, *Working-Class Experience: Rethinking the History of Canadian Labour, 1800–1991* (Toronto, 1992), 66–9.

17 For a discussion of the literature on the Mounted Police, see Walden, *Visions of Order*.

18 A.L. Haydon, *Riders of the Plains* (Rutledge, VT, 1910); R.G. MacBeth, *Policing the Plains: Being the Real-Life Record of the Famous Royal North-West Mounted Police* (London, 1921). Also see Cecil Edward Denny, *The Law Marches West* (Toronto, 1939); Ronald Atkin, *Maintain the Right: The Early History of the North-West Mounted Police* (London, 1973); R.C. Fetherstonaugh, *The Royal Canadian Mounted Police* (New York, 1938); Louis Charles Douthwaite, *The Royal Canadian Mounted Police* (London, 1939).

19 See Alison Griffiths and David Cruise, *The Great Adventure: How the Mounties Won the West* (Toronto, 1996).

20 Nora Kelly and William Kelly, *The Royal Canadian Mounted Police: A Century of History, 1873–1973* (Edmonton, 1973); William Kelly, C.W. Harvison, *The Horsemen* (Toronto, 1967); Charles Rivett-Carnac, *Pursuit in the Wilderness* (Toronto, 1965); Vernon A.M. Kemp, *Without Fear, Favour or Affection: Thirty-Five Years with the Royal Canadian Mounted Police* (Toronto, 1958), and *Scarlet and Stetson: The Royal North-West Mounted Police on the Prairies* (Toronto, 1964).

21 See R.S.S. Wilson, *Undercover for the RCMP* (Victoria, 1986); Jack Fossum, *Mancatcher: An Immigrant's Story of Logging, Policing, and Pioneering in the Canadian West* (Comox, BC, 1990); Jack Fossum, *Cop in a Closet* (Vancouver, 1981); Donovan T. Saul, ed., *The Way it Was: Fifty Years of RCMP Memories* (Victoria, 1993); Donovan T. Saul, ed., *Red Serge and Stetsons: A Hundred Years of Mountie Memories* (Victoria, 1993).

22 Nora Kelly and William Kelly, *The Royal Canadian Mounted Police: A Century of History* (Edmonton, 1973), 151.

23 S.W. Horrall, 'The Royal North-West Mounted Police and Labour Unrest in Western Canada, 1919,' *Canadian Historical Review* 61, no. 2 (1980), 170.

24 J.R. Miller, *Skyscrapers Hide the Heavens: A History of Indian-White Relations in Canada* (Toronto, 1989), 212–17; National Archives of Canada (NA), Record Group (RG) 146, Records of the Canadian Security Intelligence Service, vol. 3332, pt. 1, Communist Party Indians-Canada, 15 February 1934 to 23 November 1937; ibid., RCMP Records Related to Communists and Indians, file 94-A-00028, Memo of Leopold, 24 September 1936; Steve Hewitt, 'Royal Canadian Mounted Spy: The Secret Life of John Leopold/Jack Esselwein,' *Intelligence and National Security* 15, no. 1 (2000), 158.

25 See, for example, Rivett-Carnac, *Pursuit in the Wilderness*; Saul, *Red Serge and Stetsons,* and *The Way it Was.*

26 These definitions are complex. In this period 'race' was employed as a concept that in the modern period would be equated with ethnicity in the sense that cultural differences were taken to constitute racial differences. Thus, Ukrainians were viewed by Anglo-Canadians as a different race whereas closer to the present they would be deemed as a distinctive ethnic group. Race, of course, is a culturally constructed notion that does not exist in any sort of biological way. For more on the topic, see Stephen E. Cornell and Stephen Ellicott, *Ethnicity and Race: Making Identities in a Changing World* (London, 1998), 24.

27 Greg Marquis, *Policing Canada's Century: A History of the Canadian Association of Chiefs of Police* (Toronto, 1993), 5; R.C. Macleod, 'How They "Got Their Man,"' *The Literary Review of Canada* 5, no. 8 (1996),

19–21; R.C. Macleod, 'The RCMP and Provincial Policing,' in R.C. Macleod and David Schneiderman, eds., *Police Powers in Canada: The Evolution and Practice of Authority* (Toronto, 1994), 44–56.

28 Richard Gid Powers, *Secrecy and Power: The Life of J. Edgar Hoover* (London, 1987); Frederic Wakeman, Jr., *Policing Shanghai, 1927–1937* (Berkeley and Los Angeles, 1995), 116–77.

2. The Architect, the Era, and the State

1 Gregory S. Kealey, 'The Early Years of State Surveillance of Labour and the Left in Canada: The Institutional Framework of the Royal Canadian Mounted Police Security and Intelligence Apparatus, 1918–26,' *Intelligence and National Security* 8, no. 3 (1993), 144.

2 Carl Betke and S.W. Horrall, *Canada's Security Service: An Historical Outline, 1864–1966* (Ottawa, 1978), 1: 351; David R. Williams, *Call in Pinkerton's: American Detectives at Work in Canada* (Toronto, 1998).

3 National Archives of Canada (NA), Records of the Royal Canadian Mounted Police, Record Group (RG) 18, vol. 572, file 52-19, Perry to McLean RNWMP Comptroller, 30 October 1918.

4 Ibid., 'Memorandum re the constitution and organization of a Police force for General duty in Canada,' 3 December 1918.

5 Betke and Horrall, *Canada's Security Service,* 1: 349–51.

6 R.C. Macleod, *The North West Mounted Police, 1873–1919* (Ottawa, 1978), 6.

7 DeLloyd J. Guth, 'The Traditional Common Law Constable, 1235–1829: From Bracton to the Fieldings of Canada,' in R.C. Macleod and David Schneiderman, eds., *Police Powers in Canada: The Evolution and Practice of Authority* (Toronto, 1994), 18; T.A. Critchley, *A History of Police in England and Wales, 900–1066* (London, 1967), 6–7.

8 James Gyffon, 'The Song of a Constable,' in A.V. Judges, ed., *The Elizabethan Underworld* (London, 1930), 488–90.

9 Allan Greer, 'The Birth of the Police in Canada,' in Allan Greer and Ian Radforth, eds., *Colonial Leviathan: State Formation in Mid-Nineteenth-Century Canada* (Toronto, 1992), 17–49.

10 Clive Emsley, *Policing and Its Context, 1750–1870* (New York, 1984), 60; John J. Tobias, 'The British Colonial Police: An Alternative Police Style,' in Philip John Stead, ed., *Pioneers and Policing* (Montclair, NJ, 1977), 242–3.

11 R.C. Macleod, *The North West Mounted Police and Law Enforcement* (Toronto, 1976), 125–8, 131–42; Macleod, *The North West Mounted Police, 1873–1919,* 9–11.

12 William R. Morrison, *Showing the Flag: The Mounted Police and Canadian Sovereignty in the North, 1894–1925* (Vancouver, 1985), 17.

13 RNWMP Annual Report, 1915, 10–11, 18–26; Carolyn Strange and Tina Loo, *Making Good: Law and Moral Regulation in Canada, 1867–1939* (Toronto, 1997), 52–4, 112–13. William Beahan and Stan Horrall, *Red Coats on the Prairies: The North West Mounted Police, 1886–1900* (Regina, 1998); William Beahan, 'Abortion and Infanticide in Western Canada 1874 to 1916: A Criminal Case Study,' in William M. Baker, ed., *The Mounted Police and Prairie Society, 1873–1919* (Regina, 1998), 193–206; Tracy Lee Strom, 'When the Mounties Came: Mounted Police and Cree Relations on Two Saskatchewan Indian Reserves' (MA thesis, University of Saskatchewan, 2000).

14 RNWMP Annual Report, 1915, 7.

15 Gregory S. Kealey, 'The Surveillance State: The Origins of Domestic Intelligence and Counter-Subversion in Canada, 1914–21,' *Intelligence and National Security* 7, no. 3 (1992), 181–2. For a history of the Alberta Provincial Police, see Sean Innes Moir, 'The Alberta Provincial Police, 1917–1932' (MA thesis, University of Alberta, 1992). For a history of the Saskatchewan Provincial Police, see Duncan F. Robertson, 'The Saskatchewan Provincial Police, 1917–1928' (MA thesis, University of Saskatchewan, 1976).

16 RNWMP Annual Report, 1917, 9.

17 Robert Craig Brown and Ramsay Cook, *Canada, 1896–1921: A Nation Transformed* (Toronto, 1974), 50–64.

18 Donald Avery, *'Dangerous Foreigners': European Immigrant Workers and Labour Radicalism in Canada, 1896–1932* (Toronto, 1979).

19 Peter W. Ward, *White Canada Forever: Popular Attitudes and Public Policy toward Orientals in British Columbia* (Montreal, 1978), 12.

20 Brown and Cook, *Canada, 1896–1921*, 67, 72 ; J.S. Woodsworth, *Strangers within Our Gates, Or Coming Canadians* (Toronto, 1909); Ralph Connor, *The Foreigner: A Tale of Saskatchewan* (Toronto, 1909).

21 Brown and Cook, *Canada, 1896–1921*, 113–14.

22 Gregory S. Kealey, 'The Canadian Labour Revolt of 1919,' in Bryan D. Palmer, ed., *The Character of Class Struggle: Essays in Canadian Working-Class History, 1850–1985* (Toronto, 1986), 90–114; ibid., 94.

23 Brown and Cook, *Canada, 1896–1921*, 122–5.

24 Richard Pipes, ed., *The Unknown Lenin: From the Secret Archive* (New Haven, CT, 1996), 8.

25 For a definition of this concept of the state, see Leo Panitch, 'The Role and Nature of the Canadian State,' in Leo Panitch, ed., *The Canadian State: Political Economy and Political Power* (Toronto, 1977), 6.

26 James C. Robb, 'The Police and Politics: The Politics of Independence,' in R.C. Macleod and David Schneiderman, eds., *Police Powers in Canada: The Evolution and Practice of Authority* (Toronto, 1994), 168, 177; Phillip C. Stenning, 'Police and Politics: There and Back and There

Again?' in Macleod and Schneiderman, *Police Powers in Canada,* 210;
Robert M. Fogelson, *Big-City Police* (Cambridge, MA, 1977), 23, 29;
David E. Smith, 'The Police and Political Science in Canada,' in
McLeod and Schneiderman, *Police Powers in Canada*, 184–208.
27 For example, see Sydney L. Harring, *Policing a Class Society: The
Experience of American Cities, 1865–1915* (New Brunswick, NJ, 1983);
and Allan Greer and Ian Radforth, eds., *Colonial Leviathan: State
Formation in Mid-Nineteenth-Century Canada* (Toronto, 1992), especially Greer, 'The Birth of the Police in Canada,' 17–49.
28 J. Skolnick, 'Changing Conceptions of the Police,' *Great Ideas Today*
(Chicago, 1972), 41, as quoted in Robert Reiner, *The Politics of the
Police* (Toronto, 1992), 2.
29 Kealey, 'The Early Years of State Surveillance of Labour and the Left in
Canada,' 142–3.
30 Betke and Horrall, *Canada's Security Service* 2:426–7.
31 Ibid.
32 NA, RG 146, vol. 26, file 93-A-00086, Wood to MacBrien, 1 February
1936.
33 Canadian Security Intelligence Service (CSIS), RCMP Records Related
to J.S. Woodsworth, vol. 23, file No. 88-A-60, J.S. Woodsworth to
Ernest Lapointe, 26 May 1924; ibid., 'Memorandum for the Honourable
Minister,' 28 May 1924. For example, see House of Commons *Debates*,
12 June 1929: 3634–5.
34 NA, RG 18, vol. 572, file 52-19, Perry to McLean, 30 October 1918;
Betke and Horrall, *Canada's Security Service*, 1:349–51.
35 For an example of relations with the military, see CSIS, RCMP Records
Related to the Communist Party of Canada in Edmonton, vol. 22, file
88-A-61, Ritchie to Starnes, 21 September 1926; ibid., RCMP Records
Related to the Estevan Strike and the Mine Workers Union of Canada,
vol. 84, file 88-A-60, W.A. Gordon, Acting Minister of Justice, to
MacBrien, 16 October 1931. For instances of the Mounties initiating
contact, see NA, RG 146, vol. 6, file 1025-9-91093, pt. 2, Assistant
Commissioner T.S. Belcher to Private Secretary of the Minister of
Justice, 9 September, 1931; ibid., Superintendent R.R. Tait to M.A.
MacPherson, 15 September 1931; ibid., Belcher to H.H. Ward,
Deputy Minister of Labour, 17 September 1931; ibid., H.H. Mathews,
Deputy Minister of Defence, to Belcher, 30 September 1931.
36 NA, RG 146, RCMP Records Related to the On to Ottawa Trek and
Regina Riot, vol. 25, file 93-A-00086, pts 1–3, MacBrien to Wood,
15 June 1935. For more on the On to Ottawa Trek, see Bill Waiser,
All Hell Can't Stop Us: The On-to-Ottawa Trek and Regina Riot
(Calgary, 2003).

37 NA, RG 146, RCMP Records Related to Radicals and Transients in
Saskatchewan, vol. 27, file 92-A-00123. pt. 1, Spalding, Assistant
Commissioner Commanding Saskatchewan Division, to MacBrien,
9 November 1932. A year later MacBrien had to caution S.T. Wood, the
new commander of 'F' Division and hence all of Saskatchewan, to at
least inform the attorney general of the province before he pulled any
'troops' out of Saskatoon; ibid., pt. 4, MacBrien to Wood, 29 April 1933.

38 NA, RG 18, vol. 572, file 52-19, Perry to G.L. Jennings, 16 December
1918.

39 NA, RG 18, vol. 1003, file 'Personnel,' Order in Council of 12 December 1918, P.C. 3076, 12 December 1918.

40 R.C. Macleod, 'The RCMP and the Evolution of Provincial Policing,' in
Macleod and Schneiderman, Police Powers in Canada, 48–9.

41 Ibid., 44.

42 Greer, 'The Birth of the Police in Canada,' 18.

43 Desmond Morton, 'Aid to the Civil Power: The Canadian Militia in
Support of Social Order, 1867–1914,' Canadian Historical Review 51,
no. 4 (1970), 424.

44 See David Jay Bercuson, Confrontation at Winnipeg: Labour, Industrial
Relations, and the General Strike (Montreal, 1974), 172–4.

45 NA, RG 18, vol. 1003, file 'Personnel,' Order in Council of 7 October
1918, P.C. 2213.

46 NA, William Lyon Mackenzie King Papers, Reel C-2277, Chas. Stewart,
George H. Boivin, and King to Lapointe, 5 October 1925: 99398; ibid.,
Lapointe to King's Private Secretary, 13 October 1925: 99399; ibid.,
Reel C-2288, Gardiner to King, 27 April 1926: 111781.

47 Macleod, 'The RCMP and the Evolution of Provincial Policing,' 46;
NA, William Lyon Mackenzie King Papers, reel C-2247, Memo from
D.D. McKenzie, 10 August 1922.

48 Macleod, 'The RCMP and the Evolution of Provincial Policing,' 46.

49 General Mewburn, as quoted in Don Macgillivray, 'Military Aid to the
Civil Power: The Cape Breton Experience in the 1920's,' in Michael S.
Cross and Gregory S. Kealey, eds., The Consolidation of Capitalism,
1896–1929 (Toronto, 1983), 119.

50 Gregory S. Kealey and Reg Whitaker, Letter to the Editor, Literary
Review of Canada 5, no. 10 (1996), 22; Steve Hewitt, Spying 101:
The RCMP's Secret Activities at Canadian Universities, 1917–1997
(Toronto, 2002), 18–38.

51 Public Archives of Alberta (PAA), Papers of Premier Brownlee, Access
No. 69.289, file 77A, Brownlee to MacPherson, 5 November 1930;
ibid., file 108, Brownlee to MacPherson, 12 November 1930.

52 Ibid., MacPherson to Brownlee, 8 November 1930.

53 NA, RG 18, vol. 572, file 52-19, Memo from McLean to Rowell, 30 November 1918; NA, Robert Borden Papers, reel C-4379, R. Bishop, for the comptroller, memo to the government, 10 January 1917: 96095.

54 NA, RG 18, vol. 572, file 52-19, Perry, 'Memorandum re the constitution and organization of a Police force for General duty in Canada,' 3 December 1918.

3. Men in Scarlet

1 Vernon A.M. Kemp, *Scarlet and Stetson: The Royal North-West Mounted Police on the Prairies* (Toronto, 1964), 79.

2 Catherine Hall, *White, Male and Middle-Class: Explorations in Feminism and History* (New York, 1992), 25.

3 Ibid., 25; Matthew Frye Jacobson, *Whiteness of a Different Color: European Immigrants and the Alchemy of Race* (London, 1998), 1–7.

4 Hall, *White, Male and Middle-Class*, 207.

5 Jack Fossum to author, 9 March 1996.

6 Carl Berger, *The Sense of Power: Studies in the Ideas of Canadian Imperialism, 1867–1914* (Toronto, 1970). For an example of the importance of English values to Anglo-Canada in the interwar period, see Michiel Horn, 'Keeping Canada "Canadian": Anti-Communism and Canadianism in Toronto, 1928–29,' *Canada: An Historical Magazine* 3, no. 1 (1975), 35–47.

7 T. Bilby, *A Course of Lessons* (London, 1823), 94, as cited in James Walvin, 'Symbols of Moral Superiority: Slavery, Sport and the Changing World Order, 1800–1950,' in J.A. Mangan, and James Walvin, eds., *Manliness and Morality: Middle-Class Masculinity in Britain and America, 1800–1940* (New York, 1987), 246–7.

8 *History of England for Public Schools* (Toronto, 1923), 297, as quoted in Timothy J. Stanley, 'White Supremacy and the Rhetoric of Educational Indoctrination: A Canadian Case Study,' in J.A. Mangan, ed., *Making Imperial Mentalities: Socialization and British Imperialism* (New York, 1990), 150.

9 See J.S. Woodsworth, *Strangers within Our Gates, Or Coming Canadians* (Toronto, 1909), 46–160.

10 Canada, House of Commons, *Debates*, 12 February 1914, 709.

11 S.W. Horrall, *The Pictorial History of the Royal Canadian Mounted Police* (Toronto, 1973), 34.

12 National Archives of Canada (NA), Royal Canadian Mounted Police Records, Record Group (RG) 18, vol. 1933, file 3, pt. 8, 'Patrols made at the Short Creek Detachment from Oct. 23, 1919 to Nov. 25, 1919.'

13 Ibid., 'List of Patrols, made from North Portal Detachment, between the 24th September & the 24 October 1919.'

14 Robert Knuckle, *In the Line of Duty: The Honour Roll of the RCMP since 1873* (Burnstown, ON, 1994), 15.

15 Kemp, *Scarlet and Stetson*, 41.

16 Rules and Regulations for the Government and Guidance of the Royal Canadian Mounted Police, 1928 (Ottawa, 1928), 243; John Sawatsky, Men in the Shadows: The RCMP Security Service (Toronto, 1980), 229–37; *Montreal Gazette*, 9 June 1986, E10; *Winnipeg Free Press*, 30 September 1986, 13; *Winnipeg Free Press*, 21 October 1986, 10; *Montreal Gazette*, 1 December 1989, A5.

17 Interview with retired Mountie Stirling McNeil, 24 January 1996.

18 Robert Craig Brown and Ramsay Cook, *Canada 1896–1921: A Nation Transformed* (Toronto, 1974), 262.

19 Letter from an anonymous retired Mountie, 30 January 1996.

20 Interview with retired Mountie Stan Wight, 28 March 1996.

21 C.W. Harvison, *The Horsemen* (Toronto, 1967), 4.

22 Joy Parr, *The Gender of Breadwinners: Women, Men and Change in Two Industrial Towns, 1880–1950* (Toronto, 1990), 245.

23 Steven Maynard, 'Queer Musings on Masculinity and History,' *Labour/ Le Travail* 42, no. 2 (1998), 184–5.

24 R.W. Connell, *Masculinities* (Cambridge, 1995), 196.

25 Gail Bederman, *Manliness and Civilization: A Cultural History of Gender and Race in the U.S., 1880–1917* (Chicago, 1995), 11–13, 19.

26 J.A. Mangan and James Walvin, Introduction, in J.A. Mangan and James Walvin, eds., *Manliness and Morality: Middle-Class Masculinity in Britain and America, 1800–1940* (New York, 1987), 1.

27 Bederman, *Manliness and Civilization*, 12.

28 Mike O'Brien, 'Manhood and the Militia Myth: Masculinity, Class and Militarism in Ontario, 1902–1914,' *Labour/Le Travail* 42, no. 2 (1998), 120–2.

29 John Springhall, 'Building Character in the British Boy: The Attempt to Extend Christian Manliness to Working-Class Adolescents, 1880–1914,' in Mangan and Walvin, *Manliness and Morality*, 52–3.

30 Carl Berger, *The Sense of Power: Studies in the Ideas of Canadian Imperialism, 1867–1914* (Toronto, 1970), 255; Robert H. MacDonald, *Sons of the Empire: The Frontier and the Boy Scout Movement, 1890–1918* (Toronto, 1993), 176–202.

31 Michael Rosenthal, *The Character Factory: Baden-Powell and the Origins of the Boy Scout Movement* (New York, 1986), 9.

32 Bederman, *Manliness and Civilization*, 15–17.

33 Edward Mann and John Alan Lee, *RCMP vs. the People: Inside Canada's Security Service* (Don Mills, ON, 1979), 123.

34 Letter from anonymous, 30 January 1996.

35 RNWMP Annual Report, 1920, 17.

36 Rosenthal, *The Character Factory*, 3, 135–6.
37 Bederman, *Manliness and Civilization*, 3–7, 41–2.
38 Greg Marquis, 'Working Men in Uniform: The Early Twentieth-Century Toronto Police,' *Histoire sociale/Social History* 20, no. 40 (1987), 270.
39 Ibid.
40 Recent publications suggest that an 'exaggerated masculinity' remains in the Mounted Police and policing in general, with major implications for those who fail to conform to such a culture. For the Mounted Police, see Robert Gordon Teather, *Scarlet Tunic: Inside Our Cars, Inside Our Hearts: On Patrol with the Royal Canadian Mounted Police* (Surrey, BC, 1994), 55–6. For female members of the Pittsburgh police, see Bonnie McElhinny, 'An Economy of Affect: Objectivity, Masculinity and the Gendering of Police Work,' in Andrea Cornwall and Nancy Lindisfarne, eds., *Dislocating Masculinity: Comparative Ethnographies* (London, 1994), 7. For a discussion of the negative treatment of contemporary British policewomen by their male colleagues, see Malcolm Young, *An Inside Job: Policing and Police Culture in Britain* (Oxford, 1991), 191–252. Finally, for the details of a study that found that female police officers in Quebec had a much higher suicide rate than their male counterparts or the general populace, see *Globe and Mail*, 25 May 1995, A4.
41 Royal Canadian Mounted Police (RCMP), Personnel Records of Superintendent Walter Mortimer, 'Annual Confidential Report – Non-Commissioned Officers,' 1931.
42 James Walvin, 'Symbols of Moral Superiority: Slavery, Sport and the Changing World Order, 1800–1950,' in Mangan and Walvin, *Manliness and Morality,'* 242; Peter Bailey, *Leisure and Class in Victorian England* (Toronto, 1978), 130; Colin D. Howell, *Northern Sandlots: A Social History of Maritime Baseball* (Toronto, 1995), 5.
43 Interview with retired Mountie Stirling McNeil, 24 January 1996.
44 Letter from I.C. Shank, 15 December 1995.
45 Interview with McNeil, 24 January 1996.
46 David J. Bercuson, 'The Winnipeg General Strike,' in Irving Abella, ed., *On Strike: Six Key Labour Struggles in Canada, 1919–1949* (Toronto, 1974), 26–7; S.D. Hanson, 'Estevan 1931,' ibid., 54; Steve Hewitt, 'September 1931: A Re-Interpretation of the RCMP's Handling of the Estevan Strike and Riot,' *Labour/Le Travail* 37 (1997).
47 Interview with Wight, 29 March 1996; Donovan T. Saul, ed., *The Way It Was: Fifty Years of RCMP Memories* (Victoria, 1990), 158.
48 Graham Dawson, *Soldier Heroes: British Adventure, Empire, and the Imagining of Masculinities* (New York, 1994), 233.
49 L.V. Kelly, 'Canada's Famous Mounted Police,' *Scarlet and Gold*

(1920), 38, as quoted in Keith Walden, *Visions of Order: The Canadian Mounties in Symbol and Myth* (Toronto, 1982), 36.

50 Douglas Owram, *Promise of Eden: The Canadian Expansionist Movement and the Idea of the West, 1856–1900* (Toronto, 1992), 140.

51 As quoted in Daniel Robinson and David Kimmel, 'The Queer Career of Homosexual Security Vetting in Cold War Canada,' *Canadian Historical Review* 75, no. 3 (1994), 334.

52 Mann and Lee, *The RCMP vs. the People*, 123. A section entitled 'Married Quarters and Privileges' appears in *Rules and Regulations for the Government and Guidance of the Royal Canadian Mounted Police, 1928*, 33; Harvison, *The Horsemen*, 60–4.

53 R.C. Macleod, *The North-West Mounted Police and Law Enforcement, 1873–1905* (Toronto, 1976), 127–8.

54 William Beahan and Stan Horrall, *Red Coats on the Prairies: The North West Mounted Police, 1886–1900* (Regina, 1998), 255; Steven Maynard, 'Rough Work and Rugged Men: The Social Construction of Masculinity in Working-Class History,' *Labour/Le Travail* 23 (1989), 159–69, and '"Horrible Temptations": Sex, Men, and Working-Class Male Youth in Urban Ontario, 1890–1935,' *Canadian Historical Review* 78, no. 2 (1997), 191–235; Carolyn Strange and Tina Loo, *Making Good: Law and Moral Regulation in Canada, 1867–1939* (Toronto, 1997), 19, 84–6; Vito Russo, *The Celluloid Closet: Homosexuality in the Movies* (New York, 1981), 4–5. For more information on early-twentieth-century gay culture and life, see George Chauncey, *Gay New York: Gender, Urban Culture, and the Making of the Gay Male World, 1890–1940* (New York, 1994).

55 Jack Fossum, *Mancatcher: An Immigrant's Story of Logging, Policing, and Pioneering in the Canadian West* (Comox, BC, 1990), 59–60, 98.

56 NA, RG 18, vol. 572, file 52-19, Perry to McLean, 30 October 1918; RCMP, Personnel Records of Walter Mortimer, Annual Confidential Report- Non-Commissioned Officers, 1931.

57 *Rules and Regulations for the Royal Canadian Mounted Police, 1928*, 14.

58 Ibid., 19.

59 Ibid., 119. The ranking came from the *King's Regulations and Orders for the Canadian Militia, 1917*.

60 NA, RG 18, vol. 1003, file 'Personnel,' Memo from A.A. McLean, 10 December 1918.

61 Dawson, *Soldier Heroes*, 1.

62 Paul Maroney, '"The Great Adventure": The Context and Ideology of Recruiting in Ontario, 1914–17,' *Canadian Historical Review* 77, no. 1 (1996), 92–3; O'Brien, 'Manhood and the Militia Myth,' 119.

63 Susan Bassnett, 'Lost in the Past: A Tale of Heroes and Englishness,' in

C.E. Gittings, ed., *Imperialism and Gender: Constructions of Masculinity* (London, 1996), 48–9.

64 See Marquis, 'Working Men in Uniforms'; Clive Emsley, *The English Police: A Political and Social History* (London, 1991), 178–82.

65 Frank W. Anderson, *Sergeant Harry Morren: Royal North West Mounted Police* (Calgary, 1969), 9.

66 Larry Hannant, *The Infernal Machine: Investigating the Loyalty of Canada's Citizens* (Toronto, 1995), 41.

67 *Rules and Regulations for the Royal Canadian Mounted Police*, 105.

68 James McKenzie and Lorne McClinton, *Troop 17: The Making of Mounties* (Calgary, 1992), 75–85.

69 C.E. Rivett-Carnac, 'The Training Depot,' *R.C.M.P. Quarterly* 3, no. 1 (1933), 24.

70 For more on this, see Steve Hewitt, '"The Royal Canadian Mounted Police are above that sort of thing": Ambition, Politics and Patronage in the Mounted Police, 1896–1931,' paper presented at Law for the Buffalo, Law for the Musk-Ox, University of Calgary, 1997.

71 RCMP Annual Report, 1920, 9.

72 RCMP Annual Report, 1930, 5.

73 Cecilia Danysk, '"Bachelor's Paradise": Homesteaders, Hired Hands, and the Construction of Masculinity, 1880–1930,' in Catherine Kavanaugh and Jeremy Mouot, eds., *Making Western Canada: Essays on European Colonization and Settlement* (Toronto, 1996), 155.

74 Bederman, *Manliness and Civilization*, 25. RCMP intelligence reports in the 1920s and 1930s frequently mentioned the number of women and children in attendance at meetings and rallies.

4. Dealing with Undesirables

1 For a discussion of this concept, see Edward W. Said, *Orientalism* (New York, 2003), 1–28.

2 For more on the concept of the 'imagined community,' see Benedict Anderson, *Imagined Communities: Reflections on the Origin and Spread of Nationalism* (London, 1991); and Catherine Hall, *White, Male and Middle-Class: Explorations in Feminism and History* (New York, 1992), 25.

3 Gerald Friesen, *The Canadian Prairies: A History* (Toronto, 1987), 272–3; J.C. Lehr, 'Government and Coercion in the Settlement of Ukrainian Immigrants in Western Canada,' *Prairie Forum* 8, no. 2 (1983), 179–94.

4 Donald Avery, *'Dangerous Foreigners': European Immigrant Workers and Labour Radicalism in Canada, 1896–1932* (Toronto, 1979), 9.

5 Howard Palmer, *Patterns of Prejudice: A History of Nativism in Alberta* (Toronto, 1982), 7.

6 Ibid., 9. In his groundbreaking 1955 study of nativism in the United States, John Higham also identified three similar categories of nativism. See his *Strangers in the Land: Patterns of American Nativism, 1860– 1925* (New Brunswick, NJ, 1955).

7 Palmer, *Patterns of Prejudice*, 10.

8 Mariana Valverde, *The Age of Light, Soap, and Water: Moral Reform in English Canada, 1885–1925* (Toronto, 1991), 104–14. For the United States, see Alan M. Kraut, *The Huddled Masses: The Immigrant in American Society, 1880–1921* (Arlington Heights, IL, 1982), 148–78; and David H. Bennett, *The Party of Fear: The American Far Right from Nativism to the Militia Movement* (New York, 1995), 183–237.

9 As quoted in Robert Craig Brown and Ramsay Cook, *Canada, 1896– 1921: A Nation Transformed* (Toronto, 1974), 67.

10 As quoted in John Herd Thompson, *The Harvests of War: The Prairie West, 1914–1918* (Toronto, 1978), 86.

11 Avery, *'Dangerous Foreigners,'* 85.

12 Thompson, *Harvests of War*, 87.

13 J.S. Woodsworth, *Strangers within Our Gates, Or Coming Canadians* (Toronto, 1909), 46–160; Valverde, *The Age of Light, Soap, and Water*, 29.

14 See Martin Robin, *Shades of Right: Nativist and Fascist Politics in Canada, 1920–1940* (Toronto, 1992), 1–44.

15 As quoted in Friesen, *The Canadian Prairies*, 405; see Christopher J. Kitzan, 'The Fighting Bishop: George Exton Lloyd and the Immigration Debate' (MA thesis, University of Saskatchewan, 1996), 110–57.

16 Barbara Roberts, *Whence They Came: Deportation from Canada, 1900– 1935* (Ottawa, 1988).

17 RNWMP Annual Report, 1919, 14.

18 As quoted in Lorne Brown and Caroline Brown, *An Unauthorized History of the RCMP* (Toronto, 1978), 63.

19 National Archives of Canada (NA), Record Group (RG) 146, RCMP Records Related to Arthur Evans, vol. 6, file 1025-9-91093, pt. 1, Wood to Attorney General of Saskatchewan, 15 September 1935.

20 Canadian Security Intelligence Service (CSIS), RCMP Records Related to Annie Buller, file 117-92-53, A.E. Acland to the Commissioner, 10 February 1932.

21 NA, RG 146, RCMP Records Related to Tim Buck, vol. 21, file 92-A-00099, pt. 2, Report of Constable Buntine, 18 July 1936.

22 NA, RG 18, Records of the RCMP, vol. 1950, file 13/9, Report of Sergeant Major Edgenton, 6 June 1919.

23 RCMP, Personnel Records of Cecil Thoroton Hildyard.

24 NA, RG 146, RCMP Records Related to the Saskatoon Relief Camp Riot, vol. 27, file 92-A-00123, pt. 4, Report of Detective Cecil Hildyard, 21 December 1922.

25 NA, RG 146, RCMP Records Related to the Estevan Strike and Riot, vol. 6, file 1025-9-91093, pt. 3, Secret Report, 4 October 1931.

26 NA, RG 18, vol. 1933, file G-57-9-1, Confidential Monthly Report for April 1919 – 'K' Division, Lethbridge, 8 May 1919; ibid., Confidential Monthly Report for August 1919; ibid., Confidential Monthly Report for March 1919. For more on the construction of whiteness, see Matthew Frye Jacobson, *Whiteness of a Different Colour: European Immigrants and the Alchemy of Race* (London, 1998).

27 NA, RG 18, vol. 2169, file 16/18, Letter to Assistant Commissioner W. Routledge, 3 April 1919.

28 RCMP, Personnel Records of Special Constable J.L. Eberhardt, Assistant Commissioner J.W. Spalding to Officer Commanding 'F' Division, 28 December 1932. Eberhardt was released from service two months later.

29 RCMP, Personnel Records of Jacob M. Tatko, Obituary, 1942.

30 Ibid. Tatko had earlier allowed a prisoner to escape and apparently began to make a habit of entering Vegreville-area bars and openly discussing his police work, including his previous activities as a secret agent.

31 *Rules and Regulations for the Government and Guidance of the Royal Canadian Mounted Police, 1928* (Ottawa, 1928), 14. For more on Leopold's life and career, see Steve Hewitt, 'Royal Canadian Mounted Spy: The Secret Life of John Leopold/Jack Esselwein,' *Intelligence and National Security* 15, no. 1 (2000), 144–68.

32 Carl Betke and S.W. Horrall, *Canada's Security Service: An Historical Outline, 1864–1966* (Ottawa, 1978), 1: 449; 'Famed Former RCMP Officer Dies Suddenly,' *R.C.M.P. Quarterly* 24, no. 1 (1958), 37; RCMP, Personnel Records of John Leopold.

33 RCMP Records, Personnel Records of Franz Droeske, F.A. Blake to Officer Commanding 'A' Division, 15 September 1939; ibid., T.B. Caulkin, Officer Commanding 'A' Division, to Commissioner S.T. Wood, 4 June 1940.

34 Thompson, *Harvests of War*, 74–6; Peter Melnycky, 'The Internment of Ukrainians in Canada,' in Frances Swyripa and John Herd Thompson, eds., *Loyalties in Conflict: Ukrainians in Canada During the Great War* (Edmonton, 1983), 2–3; William Kelly and Nora Kelly, *The Royal Canadian Mounted Police: A Century of History* (Edmonton, 1973), 146.

35 RNWMP Annual Report, 1919, 13.

36 NA, RG 18 Series A1, vol. 519, file 10, pt. 1, 11 April 1917.

37 RNWMP Annual Report, 1914, 8.
38 RNWMP Annual Report, 1915, 8.
39 NA, RG 18 series A1, vol. 519, file 11, Perry to Officer Commanding Calgary, 4 August 1917.
40 Ibid., Report of Superintendent McGibbon, Regina District, 54.
41 Ibid., Report of Superintendent Horrigan, Southern Alberta District, 133.
42 Ibid., vol. 517, file 406, Horrigan to Perry, 18 May 1915.
43 Ibid., Memo from Perry, 22 May 1915.
44 Ibid.
45 Bill Waiser, *Park Prisoners: The Untold Story of Western Canada's National Parks* (Saskatoon, 1995), 6; NA, RG 18, vol. 469, file 456, Perry to Comptroller Fortescue, 24 August 1914.
46 NA, RG 18, vol. 517, file no. 1, pt.3, Perry to Comptroller, 8 February 1917.
47 Ibid., vol. 537, file 393, Report of Staff Sergeant Fyffe, 27 June 1917.
48 Ibid., Wroughton to Perry, 28 June 1917.
49 Ibid., vol. 524, file 453, Report of Hildyard, 5 January 1917.
50 Ibid., Duffus to Hildyard, 9 January 1917.
51 Ibid., vol. 537, file 432, Report of Secret Agent 25, 11 August 1917; ibid., Perry to Comptroller, 28 August 1917; ibid., Comptroller to Col. Hugh Clark, Parliamentary Under-Secretary of State for External Affairs, 1 September 1917. Thompson, *Harvests of War*, 74.
52 NA, RG 18, vol. 565, nos. 495–507, Starnes to Perry, 10 October 1919. On 27 January 1919, the government passed an Order in Council transferring the task of registering enemy aliens in western Canada from the Dominion Police to the RNWMP. Ibid., vol. 1003, file Personnel.
53 Ibid., vol. 565, RCMP 1918, Nos 495–507, Pennefather to Perry, 9 October 1918; ibid., Perry to McLean, 15 October 1918.
54 Thompson, *The Harvests of War*, 74–5; Melnycky, 'The Internment of Ukrainians in Canada,' 1–24.
55 NA, RG 24, Department of National Defence Records, vol. 2544, file H.Q. C-2501, Commissioner Perry to Comptroller McLean, 18 February 1919.
56 NA, RG 18 A1, vol. 599, files 1309-35, Circular Memo 807, 'Re: Bolshevism,' 6 January, 1919.
57 Bill Waiser and Dave De Brou, eds., *Documenting Canada: A History of Modern Canada in Documents* (Saskatoon, 1992), 272–3; Eric Lyle Dick, 'Deportation under the Immigration Act and the Canadian Criminal Code, 1919–1936' (MA thesis, University of Manitoba, 1978), 41; NA, RG 18, vol. 1933, file G-57-9-1, 'K' Division, Confidential Monthly Report for November 1919.
58 Steve Hewitt, 'Malczewski's List: A Case Study of Royal North-West

Mounted Police-Immigrant Relations,' *Saskatchewan History* 46, no. 1 (1994), 35–41.

59 For a history of the security bulletins, see Reg Whitaker, ed., 'Introduction,' in Gregory S. Kealey and Reg Whitaker, eds., *R.C.M.P. Security Bulletins: The War Series, 1939–1941* (St John's, 1989), 9–20. For the first set of security bulletins, see Gregory S. Kealey and Reg Whitaker, eds., *R.C.M.P. Security Bulletins: The Early Years, 1919–1929* (St. John's, 1994).

60 Ivan Avakumovic, *The Communist Party in Canada: A History* (Toronto, 1975), 35, 119–20.

61 CSIS, RCMP Records Related to the Communist Party in Edmonton, vol. 22, file 88-A-61, pt 7, G.L. Jennings to Commissioner Starnes, 4 April 1923.

62 Ibid., Report of Detective Staff Sergeant MacBrayne, 18 July 1922.

63 Avery, *'Dangerous Foreigners,'* 49; NA, RG 146, vol. 27, file 92-A-00123, pt 6, Ritchie to Starnes, 29 March 1927.

64 RCMP, Personnel Records of Inspector William Moorhead, S.T. Wood to MacBrien, Re: Reg. No. 10854, Constable Campbell, 21 July 1933.

65 RCMP Annual Report, 1936, 78. Some Doukhobors did belong to the Communist Party in Canada in the 1930s. Avakumovic, *The Communist Party in Canada*, 121.

66 Superintendent W.P. Lindsay, as quoted in John McLaren, 'Wrestling Spirits: The Strange Case of Peter Verigin II,' *Canadian Ethnic Studies* 27, no. 3 (1995), 101.

67 CSIS, RCMP Records Related to Peter Verigin, vol. 51, file 117-91-22, Report of Detective/Corporal A.J. Stretton, 8 August 1933.

68 Ibid., Report of Assistant Commissioner W. Mortimer, Officer Commanding F Division, 18 March 1936.

69 Valverde, *The Age of Light, Soap, and Water*; Hall, *White, Male, and Middle Class*, 25; Gail Bederman, *Manliness and Civilization: A Cultural History of Gender and Race in the U.S., 1880–1917* (New York, 1995), 13.

70 Canada, House of Commons, *Debates*, 14 March 1923, 1144–5.

71 R.C. Macleod, *The North West Mounted Police and Law Enforcement, 1873–1905* (Toronto, 1976), 125; David F. Musto, *The American Disease: Origins of Narcotic Control* (New York, 1973), 182–4; Desmond Manderson, *From Mr. Sin to Mr. Big: A History of Australian Drug Laws* (New York, 1993), 62–71, 95–104; Catherine Carstairs, 'Innocent Addicts, Dope Fiends and Nefarious Traffickers: Illegal Drug Use in 1920s English Canada,' *Journal of Canadian Studies* 33, no. 3 (1998), 146.

72 Robert Montserin, 'Criminalization of Drug Activity in Canada' (MA thesis, University of Ottawa, 1981), 40.
73 Emily Murphy, *The Black Candle* (Toronto, 1922), 210; Valverde, *The Age of Light, Soap, and Water*, 167.
74 Madge Pon, 'Like a Chinese Puzzle: The Construction of Chinese Masculinity in Jack Canuck,' in Joy Parr and Mark Rosenfeld, eds., *Gender and History in Canada* (Toronto, 1996), 88; see also Peter Ward, *White Canada Forever: Popular Attitudes and Public Policy toward Orientals in British Columbia* (Montreal, 1978), 12; Woodsworth, *Strangers within Our Gates*, 155.
75 C.W. Harvison, *The Horsemen* (Toronto, 1967), 66. Harvison, who was a foot soldier in the 1920s war against drugs, would later become commissioner of the Mounted Police.
76 Ibid., 58–96.
77 Starnes as quoted in RCMP Annual Report, 1922, 17.
78 Neil Boyd, 'The Origins of Canadian Narcotics Legislation: The Process of Criminalization in Historical Context,' in R.C. Macleod, ed., *Lawful Authority: Readings on the History of Criminal Justice in Canada* (Toronto, 1988), 203.
79 R.C. Macleod, 'The RCMP and the Evolution of Provincial Policing,' in R.C. Macleod and David Schneiderman, eds., *Police Powers in Canada: The Evolution and Practice of Authority* (Toronto, 1994), 49.
80 RCMP Annual Report, 1921, 13–14.
81 Boyd, 'The Origins of Canadian Narcotics Legislation,' 203.
82 Harvison, *The Horsemen*, 42.
83 Bederman, *Manliness and Civilization*, 25.
84 Carleton Simon, 'The Criminal and His Face,' *R.C.M.P. Quarterly* 3, no. 1 (1935), 22.
85 'R.C.M.P.,' in *R.C.M.P. Quarterly* 7, no. 3 (1940), 282.
86 RCMP Annual Report, 1922, 16.
87 Canada, House of Commons, *Debates*, 23 April 1923, 2117. Section 14 of the Opium and Narcotic Drugs Act reads: 'Where a charge is laid under either paragraphs (a), (d), or (e) of section four of this act, the onus shall be upon the accused to establish that he had lawful authority to commit the act complained of, or that he had a license from the minister authorizing such acts.'
88 Harvison, *The Horsemen*, 46–7; R.S.S. Wilson, *Undercover for the RCMP* (Victoria, 1986), 172; P.J. Giffen, Shirley Endicott, and Sylvia Lambert, *Panic and Indifference: The Politics of Canada's Drug Laws* (Ottawa, 1991), 144; RCMP Annual Report, 1922, 16; Boyd, 'The Origins of Canadian Narcotics Legislation,' 203; Giffen, Endicott, and Lambert, *Panic and Indifference*, 135.

89 RCMP Annual Report, 1923, 16.
90 NA, RG 18, Reel T-4511, 'Arrests Under the Opium and Narcotic Drug Act,' 270–332.
91 Canada, House of Commons, *Debates* (27 February 1923), 698–9; Greg Marquis, *Policing Canada's Century: A History of the Canadian Association of Chiefs of Police* (Toronto, 1993), 92.
92 Interview with retired Staff Sergeant Stan Wight, 29 March 1996; Marquis, *Policing Canada's Century*, 153. For a period study displaying ethnic stereotypes, see Charles H. Young, *The Ukrainian Canadians: A Study in Assimilation* (Toronto, 1931), 197, 265.
93 Allard as quoted in RCMP Annual Report, 1925, 29.
94 Superintendent W.P. Lindsay as quoted in RCMP Annual Report, 1927, 33; ibid., 29; RCMP Annual Report, 1923, 26–7; Wilson, *Undercover for the RCMP*; RCMP Annual Report, 1935, 26.
95 RCMP Annual Report, 1927, 28. An effort was made after the Winnipeg General Strike to construct a new Canadian citizenship, one that excluded radicals and those unwilling to be assimilated. See Tom Mitchell, '"The Manufacture of Souls of Good Quality": Winnipeg's 1919 National Conference on Canadian Citizenship, English-Canadian Nationalism, and the New Order after the Great War,' *Journal of Canadian Studies* 31, no. 4 (1996–7), 5–28.
96 RCMP Annual Report 1922, 15.
97 Superintendent Christen Junget as quoted in 'Report of the RCMP for the Year Ended September 30, 1927,' 28.
98 As quoted in Security Bulletin 42, 23 September 1920, in Kealey and Whitaker, eds., *R.C.M.P. Security Bulletins, 1919–1929*, 154–5.
99 CSIS Records, Spalding to Officer Commanding, 'K' Division, Document 57, file 88-A-75, 23 January 1925.
100 Security Bulletin 44, 7 October 1920, in Kealey and Whitaker, *R.C.M.P. Security Bulletins, 1919–1929*, 196.
101 Public Archives of Alberta (PAA), Accession no. 75.126, vol. 218, file 4618. Starnes to Brownlee, 1923.
102 Ibid., 'Revolutionary Schools' – Memo prepared by Starnes for Gouin, 30 December 1922.
103 Betke and Horrall, *Canada's Security Service,* 1: 429–30.
104 Security Bulletin 330, 5 August 1926, in Kealey and Whitaker, *R.C.M.P. Security Bulletins, 1919–1929*, 316.
105 Ibid.
106 Security Bulletin 334, 2 September 1926, in ibid., 343–51.
107 'Training Young Communists,' *R.C.M.P. Quarterly* 3, no. 2 (1935), 185, 187.

108 Security Bulletin 9, 29 January 1920, in Kealey and Whitaker, *R.C.M.P. Security Bulletins, 1919–1929*, 30.
109 Security Bulletin 331, 12 August 1926, Security Bulletin 332, 19 August 1926, in ibid., 331, 337.
110 CSIS, RCMP Records Related to the Communist Party of Canada in Edmonton, vol. 22, file 88-A-61, Document 22, pt 7, Report of [deleted], 3 April 1923.
111 R. Bruce Shepard, *Deemed Unsuitable* (Toronto, 1996); Ward, *White Canada Forever.*
112 Barbara Roberts, *Whence They Came: Deportation from Canada, 1900–1935* (Ottawa, 1988), 108.
113 Allard as quoted in RCMP Annual Report, 1924, 27.
114 RCMP Annual Report, 1925, 25–9.
115 Catherine Carstairs, 'Deporting "Ah Sin" to Save the White Race: Moral Panic, Racialization and the Creation of Canada's Drug Laws,' *Canadian Bulletin of Medical Health* 16, no. 1 (1999), 32.
116 http://www.cbc.ca/news/background/arar/; Michael Scheuer, 'A Fine Rendition,' *New York Times*, 11 March 2005.
117 NA, RG 76, Department of Immigration, vol. 627, file 961162, reel c-10443, Blair to Under Secretary of State, 9 January 1920.
118 Ibid., vol. 29, file 653, pt 2, F.C. Blair to A.L. Jolliffe, 11 March 1920.
119 NA, RG 18, vol. 1933, file G-57-9-1, 'K' Division, Lethbridge, Confidential Monthly report for July 1919. Pennefather may have been overly optimistic in his conclusion to the case as it is not clear if the individual was ever expelled from Canada.
120 Ibid., 'K' Division, Lethbridge, Confidential Monthly report for February 1920.
121 Ibid., Confidential Monthly Report for June 1919.
122 CSIS, RCMP Records Related to the Communist Party of Canada in Edmonton, vol. 7, file 88-A-61, Starnes to Department of Immigration, Department of Insurance, 9 January 1929.
123 Avery, '*Dangerous Foreigners*,' 100–1; McLaren, 'Wrestling Spirits,' 101.
124 NA, RG 76, vol. 738, file 513057, Wood to MacBrien, 3 March 1933.
125 NA, A.G.L. McNaughton Papers, Manuscript Group (MG) 30, E133, Series II, vol. 10, file 46, Memorandum, 13 October 1931.
126 NA, RG 146, RCMP Records Related to the National Association of Unemployed, vol. 21, file 92-A-00099, pt 1, T.S. Belcher to Officer Commanding 'K' Division, 29 October 1931.
127 Ibid., vol. 27, file 92-A-00123, pt 2, Walter Munday, Officer Com-

manding Saskatoon, to Superintendent J.W. Spalding, Officer Commanding 'F' Division, 5 November 1932.

128 Ibid., vol. 6, file 1025-9-91093, pt 3, Inspector Moorhead to M.A. MacPherson, Attorney General of Saskatchewan, 15 October 1931.

129 Ibid., Spalding to Officer Commanding, Weyburn Sub-District, 15 December 1931.

130 NA, RG 76, vol. 738, file 513057, Assistant Commissioner of Immigration, R.L. Munroe to Jolliffe, Commissioner of Immigration, 10 May 1932.

131 Ibid., Memo from Munroe, 25 May 1932; ibid., Memo for Commissioner of Immigration, 26 May 1933.

132 Roberts, *Whence They Came*, 45.

5. Men in Secret

1 Robert Craig Brown and Ramsay Cook, *Canada, 1896–1921: A Nation Transformed* (Toronto, 1974), 311.

2 Cahan to Borden, 14 September 1918 and 21 October 1918, as quoted in Donald Avery, *'Dangerous Foreigners': European Immigrant Workers and Labour Radicalism in Canada, 1896–1932* (Toronto, 1979), 75. See also A. Ross McCormack, *Reformers, Rebels, and Revolutionaries: The Western Canadian Radical Movement, 1899–1919* (Toronto, 1977), 151.

3 Avery, *'Dangerous Foreigners,'* 75.

4 National Archives of Canada (NA), Record Group (RG) 18, Royal Canadian Mounted Police Records, vol. 599, file 1309-1335, Circular Memo 807, Re: Bolshevism, 6 January 1919.

5 Ibid., Circular Memo 807A, Re: Bolshevism, 6 January 1919.

6 Ibid., Circular Memo 807B, 5 February 1919.

7 Ibid. For a detailed examination of the RCMP's intelligence branch's activities in Ontario in the interwar period see Michael Butt, 'Surveillance of Canadian Communists: A Case Study of Toronto RCMP Intelligence Networks, 1920–1939,' PhD diss., Memorial University of Newfoundland, 2004.

8 Elizabeth Grace and Colin Leys, 'The Concept of Subversion and its Implications,' in C.E.S. Franks, ed., *Dissent and the State* (Toronto, 1989), 62; Reg Whitaker, 'Cold War Alchemy: How America, Britain and Canada Transformed Espionage into Subversion,' *Intelligence and National Security* 15, no. 2 (2000), 177–210.

9 NA, RG 18, RCMP Records, vol. 599, file 1309-1335, Circular Memo 807, Re: Bolshevism, 6 January 1919.

10 Ibid.

11 Ibid.
12 Richard Gid Powers, *Secrecy and Power: The Life of J. Edgar Hoover* (London, 1987), 33–53.
13 Bernard Porter, *The Origins of the Vigilant State: The London Metropolitan Police Special Branch before the First World War* (London, 1987), 4–16.
14 Bernard Porter, *Plots and Paranoia: A History of Political Espionage in Britain, 1790–1988* (New York, 1992), 121–2.
15 Frank Donner, *Protectors of Privilege: Red Squads and Police Repression in Urban America* (Berkeley, 1991), 76.
16 Wesley K. Wark, 'Security Intelligence in Canada, 1864–1945: The History of a National Insecurity State,' in Keith Nelson and B.J.C. McKercher, eds., *Go Spy the Land: Military Intelligence in History* (Westport, CT, 1992), 157.
17 Carl Betke and S.W. Horrall, *Canada's Security Service: An Historical Outline, 1864–1966* (Ottawa, 1978), 1: 225; Bill Waiser, *Park Prisoners: The Untold Story of Western Canada's National Parks, 1915–1946* (Saskatoon, 1995), 6.
18 Gregory S. Kealey, 'The Surveillance State: The Origins of Domestic Intelligence and Counter-Subversion in Canada, 1914–21,' *Intelligence and National Security* 7, no. 3 (1992), 182–3. Also see McCormack, *Reformers, Rebels, and Revolutionaries*, 131.
19 Royal Canadian Mounted Police, Personnel Records of Cecil Thoroton Hildyard, Superintendent F.J.A. Demers to the Commissioner, 18 September 1924; ibid., Hildyard to the Officer Commanding Prince Albert, 5 September 1923.
20 James Dubro and Robin Rowland, *Undercover: Cases of the RCMP's Most Secret Operative* (Toronto, 1991).
21 Betke and Horrall, *Canada's Security Service*, 237–8.
22 NA, RG 146, RCMP Records Related to the Estevan Strike and Riot, vol. 27, file 92-A-00123, pt 3.
23 Ibid.
24 RCMP, Personnel Records of John Leopold, Detective-Sergeant Salt to Allard, RE: Secret Agent 30, 2 July 1921.
25 Ibid.
26 Ibid., Commissioner Perry to Allard, 6 July 1921.
27 Ibid., Leopold to Allard, 17 July 1921.
28 Canada, House of Commons, *Debates*, 20 March 1934, 1663–5.
29 Canada, House of Commons, *Debates*, 5 April 1937, 2571–2. In 1966 Coldwell became one of three appointed to a Royal Commission on Security. Ironically he proved the most conservative of the three. See John Sawatsky, *Men in the Shadows* (Toronto, 1980), 194.

30 RCMP, Personnel Records of John Leopold, Starnes to Knight, 18 October 1926.
31 Ibid., Newson, Officer Commanding 'O' Division, to Assistant Commissioner G.S. Worsley, 23 June 1927.
32 Ibid., G.L. Jennings to Starnes, 18 May 1928.
33 Gregory S. Kealey, 'The Early Years of State Surveillance of Labour and the Left in Canada: The Institutional Framework of the Royal Canadian Mounted Police Security and Intelligence Apparatus, 1918–26,' *Intelligence and National Security* 8, no. 3 (1993), 145.
34 *The Sheaf*, 26 November 1935; Steve Hewitt, 'Spying 101: The RCMP's Secret Activities at the University of Saskatchewan, 1920–1971,' *Saskatchewan History* 47, no. 2 (1995), 20–31; RCMP, Personnel Records of John Leopold, Leopold's Record-Defaulter Sheet; NA, RG 146, RCMP Records Related to the On to Ottawa Trek and Regina Riot, vol. 26, file 93-A-00086, Wood to Commissioner MacBrien, 25 January 1936; Kealey, 'The Early Years of State Surveillance of Labour and the Left in Canada,' 145.
35 S.W. Horrall, 'The Royal North-West Mounted Police and Labour Unrest in Western Canada, 1919,' *Canadian Historical Review* 61, no. 2 (1980), 174; Dubro and Rowland, *Undercover,* 24–73.
36 Canadian Security Intelligence Service (CSIS), RCMP Records Related to J.S. Woodsworth, Report of Constable T.E. Ryan, 19 September 1919. The RCMP deemed the personnel records of Ryan as not of historical value and destroyed them. His medical records, however, still exist.
37 NA, RG 146, RCMP Records Related to the Saskatoon Relief Camp Riot, vol. 27, file 92-A-00123, pt 3, Report of Constable H.M. Wilson, 26 April 1933.
38 Helen Potrebenko, *No Streets of Gold* (Vancouver, 1977), 210; NA, Prime Minister R.B. Bennett Papers, Reel M-1453, CIB Confidential Monthly Report on Edmonton Unemployed, 493667-772; Barbara Roberts, *Whence They Came: Deportation from Canada, 1900–1935* (Ottawa, 1988), 156.
39 Gregory S. Kealey supplies a partial list of secret agents from 1919–20 in 'The Surveillance State,' 205. (1) F.E. Reithdorf, Secret Agent 50 a.k.a. Frederick Edwards; (2) Roth, Secret Agent 6; (3) Dourasoff, Secret Agent 14; (4) Jones, Secret Agent 58, Vancouver; (5) A.B. Smith, Secret Agent 61, Victoria; (6) F.H. Colam; (7) F.W. Zaneth; (8) George C. Evans; (9) R.M. Gosden; (10) Devitt, Vancouver; (11) W.P. Walker, Edmonton; (12) Eccles, Vancouver; (13) Spain, Vancouver; (14) Orton Hall, Vancouver; (15) Davies, Vancouver; (16) Wilkie, Vancouver; (17) Lawrence, Vancouver; (18) Kobus; (19) Kyzlick; (20) Harry Daskaluk, Secret Agent 21; (21) Gore Kaburagi or Goro Karbarugi; (22) John

Leopold; (23) T.E. Ryan; (24) John Veloskie; (25) Julius Chmichlewski. For more on the life and career of Gosden, see Mark Leier, *Rebel Life: The Life and Times of Robert Gosden, Revolutionary, Mystic, Labour Spy* (Vancouver, 1999).

40 RCMP, Personnel Records of Mervyn Black, 1935.

41 NA, RG 146, RCMP Records Related to the Winnipeg General Strike, vol. 1, file 1025-9-9028, pt 12, Spalding to Staff Sergeant Hall, 30 May 1919.

42 Ibid., vol. 1933, file G-57-9-1, 'K' Division Confidential Monthly Report for February 1919; ibid., vol. 1, file 1025-9-9028, pt 12, Report of Detective S.R. Waugh, 29 May 1919; Gregory S. Kealey, Introduction, in Gregory S. Kealey and Reg Whitaker, eds., *R.C.M.P. Security Bulletins: The Depression Years, Part 1, 1933–1934* (St John's, 1993), 12–15.

43 NA, RG 18, 85–86/574, Box 9, G-537-1, 'Organization of the CIB,' H. Darling, Assistant Superintendent for DCI, to Commissioner MacBrien, 22 May 1934, as quoted and cited in Kealey, 'The Early Years of State Surveillance of Labour and the Left in Canada,' 144.

44 NA, RG 18, vol. 511, file 306; David Ricardo Williams, *Call in Pinkerton's: American Detectives at Work for Canada* (Toronto, 1998).

45 Porter, *Plots and Paranoia*, 8.

46 NA, RG 18, A1, vol. 599, files 1309–35, 'Circular Memorandum No. 807A: RE: Detectives and Bolshevism,' 6 January 1919.

47 Ibid., vol. 519, file 11, pt 1, Superintendent T.A. Wroughton to Perry, 31 October 1917. Wroughton lamented that a plain-clothes Mountie lacked another witness to corroborate a particularly seditious speech.

48 Ibid., vol. 537, file 409, Wroughton to Perry, 31 July 1917.

49 Ibid., vol. 2169, file 16/1–16/15, Perry to Chairman, Board of Police Commissioners.

50 Ibid., vol. 1931, file 2, pt 2, 31 January 1919. On 4 February 1919 Perry gave Wroughton permission to employ 'such special agents as might be found necessary to cope with these elements.' Ibid., vol. 572, file 52-19, Perry to McLean, 4 February 1919.

51 Ibid., vol. 1943, file 82, Pennefather to Perry, 9 August 1919; ibid., 8 September 1919. Detective S.R. Waugh, who handled Zaneth, made a similar complaint noting that he was confined to his office more than he would like because he had to transcribe every report. NA, RG 146, vol. 1, file 1025-9-9028, pt 12, Report of Detective S.R. Waugh, 29 May 1919.

52 NA, RG 18, vol. 3173, file G1030–1–23, RCMP Spending Estimates for 1923–4.

53 RCMP, Personnel Records of Mervyn Black, Wood to MacBrien, 16 October 1933; ibid., Wood to MacBrien, 8 October 1935.

54 Ibid., Wood to MacBrien, 16 October 1935; Betke and Horrall, *Canada's Security Service*, 395–6. For a more detailed description of Black's career, see Gregory S. Kealey, Introduction, in Gregory S. Kealey and Reg Whitaker, eds, *R.C.M.P. Security Bulletins: The Depression Years, Part I, 1933–1934* (St John's, 1993) 12–15.

55 RCMP, Personnel Records of Jacob M. Tatko, Memo to the Adjutant from J. Stevens, Chief Treasury Officer, 13 September 1938; ibid., W.F. Hancock to the Commissioner, 21 November 1938.

56 William Repka and Kathleen M. Repka, *Dangerous Patriots: Canada's Unknown Prisoners of War* (Vancouver, 1982), 64.

57 CSIS, RCMP Records Related to J.S. Woodsworth, Saskatoon Detachment, re: Woodsworth, 30 May 1919.

58 RCMP, Personnel Records of C.T. Hildyard, Hildyard to Officer Commanding, Prince Albert, 5 September 1923; CSIS, RCMP Records Related to the Canadian Labour Defence League and A.E. Smith, vol. 19, Report of [deleted], Regarding A.E. Smith in Edmonton, 18 April 1928. Ibid., Report of [deleted], 16 January 1928. In 1920 in Edmonton an informant or secret agent reported on his work on a labour committee. NA, RG 146, vol. 1, file 1025-9-9028, pt 6, Report of anonymous, Edmonton, 26 April 1920.

59 CSIS, RCMP Records Related to Malcolm Bruce, vol. 87, file 117-89-57, Report of Hildyard, 3 February 1922; CSIS, vol. 19, file 1, Smith, Report of C. Hildyard, 17 June 1925.

60 NA, RG 146, vol. 1, file 1025-9-9028, pt 6, Hall to Spalding, 17 April 1920. The informant demanded $10 for his work. Ibid., Pennefather to Commissioner, 10 May 1920.

61 NA, RG 18, A1, vol. 599, files 1309–35, 'Circular Memorandum No. 807A, Re: Detectives and Bolshevism,' 6 January 1919.

62 CSIS, vol. 87, file 117-89-57, Report of Detective Sergeant Moss, 14 November 1924.

63 Ibid., Report of Leopold, 5 December 1924.

64 NA, RG 18, A1, vol. 599, files 1309–35, 'Circular Memorandum No. 807A: RE: Detectives and Bolshevism,' 6 January 1919; Gregory S. Kealey, 'Filing and Defiling: The Organization of the Canadian State's Security Archives in the Interwar Years,' in Franca Iacovetta and Wendy Mitchinson, eds, *On the Case* (Toronto, 1998), 88–105.

65 CSIS, RCMP Records Related to J.S. Woodsworth, Report of Corporal W.J. Barker, 17 May 1920.

66 NA, RG 146, vol. 1, 1025-9-9028, pt 7, Assistant Commissioner W.H. Routledge to Inspector C. Prime, 27 June 1919.

67 Security Bulletin No. 45-14 October 1920, in Gregory S. Kealey and Reg Whitaker, eds., *R.C.M.P. Security Bulletins: The Early Years,*

1919–1929 (St John's, 1994), 205–36. For a study of state persecution of Jehovah's Witnesses in Canada, see William Kaplan, *State and Salvation: The Jehovah's Witnesses and Their Fight for Civil Rights* (Toronto, 1989).

68 NA, RG 18, vol. 1933, file G-57-9-1, 'K' Division Confidential Monthly Report for November 1919.

69 S.T. Wood, 'Tools for Treachery,' *R.C.M.P. Quarterly* 8, no. 4 (1941), 39.

70 NA, RG 18, A1, vol. 599, files 1309–35, 'Circular Memorandum No. 807A: RE: Detectives and Bolshevism,' 6 January 1919.

71 Ivan Avakumovic, *The Communist Party in Canada: A History* (Toronto, 1975), 22–3; Ellen Schrecker, *Many Are the Crimes: McCarthyism in America* (New York, 1998), 4.

72 Avakumovic, *The Communist Party in Canada*, 36.

73 CSIS, RCMP Records Related to the CPC in Edmonton, vol. 22, file no. 88-A-61, Ritchie to the Attorney General of Alberta and the Officer Commanding, Military District No. 13, 15 May 1925.

74 Security Bulletin 332, 19 August 1926, in Kealey and Whitaker, *R.C.M.P. Security Bulletins: The Early Years*, 337–8.

75 CSIS, RCMP Records Related to the CPC in Drumheller, vol. 57, file 88-A-75, Spalding to Corporal Taylor, Drumheller, 15 January 1925.

76 'Training Young Communists,' *R.C.M.P. Quarterly* 3, no. 2 (1935), 185.

77 F.J. Mead, 'Communism in Canada,' *R.C.M.P. Quarterly* 3, no. 1 (1935), 45, 44.

78 Desmond Morton, 'Aid to the Civil Power: The Stratford Strike of 1933,' in Irving Abella, ed., On *Strike: Six Key Labour Struggles in Canada, 1919–1949* (Toronto, 1974), 79–91. For a description of the relief camp system, see James Struthers, *No Fault of Their Own: Unemployment and the Canadian Welfare State, 1914–1941* (Toronto, 1983). Also see Lorne Brown, *When Freedom Was Lost: The Unemployed, the Agitator, and the State* (Montreal, 1987).

79 Victor Howard, *'We Were the Salt of the Earth!' A Narrative of the On-to-Ottawa Trek and the Regina Riot* (Regina, 1985); John Herd Thompson and Allen Seager, *Canada, 1922–1939: Decades of Discord* (Toronto, 1985), 228–9.

80 NA, RG 18, vol. 469, file 456, Perry to Fortescue, 24 August 1914.

81 Ibid., vol. 537, file 3939, RNWMP Comptroller to Colonel Clark, Parliamentary Under-Secretary of State for External Affairs, 9 July 1917.

82 Ibid., vol. 524, file 453, Perry to Comptroller, 10 December 1917. Perry wrote, 'I think it would be inadvisable, at present, to submit the case to the Attorney General of Alberta. We will however continue to watch

Clarke until sufficient evidence is obtained to warrant our proceeding against him.' Perry was responding to a 4 December 1917 report from a Mounted Police detective in Edmonton: 'Clark [*sic*] made a violent speech against the Union Government, although he did not actually utter sedition, one sentence that I took particular note of was, when J. Clark [*sic*] ... said "R.B. Bennett has stolen $5,000,000 from the people since 1911."' Ibid., Report of S.L. Warrior, 4 December 1917.

83 Ibid., Report of Secret Agent 50 (F.E. Reithdorf), 10 November 1917; ibid., Report of S.L. Warrior, 13 November 1917.

84 Ibid., Wroughton to Commissioner, 16 November 1917.

85 NA, RG 24, vol. 2544, file H.Q. c-2051, Bolsheviki Conditions/Edmonton, 25 March 1919. The Mountie report noted that 'Mayor Joe A Clarke who has been somewhat unrestrained in his utterances is more and more feeling the responsibilities of his official position and is assuming a more dignified position.'

86 Sometimes descriptions of audience reactions would go to ridiculous extremes. An informant covering an address by A.E. Smith in Regina in 1919 noted that 'Dr. & Mrs. Stapleford, who left at the conclusion of Smith's main address and looked upset. J.B. Musselman was also there. Two or three times he wanted to get up, but his wife put her hand on his shoulder, shook her head and held him back. However, he asked a question at one time.' CSIS, vol. 19, file 1, Report of [deleted], 7 May 1919.

87 NA, RG 24, vol. 2544, file H.Q. c-2051, A.A. McLean to Colonel F.E. Davis, Assistant Director of Military Intelligence, 6 May 1919. McLean forwarded a report by a secret agent on 'Returned Soldiers and Agitators: Southern Saskatchewan,' dated 28 April 1919; ibid., Bolsheviki Conditions – Edmonton, 25 March 1919. Ibid., 'Memorandum on Revolutionary Tendencies in Western Canada,' no date. In 1926 Starnes wrote to MacBrien, still in the military at the time, to notify him that four members of the Princess Patricia Canadian Light Infantry were spotted at a Becky Buhay rally. NA, RG 146, RCMP Records Related to Rebecca Buhay, vol. 10, file 92-A-00012, pt 2, Letter to Major General J.H. MacBrien, 23 November 1926. In a confidential memo entitled 'Revolutionary Tendencies in Western Canada,' Perry discussed the potential of returned soldiers siding with revolutionaries. A report from Edmonton on soldiers involved in Bolshevism describes them as 'neurasthenics' or mentally ill. NA, RG 24, vol. 2544, file H.Q. c-2051, pt 5, 'Bolsheviki Conditions – Edmonton,' 25 March 1919.

88 Ibid., Perry to McLean, 18 February 1919.

89 NA, RG 146, vol. 1, file 1025-9-9028, pt 1, Spalding to Pennefather, 24 September 1919.

90 NA, RG 146, RCMP Records Related to A.E. Smith, vol. 4157, file 94-a-00014, pt 1, Tait to Deputy Attorney General of Saskatchewan, 11 April 1932; ibid., Deputy Attorney General of Saskatchewan to Tait, 14 April 1932; ibid., Report of Corporal J.J. Weaver, 19 November 1930; ibid., Wood to N.C.O., Regina Town Station, 25 June 1934. For more on the career of A.E. Smith and the RCMP's interest in him, see Tom Mitchell, 'From the Social Gospel to "the Plain Bread of Leninism": A.E. Smith's Journey to the Left in the Epoch of Reaction after World War I,' *Labour/Le Travail* 33 (1994), 125–51.

91 NA, RG 146, vol. 4157, access no. 94-a-00014, pt 1, Report of Corporal A. Batos, 9 December 1930.

92 Ibid., Report of Constable J. Hudz, 9 December 1937.

93 CSIS, vol. 87, file 117-89-57, Allard to the Commissioner, 16 March 1921.

94 CSIS, vol. 22, file 88-A-61, Ritchie to the Attorney General of Alberta and the Officer Commanding Military District No. 13, 15 May 1925.

95 David Monod, 'The Agrarian Struggle: Rural Communism in Alberta and Saskatchewan, 1926–1935,' *Histoire sociale/Social History* 18, no. 35 (1985), 99–118; Ivan Avakumovic, 'The Communist Party of Canada and the Prairie Farmer: The Interwar Years,' in David J. Bercuson, ed., *Western Perspectives I* (Toronto, 1974), 78–87.

96 NA, RG 146, RCMP Records Related to the National Farmers Union of Canada, vol. 2015, file 94-A-00090, pt 1, Report of No. 30 (Leopold), 19 July 1926. For more on Partridge see Murray Knuttila, 'E.A. Partridge: The Farmers' Intellectual,' *Prairie Forum* 14, no. 1 (1989), 59–74.

97 NA, RG 146, vol. 2015, file 94-A-00090, pt 1, 'Appendix No. 1: Special Report on Communism amongst Saskatchewan Farmers,' no date. Emphasis in the original.

98 NA, RG 146, RCMP Records Related to the National Farmers Union, vol. 2023, file 94-A-00090, pt 1, Report on United Farmers' Convention, North Battleford, 17 June 1931.

99 Ibid., vol. 2015, file 94-A-00090, pt 1, Superintendent R.E. Mercer to Commissioner, 23 August 1939.

100 Mead, 'Communism in Canada,' 44.

101 NA, RG 146, vol. 27, file 93-A-00087, pt 1, Report of Constable G.M. Elder, 6 May 1932.

102 NA, RG 146, vol. 2015, file 94-A-00090, pt. 1, 'Appendix No. 1: Special Report on Communism amongst Saskatchewan Farmers,' no date.

103 For the post–World War Two anticommunist campaigns, see Reg Whitaker and Gary Marcuse, *Cold War Canada: The Making of a*

National Insecurity State, 1945–1957 (Toronto, 1994); Len Scher, *The Un-Canadians: True Stories of the Blacklist Era* (Toronto, 1992).

104 CSIS, RCMP Records Related to the Political Activities of Jeanne Corbin, vol.7, file 88-A-20, Personal History file Re: (Miss) Jean Corbin, 30 December 1925. For more on the masculine construction of intelligence work, see Fiona Capp, *Writers Defiled* (South Yarra, AU, 1993), 50–3.

105 Mead, 'Communism in Canada,' 45.

106 CSIS, RCMP Records Related to the Political Activity of Jeanne Corbin, Starnes to Ritchie, 19 September 1926.

107 Ibid., Ritchie to Starnes, 28 October 1926; ibid., Ritchie to Starnes, 10 September 1928.

108 CSIS, RCMP Records Related to Jan Lakeman, vol. 101, file 117-89-57, Starnes to Page, Chief of Investigations, CNR, 9 February 1926; ibid., Report of [deleted], 22 April 1927.

109 CSIS, vol. 87, file 117-89-57, Report of T.E. Ryan, 24 November 1919.

110 CSIS, RCMP Records Related to the Communist Party of Canada in Drumheller, Alberta, vol. 57, file 88-A-75, Spalding to Corporal Taylor, Drumheller, 15 January 1925; CSIS, vol. 22, file 88-A-61, Ritchie to Starnes, 14 March 1925.

111 CSIS, RCMP Material Related to J.S. Woodsworth, Report of Sergeant W.J. Kempson, 8 June 1919.

112 Ibid., Report of T.E. Ryan, 22 September 1919. Ryan's view was confirmed by an informant a few months later: 'There was absolutely no taint of a revolutionary thought or inciting to any kind of violence.' Ibid., Report of Informant, 4 July 1920.

113 Hewitt, 'Spying 101,' 22.

114 CSIS, RCMP Records Related to J.S. Woodsworth, Report of Detective/Constable J. Leopold, 4 July 1920. Ibid., Report and Letter of John Leopold, 24 July 1920.

115 Richard Allen, *The Social Passion; Religion and Social Reform in Canada, 1914–28* (Toronto, 1971), 170–3. For more on the career of Irvine, see Anthony Mardiros, *William Irvine: The Life of a Prairie Radical* (Toronto, 1979).

116 CSIS, RCMP Records Related to William Irvine, vol. 81, file 117-89-27, Assistant Commissioner J.A. McGibbon to the Comptroller, 17 June 1919.

117 Ibid., Pennefather to Commissioner, 20 November 1919.

118 Ibid., J. Ritchie to Starnes, 5 April 1926.

119 CSIS, RCMP Records Related to J.S. Woodsworth, Starnes to Duffus, 27 November 1925. Even then, however, when Woodsworth addressed a convention of the Canadian Labour Party a year later, included among

the records of the convention was a detailed description of his speech. NA, RG 146, vol. 27, file 92-A-00123, pt 5, 16 August 1926.

120 CSIS, RCMP Records Related to the Worker's Party and Communist Party – Regina, Saskatchewan, vol. 135, file 117-91-87, pt 1, Report of No. 30 [Leopold], 30 March 1922.

121 Ibid., Allard to the Commissioner; 30 March 1922.

122 CSIS, vol. 87, file 117-89-57, Allard to the Commissioner, 7 January 1919.

123 Ibid., Starnes to F.A. Acland, 4 April 1922.

124 Betke and Horrall, *Canada's Security Service*, 430.

125 Vernon A.M. Kemp, *Without Fear, Favour or Affection: Thirty-Five Years with the Royal Canadian Mounted Police* (Toronto, 1958), 202.

126 C.W. Harvison, *The Horsemen* (Toronto, 1967), 86; Betke and Horrall, *Canada's Security Service*, 465.

127 Charles Rivett-Carnac, *Pursuit in the Wilderness* (Toronto, 1965), 294.

128 C.E. Edgett, 'Peace, War and Communism,' as quoted in Lorne Brown and Caroline Brown, *An Unauthorized History of the RCMP* (Toronto, 1978), 82.

129 NA, Manuscript Group (MG) 30 E163, Norman Robertson Papers, vol. 12, file 137, Charles Rivett-Carnac, Memorandum Regarding Information Received from Mr. A.L. Lawes, January 1939.

130 Wood, 'Tools for Treachery,' 394.

131 David Cunningham, *There's Something Happening Here: The New Left, The Klan, and FBI Counterintelligence* (Berkeley, 2004), 12.

132 Kealey and Whitaker, *R.C.M.P. Security Bulletins: The Early Years, 1919–1929*, 622, 305–6. CSIS, RCMP Records Related to Threats to the Security of Canada by Right-Wing Extremists, vol. 109, file 88-a-34, pt 1, Superintendent G.S. Worsley to Lucien Cannon, Acting Minister of Justice, 25 June 1927.

133 See Martin Robin, *Shades of Right: Nativist and Fascist Politics in Canada, 1920–1940* (Toronto, 1992), 61, 65–84.

134 CSIS, RCMP Records Related to Threat to the Security of Canada by Right-Wing Extremists, Worsley to Under Secretary of State, 20 June 1927; Robin, *Shades of Right*, 15–16, 34–5, 44, 62–3.

135 Robin, *Shades of Right*, 50–2; David E. Smith, *Prairie Liberalism: The Liberal Party in Saskatchewan, 1905–71* (Toronto, 1975), 144.

136 RNWMP Annual Report for 1919, 14.

137 Robin, *Shades of Right*, 56, 61–84.

138 CSIS, RCMP Records related to the National Unity Party and Fascists, vol. 7, pt 4, V.A.M. Kemp to Officer Commanding 'F' Division, 27 September 1938.

139 For a study of Nazis in Saskatchewan, see Jonathan F. Wagner, 'Heim

ins Reich: The Story of Loon River's Nazis,' *Saskatchewan History* 28, no. 1 (1976), 41–50, and his *Brothers beyond the Sea: National Socialism in Canada* (Waterloo, ON, 1981), 85–94. For more on the RCMP and the right, see Michelle McBride, 'From Indifference to Internment: An Examination of RCMP Responses to Nazism and Fascism in Canada from 1934 to 1941' (MA thesis, Memorial University of Newfoundland, 1997); Reg Whitaker and Gregory S. Kealey, 'A War on Ethnicity? The RCMP and Internment,' in Franca Iacovetta, Roberto Perin, and Angelo Principe, eds., *Enemies Within: Italian and Other Internees in Canada and Abroad* (Toronto, 2000), 128–47.
140   NA, RG 146, vol. 27, file 92-a-000123, pt 1, W.F. Hancock, Officer Commanding 'K' Division, to Commissioner Wood, 21 July 1938.

6. Policing Workers

1   National Archives of Canada (NA), Record Group (RG) 146, Royal Canadian Mounted Police (RCMP) Records Related to the National Association of Unemployed, vol. 21, file 92-A-00099, pt 1, Personal History Fyle-James Bryson.
2   Mariana Valverde, *The Age of Light, Soap, and Water* (Toronto, 1991), 129–55.
3   Rodney Stark as quoted in Dominique Wisler and Marko Tackenberg, 'The Role of the Police: Image or Reality?' in Richard Bessel and Clive Emsley, eds., *Patterns of Provocation: Police and Public Disorder* (Oxford, 2000), 121. For more on violence in Canada, see Judy Torrance, *Public Violence in Canada* (Montreal, 1986).
4   Frank Donner, *Protectors of Privilege: Red Squads and Police Repression in Urban America* (Berkeley, 1991), 76. See also Richard Bessel and Clive Emsley, Introduction, in Richard Bessel and Clive Emsley, eds., *Patterns of Provocation: Police and Public Disorder* (Oxford, 2000).
5   For a study of the Prairie working class at this time, see David Bright, *The Limits of Labour: Class Formation and the Labour Movement in Calgary, 1883–1929* (Vancouver, 1998); Joe Cherwinski, 'Early Working-Class Life on the Prairies,' in R. Douglas Francis and Howard Palmer, eds., *The Prairie West: Historical Readings* (Edmonton, 1992), 544–56; Cecilia Danysk, *Hired Hands: Labour and the Development of Prairie Agriculture, 1880–1930* (Toronto, 1995); Glen Makahonuk, 'The Labouring Class in Saskatchewan's Economy, 1850 to 1912,' *Saskatchewan History* 46, no. 1 (1994), 22–34.
6   David J. Bercuson, *Fools and Wise Men: The Rise and Fall of the One Big Union* (Toronto, 1978), 88.

7 NA, Records of the RCMP, RG 18, vol. 537, file 439, Report of Waugh, 25 August 1917.

8 Jane Morgan, *Conflict and Order: The Police and Labour Disputes in England and Wales, 1900–1939* (London, 1987), 43; Desmond Morton, 'Aid to the Civil Power: The Canadian Militia in Support of Social Order, 1867–1914,' *Canadian Historical Review* 51, no. 4 (1970), 407–25.

9 Gerda Ray, '"We Can Stay Until Hell Freezes Over": Strike Control and the State Police in New York, 1919–1923,' *Labor History* 37, no. 3 (1995), 404.

10 NA, RG 146, RCMP Records Related to the Saskatoon Relief Camp Riot, vol. 27, file 92-A-00123, pt 4, Alex Blackwood, Saskatchewan Deputy Attorney General, to G.M. Donald, Saskatoon Chief Constable, 29 April 1933.

11 Ibid., pt 2, J.W. Spalding to MacPherson, Saskatchewan Attorney General, 3 November 1932.

12 NA, RG 146, vol. 26, file 93-A-00086, pts 1–3, MacBrien to Wood, 15 June 1935; Canadian Security Intelligence Service (CSIS), RCMP Records Related to the Estevan Strike and Riot, vol. 94, file 88-A-60, H.H. Mathews, Deputy Minister of National Defence, to Belcher, 30 September 1931.

13 NA, RG 146, RCMP Records Related to the Regina Riot, vol. 26, file 93-A-00086, pts 1–3, Wood to MacBrien, 'Re: Training,' July 1935; NA, RG 18 A-1, vol. 517, file 1, pt 4, Memorandum on Redistribution of Force, 6 January 1917; Report of 'K' Division, RCMP Annual Report, 1932, 54; Donovan T. Saul, ed., *The Way It Was: Fifty Years of RCMP Memories* (Victoria, 1990), 30–1; Donovan T. Saul, ed., *Red Serge and Stetsons: A Hundred Years of Mountie Memories* (Victoria, 1993), 36.

14 RCMP Annual Report, 1932, 32.

15 RG 18, vol. 572, file 52-19, Memo on 'The Constitution and Organization of a Police Force for General Duty in Canada,' 3 December 1918.

16 R.S.S. Wilson, *Undercover for the RCMP* (Victoria, 1986), 12. For a modern study of RCMP training, see James McKenzie and Lorne McClinton, *Troop 17: The Making of Mounties* (Calgary, 1992).

17 C.W. Harvison, *The Horsemen* (Toronto, 1967), 19.

18 NA, RG 18, vol. 1931, file 2, pt 2, Monthly Report for 'G' Division, 30 April 1919; NA, Manuscript Group (MG) 30 E133 Series II, A.G.L. McNaughton Papers, vol. 10, file 46, Memorandum, 14 October 1931.

19 NA, Manuscript Group (MG) 30 E133 Series II, A.G.L. McNaughton Papers, vol. 10, file 46, Memorandum for the Honourable Minister, 16 October 1931.

20 NA, RG 146, vol. 26, file 93-A-00086, pts 1–3, Wood to MacBrien, 'Re: Training,' July 1935.

21 Gregory S. Kealey, 'State Repression of Labour and the Left in Canada, 1914–20: The Impact of the First World War,' *Canadian Historical Review* 73, no. 3 (1992), 288.

22 E.P. Thompson, *The Making of the English Working Class* (London, 1980), 539–40. Woodsworth as quoted in Canada, House of Commons, *Debates*, 3 May 1932, 2591–2.

23 As quoted in Morgan, *Conflict and Order*, 65.

24 Sidney L. Harring, *Policing a Class Society: The Experience of American Cities, 1865–1915* (New Brunswick, NJ, 1983), 145–6; Elizabeth Grace and Colin Leys, 'The Concept of Subversion and Its Implications,' in C.E.S. Franks, ed., *Dissent and the State* (Toronto, 1989), 66; Clive Emsley, *Policing and Its Context, 1750–1870* (London, 1984), 86.

25 NA, RG 18, series A1, vol. 599, files 1309–35, 'Circular Memorandum No. 807A: RE: Detectives and Bolshevism,' 6 January 1919.

26 CSIS, RCMP Records Related to the Canadian Labour Defence League and A.E. Smith, vol. 19, file 1, Staff Sergeant J.J. Wilson to Officer Commanding Maple Creek, 'A' Div, 23 June 1919.

27 CSIS, RCMP Records Related to Mathew Popovich, vol. 77, file 1, MacBrien to Winnipeg Mayor Ralph Webb, 27 October 1934.

28 NA, RG 18, vol. 525, file 494, Report of Sergeant McLauchlan, 1 December 1916.

29 For more information on strikes in 1919, see Gregory S. Kealey, '1919: The Canadian Labour Revolt,' in Bryan D. Palmer, ed., *The Character of Class Struggle: Essays in Canadian Working–Class History, 1850–1985* (Toronto, 1986), 90–114.

30 NA, Sir Robert Borden Papers, MG 26 H1, vol. 112, reel c-4340, Secret Agent report, 7 June 1919: 60970; ibid., Lea to Yates, 19 June 1919; Mark Leier, 'Portrait of a Labour Spy: The Case of Robert Gosden, 1882–1961,' *Labour/Le Travail* 42 (fall 1998). See also Mark Leier, *Rebel Life: The Life and Times of Robert Gosden, Revolutionary, Mystic, Labour Spy* (Vancouver, 1999).

31 NA, RG 18, vol. 1933, file G-57-9-1, Confidential Monthly Reports – 'K' Division, Lethbridge December 1919.

32 CSIS, RCMP Records Related to Arthur Evans and the One Big Union, Report of Detective/Sergeant F. Lobb, 8 October 1920, Report of Corporal Paris, 4 March 1920.

33 Ibid., Inspector A. Mellor, Superintendent Commanding Southern Alberta District, to the Commissioner, 6 October 1920.

34 Security Bulletin No. 48-4 November 1920, in Gregory S. Kealey and Reg Whitaker, eds., *R.C.M.P. Security Bulletins: The Early Years, 1919–1929* (St John's, 1994), 260.

35 CSIS, RCMP Records Related to Malcolm Bruce, vol. 87, file 117-89-57, pt 1, Report of Hildyard, 11 November 1924.
36 CSIS, RCMP Records Related to the Mine Workers Union of Canada, vol. 84, file 88-A-60, H.M. Newson, Assistant Commissioner, Commanding 'K' Division, to MacBrien, Re: Mine Workers Union of Canada, 4 January 1935; Security Bulletin 330 – 5 August 1926, in Kealey and Whitaker, eds., *R.C.M.P. Security Bulletins, The Early Years*, 314; NA, RG 146, vol. 27, file 92-A-00123, pt 4, Inspector F. Humby to the Commissioner, 25 April 1922; NA, RG 18, vol. 603, file 24/1920, pt 1, Report of Constable W. Craig, 27 September 1920; Security Bulletin 36 – 12 August 1920, in Kealey and Whitaker, *R.C.M.P. Security Bulletins: The Early Years*, 33. The Mounted Police frequently kept an eye on the activities of American IWW agitators among harvesters. Danysk, *Hired Hands*, 108, 127–8
37 NA, RG 146, vol. 10, file 92-A-00012, pt 1, Report of Detective Staff Sergeant S.R. Waugh, 28 December 1922.
38 Ian Angus, *Canadian Bolsheviks: The Early Years of the Communist Party of Canada* (Montreal, 1981), 265–9.
39 NA, RG 146, vol. 13, file 92-A-00056, S.T. Wood to Officer Commanding Weyburn, 25 October 1934; CSIS, RCMP Records Related to the Estevan Strike and Riot, vol. 84, file 88-A-60, H.M. Newson, Assistant Commissioner, Commanding K Division to Commissioner, 4 January 1935; NA, RG 146, RCMP Records Related to the Estevan Strike and Riot, vol. 6, file 1025-9-91093, Spalding to Officer Commanding Southern Alberta District, Re: James Sloan, 12 February 1932.
40 Public Archives of Alberta (PAA), Premiers' Papers, accession no. 69.289, file 108, Confidential. Report from Newson to Alberta Deputy Attorney General, re: Confidential C.I.B. Monthly Report, 'K' Division – October 1932.
41 CSIS, vol. 84, file 88-A-60, Private Secretary, Department of Trade and Commerce to MacBrien, 4 July 1934; NA, RG 146, RCMP Records Related to A.E. Smith, vol. 4157, file 94-A-00014, pt 2, William Dickson, Deputy Minister of Labour, to MacBrien, 18 April 1934; NA, R.B. Bennett Papers, reel M-988, William Dickson to Gideon Robertson, 10 October 1931, 92760; NA, RG 146, vol. 13, file 92-A-00056.
42 CSIS, RCMP Records Related to J.S. Woodsworth, Memorandum for the Honourable Minister, 28 May 1924.
43 CSIS, RCMP Records Related to Sam Scarlett, vol. 78, file 117-89-57, Sergeant Drysdale to Officer Commanding Prince Albert, 29 September 1925.
44 Greg Marquis, 'Working Men in Uniform: The Early Twentieth-Century Toronto Police,' *Histoire sociale/Social History* 20, no. 40 (1987), 259–77.

45 Interview with retired Staff Sergeant Stan Wight, 29 March 1996.
46 NA, RG 146, RCMP Records Related to the Winnipeg General Strike, vol. 1, file 1025-9-9028, pt 12, Report by Zaneth, 3 June 1919; ibid., Spalding to Pennefather, 30 May 1919.
47 As quoted in Security Bulletin 46 – 21 October 1920, Kealey and Whitaker, *R.C.M.P. Security Bulletins: The Early Years*, 229.
48 Lorne Brown and Caroline Brown, *An Unauthorized History of the RCMP* (Toronto, 1978); Nora Kelly and William Kelly, *The Royal Canadian Mounted Police: A Century of History, 1873–1973* (Edmonton, 1973); R.C. Macleod, *The North West Mounted Police and Law Enforcement, 1873–1905* (Toronto, 1976); William M. Baker, 'The Miners and the Mounties: The Royal North West Mounted Police and the 1906 Lethbridge Strike,' *Labour/Le Travail* 27 (1991), 63.
49 Harring, *Policing a Class Society,* 103.
50 Baker, 'The Miners and the Mounties,' 90–1; Macleod, *The North West Mounted Police and Law Enforcement*, 157; Kelly and Kelly, *The Royal Canadian Mounted Police*, 151; Brown and Brown, *An Unauthorized History of the RCMP*, 71–6, 85; Allen Seager, 'A History of the Mine Workers' Union of Canada' (MA thesis, McGill University, 1978), 260.
51 'RCMP Annual Report for the Year Ended September 30, 1923,' 24.
52 PAA, Records of the Alberta Provincial Police, accession no. 75.126, vol. 218, file 4598, APP Report, 'C' Division, 5 September 1923.
53 Ibid., APP Commissioner to Premier Brownlee, 7 September 1923.
54 NA, RG 18, vol. 1931, file 2, pt. 2, Monthly report for 'G' Division, 7 July 1919.
55 Security Bulletin No. 49 – 11 November 1920, in Kealey and Whitaker, *R.C.M.P. Security Bulletins: The Early Years*, 273–94.
56 CSIS, RCMP Records Related to Arthur Evans and the One Big Union, Report of Corporal Paris, 24 October 1919.
57 NA, RG 146, vol. 27, file 92-A-000123, pt 4, Report of C. Hildyard, 20 April 1922.
58 S.D. Hanson, 'The Estevan Strike and Riot, 1931' (MA thesis, University of Saskatchewan, 1971), 32–49, 80, 79. Also see Stephen Lyon Endicott, *Bienfait: The Saskatchewan Miners' Struggle of '31* (Toronto, 2002).
59 NA, RG 146, vol. 6, file 1025-9-91093, pt 1, Report of Sergeant W. Mulhall, 5 September 1931.
60 Ibid., Report of Constable F.H. Steele, 3 September 1931.
61 Brown and Brown, *An Unauthorized History of the RCMP*, 76; NA, RG 146, vol. 6, file 1025-9-91093, pt 2, Report of Mulhall, 11 September 1931.
62 NA, RG 146, vol. 6, file 1025-9-91093, pt 2, Detective/Sergeant J. Metcalfe to Mulhall, 7 September 1931; ibid., Superintendent R.R.

Tait to M.A. MacPherson, Attorney General of Saskatchewan, 8 September 1931; NA, CSIS Records, RG 146, vol. 6, file 1025-9-91093, pt 3, Report of Secret Agents at Estevan Detachment, 18 October 1931; ibid., Tait to MacPherson, 15 September 1931; ibid., Report of Mulhall, 17 September 1931; ibid., Tait to Spalding, 28 September 1931.

63 NA, RG 146, Report of Detective/Staff-Sergeant W. Mortimer, 19 September 1931.

64 Ibid., Report of Sergeant C. Richardson, 18 September 1931.

65 Ibid., Schutz to Tait, 22 September 1931; Hanson, 'The Estevan Strike and Riot, 1931,' 114.

66 *Regina Leader-Post*, 16 September 1931, as cited in Hanson, 'The Estevan Strike and Riot, 1931,' 114; S.D. Hanson, 'Estevan 1931,' in Irving Abella, ed., *On Strike: Six Key Labour Struggles in Canada, 1919–1949* (Toronto, 1974), 63–4.

67 NA, RG 146, vol. 6, file 1025-9-91093, pt 2, Tait to MacPherson, 23 September 1931.

68 Ibid., Spalding to MacBrien and MacPherson, 21 September 1931.

69 Ibid.

70 Hanson, 'Estevan 1931,' 54.

71 For the Mounted Police perspective on the Winnipeg General Strike, see Vernon A.M. Kemp, *Without Fear, Favour or Affection* (Toronto, 1958), 66–8; for a Mountie interpretation of the Regina Riot, see NA, RG 146, vol. 26, file 93-A-00086, Assistant Commissioner S.T. Wood to MacBrien, 4 July 1935.

72 Brown and Brown, *An Unauthorized History of the RCMP*, 73–4; RCMP, Personnel Records of William Mulhall, Report by Assistant Commissioner J.W. Spalding, 20 October 1931.

73 NA, RG 146, vol. 6, file 1025-9-91093, pt 3, Report of Metcalfe, 3 December 1931.

74 John Herd Thompson, with Allen Seager, *Canada, 1922–1939: Decades of Discord* (Toronto, 1985), 351.

75 See James Struthers, *No Fault of Their Own: Unemployment and the Canadian Welfare State, 1914–1941* (Toronto, 1983), 79–80.

76 'Report of the Royal Canadian Mounted Police for the Year Ended March 31, 1935,' 14.

77 'Report of the Royal Canadian Mounted Police for the Year Ended March 31, 1921,' 47.

78 NA, RG 146, RCMP Records Related to Rebecca Buhay, vol. 10, file 92-A-00012, pt 2, J. Ritchie, Superintendent Commanding 'G' Division, to the Commissioner, 20 December 1927.

79 NA, RG 146, vol. 27, file 92-A-00123, pt 4; Spalding to Attorney General of Saskatchewan MacPherson, 30 January 1931.

80 Ibid., T.S. Belcher to Officer Commanding 'K' Division, 29 October
    1931; NA, RG 146, RCMP Records Related to Harvey Murphy, vol. 27,
    file 93-A-00087, pt 2, Hancock to the Commissioner, 30 September
    1932.
81 NA, R.B. Bennett Papers, reel M-1453, 493667-772.
82 PAA, accession no. 69.289, file 517B, Newson to Alberta Attorney
    General, 22 November 1932.
83 Glen Makahonuk, 'The Saskatoon Relief Camp Workers' Riot of May 8,
    1933: An Expression of Class Conflict,' *Saskatchewan History* 37, no. 2
    (1984), 56.
84 NA, RG 146, vol. 27, file 92-A-00123, pt 2, Munday to Spalding, 5 No-
    vember 1932.
85 Ibid., pt 4, S.T. Wood to Deputy Attorney General of Saskatchewan,
    22 April 1933; ibid., pt 3 , Wood to Commissioner, 26 April 1933.
86 Ibid., pt 3, Munday to Commissioner MacBrien, 9 April 1933.
87 Ibid., Report by A.S. Acland, 10 April 1933.
88 *Saskatoon Star-Phoenix*, 9 May 1933, 7, as quoted in Makahonuk, 'The
    Saskatoon Relief Camp Workers' Riot,' 63.
89 NA, RG 146, vol. 27, file 92-A-00123, pt 3 Wood to Commissioner,
    12 May 1933.
90 There are numerous works on the Trek. See, for example, Lorne Brown,
    When Freedom Was Lost: The Unemployed, the Agitator, and the State
    (Montreal, 1987); Victor Howard, *'We Were the Salt of the Earth! A
    Narrative of the On-to-Ottawa Trek and the Regina Riot* (Regina, 1985);
    Michael Lonardo, 'Under a Watchful Eye: A Case Study of Police Sur-
    veillance during the 1930s,' *Labour/Le Travail* 35 (1995), 11–41. The
    previous definitive work on the actual events surrounding the Regina
    Riot by Gladys May Stone, 'The Regina Riot: 1935' (MA thesis, Uni-
    versity of Saskatchewan, 1967) has now been surpassed by Bill Waiser,
    All Hell Can't Stop Us: The On-to-Ottawa Trek and Regina Riot
    (Calgary, 2003).
91 Steve Hewitt, '"We Are Sitting at the Edge of a Volcano": Winnipeg
    during the On to Ottawa Trek,' *Prairie Forum* 19, no. 1 (1994),
    51–64.
92 NA, RG 146, vol. 26, file 93-A-00086, Wood to Inspectors and Ser-
    geants, 12 June 1935.
93 Ibid., Report of Wood, 19 July 1935.
94 Waiser, *All Hell Can't Stop Us*, 172–3.
95 Lonardo, 'Under a Watchful Eye,' 24.
96 NA, RG 146, vol. 26, file 93-A-00086, Wood to MacBrien, 12 Decem-
    ber 1935; Waiser, *All Hell Can't Stop Us*, 172.

97 NA, RG 146, vol. 26, file 93-A-00086, Wood to MacBrien, 2 July 1935.
98 Ibid., Wood to MacBrien, 24 June 1935.
99 Ibid., Wood to MacBrien, 25 June 1935.
100 Ibid., Wood to MacBrien, 23 July 1935.
101 Ibid., Wood to the Commissioner, 4 July 1935; ibid., Wood to MacBrien regarding firearms, 24 July 1935; ibid., Report of Inspector A.S. Cooper, July 24, 1935.
102 Ibid., Deputy Commissioner J.W. Spalding to Wood, 15 July 1935.
103 Ibid., Wood to Commissioner, 25 January 25 1936.
104 Ibid., Wood to MacBrien, 1 February 1936.
105 Ibid., MacBrien to Wood, 'Re: Responsibility,' 31 January 1936.
106 NA, RG 146, vol. 6, file 1025-9-91093, pt 4, 'Memo Re: Sask. refusing to pay Estevan expenses,' 9 January 1932.
107 NA, RG 146, vol. 26, file 93-A-00086., MacBrien to Guthrie, 20 June 1935.
108 Thompson and Seager, *Decades of Discord*, 293–4; NA, RG 146, RCMP Records Related to Radicals and Unemployed in Edmonton, vol. 27, file 92-A-000123, pt 1, Report of Detective Constable A.W. Parsons, 26 July 1938.

7. Conclusion

1 S.T. Wood, 'Tools for Treachery,' *R.C.M.P. Quarterly* 8, no. 4 (1941), 394.
2 For more information on the Defence of Canada Regulations and the RCMP role in its creation, see Daniel Robinson, 'Planning for the "Most Serious Contingency": Alien Internment, Arbitrary Detention, and the Canadian State, 1938–39,' *Journal of Canadian Studies* 28, no. 2 (1993), 5–20.
3 William Repka and Kathleen Repka, *Dangerous Patriots: Canada's Unknown Prisoners of War* (Vancouver, 1982), 34–5.
4 National Archives of Canada (NA), Record Group (RG) 18, series A-1, Royal Canadian Mounted Police (RCMP), Records, vol. 519, file 11, pt 1, 'Crime Report Re Nels Bakkene Ranfurly, Alberta,' 23 October 1917.
5 For a good study of the symbolism of the CPC, see Michiel Horn, 'Keeping Canada "Canadian": Anti-Communism and Canadianism in Toronto, 1928–29,' *Canada: An Historical Magazine* 3, no. 1 (1975), 35–47.
6 R.C. Macleod, 'The RCMP and the Evolution of Provincial Policing,' in R.C. Macleod and David Schneiderman, eds., *Police Powers in Canada: The Evolution and Practice of Authority* (Toronto, 1994), 44.

7 Horn, 'Keeping Canada "Canadian,"' 46.

8 Emily Murphy, *The Black Candle* (Toronto, 1922), 210.

9 NA, RG 18, A1, vol. 599, file 1309-1335, 'Circular Memorandum No. 807A: RE: Detectives and Bolshevism,' 6 January 1919. The emphasis is in the original.

10 Richard Bessel and Clive Emsley, Introduction, in Richard Bessel and Clive Emsley, eds., *Patterns of Provocation: Police and Public Disorder* (Oxford, 2004), 4.

11 Carl Betke and S.W. Horrall, *Canada's Security Service: A Historical Outline, 1864–1966* (Ottawa, 1978) 1: 429–3

12 Lorne Brown and Caroline Brown, *An Unauthorized History of the RCMP* (Toronto, 1978), 63.

13 Walter Hildebrandt, *Views from Fort Battleford: Constructed Visions of an Anglo-Canadian West* (Regina, 1994), 111.

14 Letter from retired Superintendent I.C. Shank, February 1996.

15 Jeff Sallot, *Nobody Said No: The Real Story about How the Mounties Always Get Their Man* (Toronto, 1979), 184. Emphasis added.

16 NA, RG 18, vol. 492, file 476, Graham Moon, Secretary, Post Office Department, to Comptroller, 31 Oct. 1914.

17 Wood, 'Tools for Treachery,' 395–7.

18 For more on the anticommunist witch-hunts in Canada, see Len Scher, *The Un-Canadians: True Stories of the Blacklist Era* (Toronto, 1992); Reg Whitaker and Steve Hewitt, *Canada and the Cold War* (Toronto, 2003), 18–57.

19 Sallot, *Nobody Said No*, 42–3.

20 Gregory S. Kealey and Reg Whitaker, Letter to the Editor, *Literary Review of Canada* 5, no. 10 (1996), 22.

21. C.W. Harvison, *The Horseman* (Toronto, 1967), 155.

22 For more on the Canadian Security Intelligence Service, see Richard Cleroux, *Official Secrets: The Story behind the Canadian Security Intelligence Service* (Toronto, 1990); Andrew Mitrovica, *Covert Entry: Spies, Lies and Crimes inside Canada's Secret Service* (Toronto, 2002).

Bibliography

Primary Sources

Archives
Canadian Security Intelligence Service
  Royal Canadian Mounted Police Security Records

National Archives of Canada
  R.B. Bennett Papers
  Robert Borden Papers
  William Lyon Mackenzie King Papers
  Arthur Meighen Papers
  A.G.L. McNaughton Papers
  Norman Robertson Papers
  RG 18, Records of the Royal Canadian Mounted Police
  RG 24, Records of the Department of National Defence
  RG 76, Records of the Department of Immigration
  RG 146, Records of the Canadian Security Intelligence Service

Public Archives of Alberta
  Papers of Premier J.E. Brownlee
  Papers of Premier William Aberhart
  Records of the Alberta Provincial Police

Royal Canadian Mounted Police
  Personnel Records of:
    Black, Mervyn
    Droeske, Franz
    Eberhardt, J.L.

Hildyard, C.T.
Jennings, G.L.
Koyich, Roy
Leopold, John
MacBrien, J.H.
Moorhead, William
Mortimer, Walter
Moss, Arthur
Mulhall, William
Perry, A.B.
Spalding, J.W.
Starnes, Cortlandt
Tatko, Jacob M.
Zaneth, Frank

Saskatchewan Archives Board
Records of the Saskatchewan Provincial Police
W.F.A. Turgeon Papers

Government Publications
1931 Census
Hansard
Mounted Police Annual Reports, 1913–40
Rules and Regulations for the Government and Guidance of the Royal Canadian Mounted Police 1928. Ottawa, 1928.

Periodicals
R.C.M.P. Quarterly, 1933–90.

Interviews and Correspondence with Former Mounted Policemen
Correspondence with anonymous
Correspondence with J.W. Duggan
Correspondence with Jack Fossum
Correspondence with I.C. Shank
Correspondence with Ted Turner
Interview with Stirling McNeil
Interview with Stan Wight

Secondary Sources

Books
Abella, Irving, ed. *On Strike: Six Key Labour Struggles in Canada, 1919–1949.* Toronto, 1974.

Abella, Irving, and Harold Troper. *None Is Too Many: Canada and the Jews of Europe, 1933–1948.* Toronto, 1982.

Allen, Richard. *The Social Passion: Religion and Social Reform in Canada, 1914–28.* Toronto, 1971.

Anderson, Benedict. *Imagined Communities – Reflections on the Origin and Spread of Nationalism.* London, 1991.

Anderson, Frank W. *Sergeant Harry Morren: Royal North West Mounted Police.* Calgary, 1969.

Angus, Ian. *Canadian Bolsheviks: The Early Years of the Communist Party of Canada.* Montreal, 1981.

Atkin, Ronald. *Maintain the Right: The Early History of the North-West Mounted Police.* London, 1973.

Avakumovic, Ivan. *The Communist Party in Canada: A History.* Toronto, 1975.

Avery, Donald. *'Dangerous Foreigners': European Immigrant Workers and Labour Radicalism in Canada, 1896–1932.* Toronto, 1979.

Bailey, Peter. *Leisure and Class in Victorian England.* Toronto, 1978.

Baker, William M., ed. *Pioneer Policing in Southern Alberta: Deane of the Mounties, 1888–1914.* Calgary, 1993.

– (ed.). *The Mounted Police and Prairie Society, 1873–1919.* Regina, 1998.

Beahan, William, and Stan Horrall. *Red Coats on the Prairies: The North West Mounted Police, 1886–1900.* Regina, 1998.

Bederman, Gail. *Manliness and Civilization: A Cultural History of Gender and Race in the U.S., 1880–1917.* Chicago, 1995.

Bennett, David H. *The Party of Fear: The American Far Right from Nativism to the Militia Movement.* New York, 1995.

Bercuson, David J. *Confrontation at Winnipeg: Labour, Industrial Relations, and the General Strike.* Montreal, 1974.

– *Fools and Wise Men: The Rise and Fall of the One Big Union.* Toronto, 1978.

Berger, Carl. *The Sense of Power: Studies in the Ideas of Canadian Imperialism, 1867–1914.* Toronto, 1970.

Bessel, Richard, and Clive Emsley, eds. *Patterns of Provocation: Police and Public Disorder.* Oxford, 2000.

Betke, Carl, and S.W. Horrall. *Canada's Security Service: An Historical Outline, 1864–1966.* 2 vols. Ottawa, 1978.

Bright, David. *The Limits of Labour: Class Formation and the Labour Movement in Calgary, 1883–1929.* Vancouver, 1998.

Brogden, Mike. *On the Mersey Beat: Policing Liverpool between the Wars.* London, 1991.

Brown, Lorne. *When Freedom Was Lost: The Unemployed, the Agitator, and the State.* Montreal, 1987.

Brown, Lorne, and Caroline Brown. *An Unauthorized History of the RCMP.* Toronto, 1978.

Brown, Robert Craig, and Ramsay Cook. *Canada, 1896–1921: A Nation Transformed.* Toronto, 1974.

Chauncey, George. *Gay New York: Gender, Urban Culture, and the Making of the Gay Male World, 1890–1940.* New York, 1994.

Christie, Nils. *Crime Control as Industry: Towards Gulags, Western Style.* London, 1993.

Cleroux, Richard. *Official Secrets: The Story behind the Canadian Security Intelligence Service.* Toronto, 1990.

Cobban, William. *Mountie: Canada's Mightiest Myth.* Ottawa, 1998.

Connell, R.W. *Masculinities.* Cambridge, 1995.

Connor, Ralph. *The Foreigner: A Tale of Saskatchewan.* Toronto, 1909.

Cornell, Stephen E., and Stephen Ellicott. *Ethnicity and Race: Making Identities in a Changing World.* London, 1998.

Critchley, T.A. *A History of Police in England and Wales, 900–1966.* London, 1967.

Cunningham, David. *There's Something Happening Here: The New Left, the Klan, and FBI Counterintelligence.* Berkeley, 2004.

Danysk, Cecilia. *Hired Hands: Labour and the Development of Prairie Agriculture, 1880–1930.* Toronto, 1995.

Dawson, Graham. *Soldier Heroes: British Adventure, Empire, and the Imagining of Masculinities.* New York, 1994.

Dawson, Michael. *The Mountie: From Dime Novel to Disney.* Toronto, 1998.

Dempsey, Hugh A. *Men in Scarlet.* Calgary, 1974.

Denny, Cecil Edward. *The Law Marches West.* Toronto, 1939.

Dion, Robert. *Crimes of the Secret Police.* Montreal, 1982.

Donner, Frank. *Protectors of Privilege: Red Squads and Police Repression in Urban America.* Berkeley, 1991.

Douthwaite, Louis Charles. *The Royal Canadian Mounted Police.* London, 1939.

Dubro, James, and Robin Rowland. *Undercover: Cases of the RCMP's Most Secret Operative.* Toronto, 1991.

Emsley, Clive. *The English Police: A Political and Social History.* London, 1991.

– *Policing and Its Context, 1750–1870.* New York, 1983.

Endicott, Stephen Lyon. *Bienfait: The Saskatchewan Miners' Struggle of '31.* Toronto, 2002.

Fetherstonhaugh, R.C. *The Royal Canadian Mounted Police.* New York, 1938.

Fidler, Richard. *RCMP: The Real Subversives.* Toronto, 1978.

Fogelson, Robert M. *Big-City Police.* Cambridge, MA, 1977.

Fossum, Jack. *Cop in a Closet.* Vancouver, 1981.

– *Mancatcher: An Immigrant's Story of Logging, Policing and Pioneering in the Canadian West.* Comox, BC, 1990.

Foucault, Michel. *Discipline and Punish: The Birth of the Prison.* London, 1977.

Franks, C.E.S., ed. *Dissent and the State.* Toronto, 1989.

Friesen, Gerald. *The Canadian Prairies: A History.* Toronto, 1987.

Giffen, P.J., Shirley Endicott, and Sylvia Lambert. *Panic and Indifference: The Politics of Canada's Drug Laws.* Ottawa, 1991.

Gramsci, Antonio. *Selections from the Prison Notebooks of Antonio Gramsci.* London, 1971.

Greer, Allan, and Ian Radforth, eds. *Colonial Leviathan: State Formation in Mid-Nineteenth-Century Canada.* Toronto, 1992.

Griffiths, Alison, and David Cruise. *The Great Adventure: How the Mounties Won the West.* Toronto, 1996.

Hall, Catherine. *White, Male and Middle-Class: Explorations in Feminism and History.* New York, 1992.

Hannant, Larry. *The Infernal Machine: Investigating the Loyalty of Canada's Citizens.* Toronto, 1995.

Harring, Sidney L. *Policing a Class Society: The Experience of American Cities, 1865–1915.* New Brunswick, NJ, 1983.

Harris, Michael. *The Judas Kiss: The Undercover Life of Patrick Kelly.* Toronto, 1995.

Hay, Douglas, Peter Linebaugh, John G. Rule, E.P. Thompson, and Cal Winslow. Albion's *Fatal Tree: Crime and Society in Eighteenth-Century England.* New York, 1975.

Harvison, C.W. *The Horsemen.* Toronto, 1967.

Haydon, A.L. *Riders of the Plains: A Record of the Royal North-West Mounted Police, 1873–1910.* Rutledge, VT, 1910.

Hewitt, Steve. *Spying 101: The RCMP's Secret Activities at Canadian Universities, 1917–1997.* Toronto, 2002.

Higham, John. *Strangers in the Land: Patterns of American Nativism, 1860–1925.* New Brunswick, NJ, 1955.

Hildebrandt, Walter. *Views from Fort Battleford: Constructed Visions of an Anglo-Canadian West.* Regina, 1994.

Horrall, S.W. *The Pictorial History of the Royal Canadian Mounted Police.* Toronto, 1973.

Howard, Victor. *We were the salt of the earth!: A Narrative of the On-to-Ottawa Trek and the Regina Riot.* Regina, 1985.

Howell, Colin D. *Northern Sandlots: A Social History of Maritime Baseball.* Toronto, 1995.

Jackson, David. *Unmasking Masculinity: A Critical Autobiography.* London, 1990.

Jacobson, Matthew Frye. *Whiteness of a Different Colour: European Immigrants and the Alchemy of Race.* London, 1998.

Kaplan, William. *State and Salvation: The Jehovah's Witnesses and Their Fight for Civil Rights.* Toronto, 1989.

Kealey, Gregory S., and Reg Whitaker, eds. *R.C.M.P. Security Bulletins: The Early Years, 1919–1929.* St John's, 1994.

– *R.C.M.P. Security Bulletins: The War Series, 1939–1941.* St John's, 1989.

– *R.C.M.P. Security Bulletins: The Depression Years, Part I, 1933–1934.* St John's, 1993.

– *R.C.M.P. Security Bulletins: The Depression Years, Part II, 1935.* St John's, 1995.

Kelly, Nora Hickson. *My Mountie and Me: A True Story.* Regina, 1999.

Kelly, Nora, and William Kelly. *The Royal Canadian Mounted Police: A Century of History, 1873–1973.* Edmonton, 1973.

Kemp, Vernon A.M. *Scarlet and Stetson: The Royal North-West Mounted Police on the Prairies.* Toronto, 1964.

– *Without Fear, Favour or Affection: Thirty-Five Years with the Royal Canadian Mounted Police.* Toronto, 1958.

Knuckle, Robert. *In the Line of Duty: The Honour Roll of the RCMP Since 1873.* Burnstown, ON, 1994.

Kraut, Alan M. *The Huddled Masses: The Immigrant in American Society, 1880–1921.* Arlington Heights, IL, 1982.

Leier, Mark. *Rebel Life: The Life and Times of Robert Gosden, Revolutionary, Mystic, Labour Spy.* Vancouver, 1999.

Lorimer, Douglas. *Color, Class and the Victorians: English Attitudes to the Negro in the Mid-Nineteenth Century.* New York, 1978.

Lowman, John, and Brian D. MacLean, eds. *Realist Criminology: Crime Control and Policing in the 1990s.* Toronto, 1992.

Luciuk, Lubomyr, and Stella Hryniuk. *Canada's Ukrainians: Negotiating an Identity.* Toronto, 1991.

MacBeth, R.G. *Policing the Plains: Being the Real-Life Records of the Famous Royal North-West Mounted Police.* London, 1921.

MacDonald, Robert H. *Sons of the Empire: The Frontier and the Boy Scout Movement, 1890–1918.* Toronto, 1993.

Macleod, R.C. *The North West Mounted Police and Law Enforcement, 1873–1905.* Toronto, 1976.

– *The North West Mounted Police, 1873–1919.* Ottawa, 1978.

Macleod, R.C., and David Schneiderman, eds. *Police Powers in Canada: The Evolution and Practice of Authority.* Toronto, 1994.

Manderson, Desmond. *From Mr. Sin to Mr. Big: A History of Australian Drug Laws.* New York, 1993.

Mangan, J.A., and James Walvin, eds. *Manliness and Morality: Middle-Class Masculinity in Britain and America, 1800–1940.* New York, 1987.

Mann, Edward, and John Alan Lee. *The RCMP vs. The People: Inside Canada's Security Service.* Don Mills, ON, 1979.

Mardiros, Anthony. *William Irvine: The Life of a Prairie Radical.* Toronto, 1979.

Marquis, Greg. *Policing Canada's Century: A History of the Canadian Association of Chiefs of Police.* Toronto, 1993.

Martynowych, Orest T. *Ukrainians in Canada: The Formative Period, 1891–1924.* Edmonton, 1991.

McCormack, A. Ross. *Reformers, Rebels, and Revolutionaries: The Western Canadian Radical Movement, 1899–1919.* Toronto, 1977.

McKenzie, James, and Lorne McClinton. *Troop 17: The Making of Mounties.* Calgary, 1992.

Michels, Robert. *Political Parties: A Sociological Study of the Oligarchical Tendencies of Modern Democracy.* Gloucester, 1915.

Miller, J.R. *Skyscrapers Hide the Heavens: A History of Indian–White Relations in Canada.* Toronto, 1989.

Mitrovica, Andrew. *Covert Entry: Spies, Lies and Crimes inside Canada's Secret Service.* Toronto, 2002.

Monkkonen, Eric. *Police in Urban America, 1860–1920.* Cambridge, 1981.

Morgan, Jane. *Conflict and Order: The Police and Labour Disputes in England and Wales, 1900–1939.* London, 1987.

Morrison, William R. *Showing the Flag: The Mounted Police and Canadian Sovereignty in the North, 1894–1925.* Vancouver, 1985.

Murphy, Emily. *The Black Candle.* Toronto, 1922.

Musto, David F. *The American Disease: Origins of Narcotic Control.* New York, 1973.

Owram, Douglas. *Promise of Eden: The Canadian Expansionist Movement and the Idea of the West, 1856–1900.* Toronto, 1992.

Pagels, Elaine. *The Origin of Satan.* New York, 1995.

Palango, Paul. *Above the Law.* Toronto, 1994.

Palmer, Bryan D. *Working-Class Experience: Rethinking the History of Canadian Labour, 1800–1991.* Toronto, 1992.

Palmer, Howard. *Patterns of Prejudice: A History of Nativism in Alberta.* Toronto, 1982.

Parr, Joy. *The Gender of Breadwinners: Women, Men and Change in Two Industrial Towns, 1880–1950.* Toronto, 1990.

Pipes, Richard, ed. *The Unknown Lenin: From the Secret Archive.* New Haven, CT, 1996.

Porter, Bernard. *The Origins of the Vigilant State: The London Metropolitan Police Special Branch before the First World War.* London, 1987.

– *Plots and Paranoia: A History of Political Espionage in Britain, 1790–1988.* New York, 1992.

Potrebenko, Helen. *No Streets of Gold.* Vancouver, 1977.

Powers, Richard Gid. *Secrecy and Power: The Life of J. Edgar Hoover.* London, 1987.

Preston, William. *Aliens and Dissenters: Federal Suppression of Radicals, 1903–1933.* Chicago, 1994.

Reiner, Robert. *The Politics of the Police.* 2nd ed. Toronto, 1992.

Reith, Charles. *The Police Idea: Its History and Evolution in England in the Eighteenth Century and After.* London, 1938.

Repka, William, and Kathleen M. Repka. *Dangerous Patriots: Canada's Unknown Prisoners of War.* Vancouver, 1982.

Rivett-Carnac, Charles. *Pursuit in the Wilderness.* Toronto, 1965.

Roberts, Barbara. *Whence They Came: Deportation from Canada, 1900–1935.* Ottawa, 1988.

Robin, Martin. *Shades of Right: Nativist and Fascist Politics in Canada, 1920–1940.* Toronto, 1992.

Rosenthal, Michael. *The Character Factory: Baden-Powell and the Origins of the Boy Scout Movement.* New York, 1986.

Roy, Patricia. *A White Man's Province: British Columbia Politicians and Chinese and Japanese Immigrants, 1858–1914.* Vancouver, 1989.

Rude, George. *The Crowd in History: A Study of Popular Disturbances in France and England, 1730–1848.* New York, 1964.

Russo, Vito. *The Celluloid Closet: Homosexuality in the Movies.* New York, 1981.

Said, Edward W. *Orientalism.* New York, 2003.

Sallot, Jeff. *Nobody Said No: The Real Story about How the Mounties Always Get Their Man.* Toronto, 1979.

Saul, Donovan T., ed. *Red Serge and Stetsons: A Hundred Years of Mountie Memories.* Victoria, 1993.

Saul, Donovan T. *The Way It Was: Fifty Years of RCMP Memories.* Victoria, 1993.

Sawatsky, John. *Men in the Shadows: The RCMP Security Service.* Toronto, 1980.

Scher, Len. *The Un-Canadians: True Stories of the Blacklist Era.* Toronto, 1992.

Schrecker, Ellen. *Many Are the Crimes: McCarthyism in America.* New York, 1998.

Segal, Lynne. *Slow Motion: Changing Masculinities, Changing Men.* London, 1990.

Shepard, R. Bruce. *Deemed Unsuitable.* Toronto, 1996.

Smith, David E. *Prairie Liberalism: The Liberal Party in Saskatchewan, 1905–71.* Toronto, 1975.

Strange, Carolyn, and Tina Loo. *Making Good: Law and Moral Regulation in Canada, 1867–1939.* Toronto, 1997.

Struthers, James. *No Fault of Their Own: Unemployment and the Canadian Welfare State, 1914–1941.* Toronto, 1983.

Talbot, C.K., C.H.S. Jayewardene, and T.J. Juliani. *Canada's Constables: The Historical Development of Policing in Canada.* Ottawa, 1985.

Teather, Robert Gordon. *Mountie Makers: Putting the CANADIAN in RCMP.* Surrey, BC, 1997.

– *Scarlet Tunic: Inside Our Cars – Inside our Hearts. On Patrol with the Royal Canadian Mounted Police.* Surrey, BC, 1994.

Thompson, E.P. *The Making of the English Working Class.* London, 1980.

Thompson, John Herd, and Allen Seager. *Canada 1922–1939: Decades of Discord.* Toronto, 1985.

– *The Harvests of War: The Prairie West, 1914–1918.* Toronto, 1978.

Torrance, Judy. *Public Violence in Canada.* Montreal and Kingston, 1986.

Turner, John Peter. *The North-West Mounted Police, 1873–1893.* Ottawa, 1950.

Valverde, Mariana. *The Age of Light, Soap, and Water: Moral Reform in English Canada, 1885–1925.* Toronto, 1991.

Wagner, Jonathan F. *Brothers Beyond the Sea: National Socialism in Canada.* Waterloo, ON, 1981.

Waiser, Bill. *All Hell Can't Stop Us: The On-to-Ottawa Trek and Regina Riot.* Calgary, 2003.

– *Park Prisoners: The Untold Story of Western Canada's National Parks, 1915–1946.* Saskatoon, 1995.

Waiser, Bill, and Dave De Brou, eds. *Documenting Canada: A History of Modern Canada in Documents.* Saskatoon, 1992.

Wakeman, Jr, Frederic. *Policing Shanghai, 1927–1937.* Berkeley and Los Angeles, 1996.

Walden, Keith. *Visions of Order: The Canadian Mounties in Symbol and Myth.* Toronto, 1982.

Ward, W. Peter. *White Canada Forever: Popular Attitudes and Public Policy toward Orientals in British Columbia.* Montreal, 1978.

Weaver, John C. *Crimes, Constables and Courts: Order and Transgression in a Canadian City, 1816–1970.* Montreal, 1995.

Whitaker, Reg, and Gary Marcuse. *Cold War Canada: The Making of a National Insecurity State, 1945–1957.* Toronto, 1994.

Whitaker, Reg, and Steve Hewitt. *Canada and the Cold War.* Toronto, 2003.

Williams, David R. *Call in Pinkerton's: American Detectives at Work in Canada.* Toronto, 1998.

Wilson, R.S.S. *Undercover for the RCMP.* Victoria, 1986.

Woodsworth, J.S. *Strangers within Our Gates, Or Coming Canadians.* Toronto, 1909.

Young, Charles H. *The Ukrainian Canadians: A Study in Assimilation.* Toronto, 1931.

Young, Malcolm. *An Inside Job: Policing and Police Culture in Britain.* Oxford, 1991.

Articles

Avakumovic, Ivan. 'The Communist Party of Canada and the Prairie Farmer: The Interwar Years.' Pp. 78–87 in David J. Bercuson, ed., *Western Perspectives 1.* Toronto, 1974.

Avery, Donald. 'Ethnic Loyalties and the Proletarian Revolution: A Case Study of Communist Political Activity in Winnipeg, 1923–1936.' Pp. 68–91 in Jorgen Dahlie and Tissa Fernando, eds. *Ethnicity, Power and Politics in Canada.* Toronto, 1981.

Axelrod, Paul. 'Spying on the Young in Depression and War: Students, Youth Groups and the RCMP.' *Labour/Le Travail* 35 (1995), 43–63.

Baker, William M. 'The Miners and the Mounties: The Royal North West Mounted Police and the 1906 Lethbridge Strike.' *Labour/Le Travail* 27 (1991), 55–96.

Bassnett, Susan. 'Lost in the Past: A Tale of Heroes and Englishness.' Pp. 47–61 in C.E. Gittings, ed., *Imperialism and Gender: Constructions of Masculinity.* London, 1996.

Beahan, William. 'Abortion and Infanticide in Western Canada 1874 to 1916: A Criminal Case Study.' In William M. Baker, ed., *The Mounted Police and Prairie Society, 1873–1919.* Regina, 1998.

Boyd, Neil. 'The Origins of Canadian Narcotics Legislation: The Process of Criminalization in Historical Context.' Pp. 192–218 in R.C. Macleod, ed., *Readings in the History of Criminal Justice in Canada.* Toronto, 1988.

Carstairs, Catherine. 'Deporting "Ah Sin" to Save the White Race: Moral Panic, Racialization and the Creation of Canada's Drug Laws.' *Canadian Bulletin of Medical Health* 16, no. 1 (1999), 65–88.

– 'Innocent Addicts, Dope Fiends and Nefarious Traffickers: Illegal Drug Use in 1920s English Canada.' *Journal of Canadian Studies* 33, no. 3 (1998), 145–62.

Cherwinski, Joe. 'Early Working-Class Life on the Prairies.' Pp. 544–56 in R. Douglas Francis and Howard Palmer, eds, *The Prairie West: Historical Readings.* Edmonton, 1992.

Curtis, T.C. 'Quarter Sessions Appearances and their Background: A Seventeenth-Century Regional Study.' Pp. 135–54 in J.S. Cockburn, ed., *Crime in England, 1550–1800.* Princeton, NJ, 1977.

Danysk, Cecilia. '"A Bachelor's Paradise": Homesteaders, Hired Hands, and
the Construction of Masculinity, 1880–1930.' Pp. 154–85 in Catherine
Cavanaugh and Jeremy Mouat, eds, *Making Western Canada: Essays on
European Colonization and Settlement.* Toronto, 1996.

Finkel, Alvin. 'Alberta Social Credit Reappraised: The Radical Character
of the Early Social Credit Movement.' *Prairie Forum* 11, no. 1 (1986),
69–86.

Gyffon, James. 'The Song of a Constable.' Pp. 488–90 in A.V. Judges, ed.,
The Elizabethan Underworld. London, 1930.

Hannant, Larry. 'Access to the Inside: An Assessment of Canada's Security
Service: A History.' *Intelligence and National Security* 8, no. 3 (1993),
149–59.

– The Calgary Working Class and the Social Credit Movement in Alberta,
1932–35.' *Labour/Le Travail* 16 (1985), 97–116.

Hewitt, Steve. 'Malczewski's List: A Case Study of Royal North-West
Mounted Police-Immigrant Relations.' *Saskatchewan History* 46, no. 1
(1994), 35–41.

– 'Re-Inventing the Mounties.' Pp. 247–56 in Michèle Kaltemback, ed.,
Le Canada face à ses nouveaux défis/Canada Revisited. Toulouse, France,
2005.

– 'Royal Canadian Mounted Spy: The Secret Life of John Leopold/Jack
Esselwein.' *Intelligence and National Security* 15, no. 1 (2000), 41–68.

– 'September 1931: A Re-Interpretation of the RCMP's Handling of the
Estevan Strike and Riot.' *Labour/Le Travail* 37 (1997), 254–71.

– 'Spying 101: The RCMP's Secret Activities at the University of Saskatchewan, 1920–1971.' *Saskatchewan History* 47, no. 2 (1995), 35–44.

– '"We Are Sitting at the Edge of a Volcano": Winnipeg during the On to
Ottawa Trek.' *Prairie Forum* 19, no. 1 (1994), 51–64.

Horn, Michiel. 'Keeping Canada "Canadian": Anti-Communism and
Canadianism in Toronto, 1928–29.' *Canada: An Historical Magazine* 3,
no. 1 (1975), 35–47.

Horrall, S.W. 'The Royal North-West Mounted Police and Labour Unrest in
Western Canada, 1919.' *Canadian Historical Review* 61, no. 2 (1980),
169–90.

Kealey, Gregory S. '1919: The Canadian Labour Revolt.' Pp. 90–114 in
Bryan D. Palmer, ed., *The Character of Class Struggle: Essays in Canadian Working-Class History, 1850–1985.* Toronto, 1986.

– 'The Early Years of State Surveillance of Labour and the Left in Canada:
The Institutional Framework of the Royal Canadian Mounted Police
Security and Intelligence Apparatus, 1918–26.' *Intelligence and National
Security* 8, no. 3 (1993), 129–48.

– 'Filing and Defiling: The Organization of the Canadian State's Security

Archives in the Interwar Years.' Pp. 88–105 in Franca Iacovetta and Wendy Mitchinson, eds., *On the Case: Explorations in Social History.* Toronto, 1998.

– 'State Repression of Labour and the Left in Canada, 1914–20: The Impact of the First World War.' *Canadian Historical Review* 73, no. 3 (1992), 281–314.

– 'The Surveillance State: The Origins of Domestic Intelligence and Counter-Subversion in Canada, 1914–21.' *Intelligence and National Security* 7, no. 3 (1992), 179–210.

Kealey, Gregory S., and Reg Whitaker. Letter to the Editor. *Literacy Review of Canada* 5, no. 10 (1996), 72.

Keshen, Jeff. 'All the News That Was Fit to Print: Ernest J. Chambers and Information Control in Canada, 1914–19.' *Canadian Historical Review* 73, no. 3 (1992), 315–43.

Kinsman, Gary. '"Character Weaknesses" and "Fruit Machines": Towards an Analysis of the Anti-Homosexual Security Campaign in the Canadian Civil Service.' *Labour/Le Travail* 35 (1995), 133–61.

Knuttila, Murray. 'E.A. Partridge: The Farmers' Intellectual.' *Prairie Forum* 14, no. 1 (1989), 59–74.

Laine, Edward W. 'Finnish Canadian Radicalism and Canadian Politics: The First Forty Years, 1900–1940.' Pp. 94–112 in Jorgen Dahlie and Tissa Fernando, eds, *Ethnicity, Power and Politics in Canada.* Toronto, 1981.

Lehr, J.C. 'Government and Coercion in the Settlement of Ukrainian Immigrants in Western Canada.' *Prairie Forum* 8, no. 2 (1983), 179–94.

Leier, Mark. 'Portrait of a Labour Spy: The Case of Robert Gosden, 1882–1961.' *Labour/Le Travail* 42 (1998), 55–84.

Lonardo, Michael. 'Under a Watchful Eye: A Case Study of Police Surveillance during the 1930s.' *Labour/Le Travail* 35 (1995), 11–41.

Macgillivray, Don. 'Military Aid to the Civil Power: The Cape Breton Experience in the 1920's.' Pp. 116–40 in Michael S. Cross and Gregory S. Kealey, eds, *The Consolidation of Capitalism, 1896–1929.* Toronto, 1983.

Macleod, R.C. 'Canadianizing the West: The North-West Mounted Police as Agents of the National Policy, 1873–1905.' Pp. 187–99 in R. Douglas Francis and Howard Palmer, eds, *The Prairie West: Historical Readings.* Edmonton, 1985.

– 'How They "Got Their Man."' *Literary Review of Canada* 5, no. 8 (1996), 19–21.

Makahonuk, Glen. 'The Labouring Class in Saskatchewan's Economy, 1850 to 1912.' *Saskatchewan History* 46, no. 1 (1994), 22–34.

– 'The Saskatchewan Coal Strikes of 1932: A Study in Class Relations.' *Prairie Forum* 9, no. 1 (1984), 79–99.

– 'The Saskatoon Relief Camp Workers' Riot of May 8, 1933: An Expression of Class Conflict.' *Saskatchewan History* 37, no. 2 (1984), 55–72.
– 'The Working and Living Conditions of the Saskatchewan Deep Seam Coal Miners, 1930–1939.' *Saskatchewan History* 33, no. 2 (1980), 41–55.

Maroney, Paul. '"The Great Adventure": The Context and Ideology of Recruiting in Ontario, 1914–17.' *Canadian Historical Review* 77, no. 1 (1996), 62–98.

Marquis, Greg. 'The History of Policing in the Maritime Provinces: Themes and Prospects.' *Urban History Review* 29, no. 2 (1990), 84–99.
– 'Working Men in Uniform: The Early Twentieth-Century Toronto Police.' *Histoire sociale/Social History* 20, no. 40 (1987), 259–77.

Maynard, Steven. '"Horrible Temptations": Sex, Men, and Working-Class Male Youth in Urban Ontario, 1890–1935.' *Canadian Historical Review* 78, no. 2 (1997), 191–235.
– 'Queer Musings on Masculinity and History.' *Labour/Le Travail* 42, no. 2 (1998), 183–97.
– 'Rough Work and Rugged Men: The Social Construction of Masculinity in Working-Class History.' *Labour/Le Travail* 23 (1989), 159–69.

McCormack, A. Ross. 'Cloth Caps and Jobs: The Ethnicity of English Immigrants in Canada, 1900–1914.' Pp. 38–55 in Jorgen Dahlie and Tissa Fernando, eds, *Ethnicity, Power and Politics in Canada*. Toronto, 1981.

McCulloch, Michael. 'Most Assuredly Perpetual Motion: Police and Policing in Quebec City, 1838–58.' *Urban History Review* 29, no. 2 (1990), 100–12.

McElhinny, Bonnie. 'An Economy of Affect: Objectivity, Masculinity and the Gendering of Police Work.' Pp. 159–72 in Andrea Cornwall and Nancy Lindisfarne, eds, *Dislocating Masculinity: Comparative Ethnographies*. London, 1994.

McLaren, John. 'Wrestling Spirits: The Strange Case of Peter Verigin II.' *Canadian Ethnic Studies* 27, no. 3 (1995), 95–130.

Mead, F.J. 'Communism in Canada.' *R.C.M.P. Quarterly* 3, no. 1 (1935), 44–5.

Melnycky, Peter. 'The Internment of Ukrainians in Canada.' Pp. 1–24 in Frances Swyripa and John Herd Thompson, eds, *Loyalties in Conflict: Ukrainians in Canada during the Great War*. Edmonton, 1983.

Mitchell, Tom. 'From the Social Gospel to the "Plain Bread of Leninism": A.E. Smith's Journey to the Left in the Epoch of Reaction after World War I.' *Labour/Le Travail* 33 (1993), 125–51.
– '"The Manufacture of Souls of Good Quality": Winnipeg's 1919 National Conference on Canadian Citizenship, English-Canadian Nationalism, and the New Order after the Great War.' *Journal of Canadian Studies* 31, no. 4 (1996–7), 5–28.

Monod, David. 'The Agrarian Struggle: Rural Communism in Alberta and Saskatchewan, 1926–1935.' *Histoire sociale/Social History* 18, no. 35 (1985), 99–118.

Morton, Desmond. 'Aid to the Civil Power: The Canadian Militia in Support of Social Order, 1867–1914.' *Canadian Historical Review* 51, no. 4 (1970), 407–25.

O'Brien, Mike. 'Manhood and the Militia Myth: Masculinity, Class and Militarism in Ontario, 1902–1914.' *Labour/Le Travail* 42, no. 2 (1998), 115–41.

Panitch, Leo. 'The Role and Nature of the Canadian State.' Pp. 3–27 in Leo Panitch, ed., *The Canadian State: Political Economy and Political Power.* Toronto, 1977.

Philips, David. '"A New Engine of Power and Authority": The Institutionalization of Law-Enforcement in England 1780–1830.' Pp. 155–89 in V.A.C. Gatrell, Bruce Lenman, and Geoffrey Parker, eds, *Crime and the Law: The Social History of Crime in Western Europe since 1500.* London, 1980.

Pon, Madge. 'Like a Chinese Puzzle: The Construction of Chinese Masculinity in Jack Canuck.' Pp. 88–100 in Joy Parr and Mark Rosenfeld, eds, *Gender and History in Canada.* Toronto, 1996.

Ray, Gerda. '"We Can Stay Until Hell Freezes Over": Strike Control and the State Police in New York, 1919–1923.' *Labor History* 37, no. 3 (1995), 403–25.

Rivett-Carnac, C.E. 'The Training Depot.' *R.C.M.P. Quarterly* 3, no. 1 (1933), 24.

Robinson, Daniel. 'Planning for the "Most Serious Contingency": Alien Internment, Arbitrary Detention, and the Canadian State, 1938–39.' *Journal of Canadian Studies* 28, no. 2 (1993), 5–20.

Robinson, Daniel, and David Kimmel. 'The Queer Career of Homosexual Security Vetting in Cold War Canada.' *Canadian Historical Review* 75, no. 3 (1994), 319–45.

Scheuer, Michael. 'A Fine Rendition.' *New York Times*, 11 March 2005.

Shepard, R.B. 'Plain Racism: The Reaction against Oklahoma Black Immigration to the Canadian Prairies.' *Prairie Forum* 10, no. 2 (1985), 365–82.

Stanley, Timothy J. 'White Supremacy and the Rhetoric of Educational Indoctrination: A Canadian Case Study.' Pp. 70–105 in J.A. Mangan, ed., *Making Imperial Mentalities: Socialization and British Imperialism.* New York, 1990.

Stone, Thomas. 'The Mounties as Vigilantes: Perceptions of Community and the Transformation of Law in the Yukon, 1885–1897.' *Law and Society Review* 14, no. 1 (1979), 83–113.

Tobias, John J. 'The British Colonial Police: An Alternative Police Style.'
Pp. 135–60 in Philip John Stead, ed., *Pioneers and Policing*. Montclair,
NJ, 1977.

Wagner, Jonathan F. 'Heim ins Reich: The Story of Loon River's Nazis.'
Saskatchewan History 28, no. 1 (1976), 41–50.

Wark, Wesley K. 'Security Intelligence in Canada, 1864–1945: The History
of a National Insecurity State.' Pp. 153–78 in Keith Nelson and B.J.C.
McKercher, eds, *Go Spy the Land: Military Intelligence in History.*
Westport, CT, 1992.

Weaver, John C. 'Social Control, Martial Conformity, and Community
Entanglement: The Varied Beat of the Hamilton Police, 1895–1920.'
Urban History Review 29, no. 2 (1990), 113–27.

Whitaker, Reg. 'Cold War Alchemy: How America, Britain and Canada
Transformed Espionage into Subversion.' *Intelligence and National
Security* 15, no. 2 (2000), 177–210.

Whitaker, Reg, and Gregory S. Kealey. 'A War on Ethnicity? The RCMP
and Internment.' Pp. 128–47 in Franca Iacovetta, Roberto Perin, and
Angelo Principe, eds, *Enemies Within: Italian and Other Internees in
Canada and Abroad.* Toronto, 2000.

Wood, S.T. 'Tools for Treachery.' *R.C.M.P. Quarterly* 8, no. 4 (1941), 39.

Papers

Dawson, Michael. '"That Nice Red Coat Goes to My Head Like Cham-
pagne": Popular Images of the Mountie, 1880–1960.' Presented at the
Annual Meeting of the Canadian Historical Association, Brock University, June 1996.

Hewitt, Steve. '"The Royal Canadian Mounted Police Are Above That Sort
of Thing": Ambition, Politics and Patronage in the Mounted Police, 1896–
1931.' Presented at Law for the Buffalo, Law for the Musk-Ox. Law and
Society in the Middle Kingdom: Canada's North-West Territories and
Prairie Provinces, 1670–1970, University of Calgary, 1997.

Lin, Zhiqiu, and Augustine Brannigan. 'The Implications of a Provincial
Police Force: The Cases of Alberta and Saskatchewan.' Presented at Law
for the Buffalo, Law for the Musk-Ox. Law and Society in the Middle
Kingdom: Canada's North-West Territories and Prairie Provinces, 1670–
1970, University of Calgary, 1997.

Master's Theses

Dick, Eric Lyle. 'Deportation under the Immigration Act and the Canadian
Criminal Code, 1919–1936.' University of Manitoba, 1978.

Hanson, S.D. 'The Estevan Strike and Riot, 1931.' University of Saskatchewan, 1971.

Hewitt, Steven. 'Beyond Regina: The On to Ottawa Trek in Manitoba and Ontario.' University of Saskatchewan, 1992.

Kitzan, Christopher J. 'The Fighting Bishop: George Exton Lloyd and the Immigration Debate.' University of Saskatchewan, 1996.

McBride, Michelle. 'From Indifference to Internment: An Examination of RCMP Responses to Nazism and Fascism in Canada from 1934 to 1941.' Memorial University of Newfoundland, 1997.

Moir, Sean Innes. 'The Alberta Provincial Police, 1917–1932.' University of Alberta, 1992.

Montserin, Robert. 'Criminalization of Drug Activity in Canada.' University of Ottawa, 1981.

Robertson, Duncan Francis. 'The Saskatchewan Provincial Police, 1917–1928.' University of Saskatchewan, 1976.

Seager, Allen. 'A History of the Mine Workers' Union of Canada.' McGill University, 1978.

Stone, Gladys May. 'The Regina Riot: 1935.' University of Saskatchewan, 1967.

Strom, Tracy Lee. 'When the Mounties Came: Mounted Police and Cree Relations on Two Saskatchewan Indian Reserves.' University of Saskatchewan, 2000.

PhD Dissertations

Butt, Michael. 'Surveillance of Canadian Communists: A Case Study of Toronto RCMP Intelligence Networks, 1920–1939.' Memorial University of Newfoundland, 2004.

Illustration Credits

Department of the Interior/Library and Archives Canada: Inspection by the Prince of Wales, PA-041412.

Felix H. Man/Library and Archives Canada: Masculine Mounties, PA-0150558.

Library and Archives Canada: Commissioner A.B. Perry, PA-0201242; Uniforms, C-027093; Yorkton, C-01314; Recruits on parade, PA-032588; Barracks and drill parade, PA-032584; Regina 3 July 1935, PA-0204459.

***R.C.M.P. Quarterly*:** 1873–1933, vol. 1, no. 2 (1933); a light-hearted but revealing look, vol. 1, no. 4 (1933).

Index

THE CANADIAN SOCIAL HISTORY SERIES

Terry Copp,
The Anatomy of Poverty: The Condition of the Working Class in Montreal, 1897–1929, 1974.
ISBN 0–7710–2252–2

Alison Prentice,
The School Promoters: Education and Social Class in Mid-Nineteenth Century Upper Canada, 1977.
ISBN 0–7710–7181–7

John Herd Thompson,
The Harvests of War: The Prairie West, 1914–1918, 1978.
ISBN 0–7710–8560–5

Joy Parr, Editor,
Childhood and Family in Canadian History, 1982.
ISBN 0–7710–6938–3

Alison Prentice and
Susan Mann Trofimenkoff, Editors,
The Neglected Majority: Essays in Canadian Women's History, Volume 2, 1985.
ISBN 0–7710–8583–4

Ruth Roach Pierson,
'They're Still Women After All': The Second World War and Canadian Womanhood, 1986.
ISBN 0–7710–6958–8

Bryan D. Palmer,
The Character of Class Struggle: Essays in Canadian Working Class History, 1850–1985, 1986.
ISBN 0–7710–6946–4

Alan Metcalfe,
Canada Learns to Play: The Emergence of Organized Sport, 1807–1914, 1987.
ISBN 0–7710–5870–5

Marta Danylewycz,
Taking the Veil: An Alternative to Marriage, Motherhood, and Spinsterhood in Quebec, 1840–1920, 1987.
ISBN 0–7710–2550–5

Craig Heron,
Working in Steel: The Early Years in Canada, 1883–1935, 1988.
ISBN 0–7710–4086–5

Wendy Mitchinson and
Janice Dickin McGinnis, Editors,
Essays in the History of Canadian Medicine, 1988.
ISBN 0–7710–6063–7

Joan Sangster,
Dreams of Equality: Women on the Canadian Left, 1920–1950, 1989.
ISBN 0–7710–7946–X

Angus McLaren,
Our Own Master Race: Eugenics in Canada, 1885–1945, 1990.
ISBN 0–7710–5544–7

Bruno Ramirez,
On the Move: French-Canadian and Italian Migrants in the North Atlantic Economy, 1860–1914, 1991.
ISBN 0–7710–7283–X

Mariana Valverde,
'The Age of Light, Soap and Water': Moral Reform in English Canada, 1885–1925, 1991.
ISBN 0–7710–8689–X

Bettina Bradbury,
Working Families: Age, Gender, and Daily Survival in Industrializing Montreal, 1993.
ISBN 0–19–541211–7

Andrée Lévesque,
Making and Breaking the Rules: Women in Quebec, 1919–1939, 1994.
ISBN 0–7710–5283–9

Cecilia Danysk,
Hired Hands: Labour and the Development of Prairie Agriculture, 1880–1930, 1995.
ISBN 0–7710–2552–1

Kathryn McPherson,
Bedside Matters: The Transformation of Canadian Nursing, 1900–1990, 1996.
ISBN 0–8020-8679-9

Edith Burley,
Servants of the Honourable Company: Work, Discipline, and Conflict in the Hudson's Bay Company, 1770–1870, 1997.
ISBN 0–19–541296–6

Mercedes Steedman,
Angels of the Workplace: Women and the Construction of Gender Relations in the Canadian Clothing Industry, 1890–1940, 1997.
ISBN 0–19–54308–3

**Angus McLaren and
Arlene Tigar McLaren,**
The Bedroom and the State: The Changing Practices and Politics of Contraception and Abortion in Canada, 1880–1997, 1997.
ISBN 0–19–541318–0

Kathryn McPherson, Cecilia Morgan, and Nancy M. Forestell, Editors,
Gendered Pasts: Historical Essays in Feminity and Masculinity in Canada, 1999.
ISBN 0–19–541449–7

Gillian Creese,
Contracting Masculinity: Gender, Class, and Race in a White-Collar Union, 1944–1994, 1999.
ISBN 0–19–541454–3

Geoffrey Reaume,
Remembrance of Patients Past: Patient Life at the Toronto Hospital for the Insane, 1870–1940, 2000.
ISBN 0–19–541538–8

Miriam Wright,
A Fishery for Modern Times: The State and the Industrialization of the New-foundland Fishery. 1934–1968, 2001.
ISBN 0–19–541620–1

Judy Fudge and Eric Tucker,
Labour Before the Law: The Regulation of Workers' Collective Action in Canada, 1900–1948, 2001.
ISBN 0–19–541633–3

Mark Moss,
Manliness and Militarism: Educating Young Boys in Ontario for War, 2001.
ISBN 0–19–541594–9

Joan Sangster,
Regulating Girls and Women: Sexuality, Family, and the Law in Ontario 1920–1960, 2001.
ISBN 0–19–541663–5

Reinhold Kramer and Tom Mitchell,
Walk Towards the Gallows: The Tragedy of Hilda Blake, Hanged 1899, 2002.
ISBN 0–19–541686–4

Mark Kristmanson,
Plateaus of Freedom: Nationality, Culture, and State Security in Canada, 1940–1960, 2002.
ISBN 0–19–541866–2

Steve Hewitt,
Riding to the Rescue: The Transformation of the RCMP in Alberta and Saskatchewan, 1914–1939, 2006.
ISBN-13: 978–0–8020–9021–8 (cloth)
ISBN-10: 0–8020–9021–4
ISBN-13: 978–0–8020–4895–0 (paper)
ISBN-10: 0–8020–4895–1